Nations, Language and Citizenship

Nations, Language and Citizenship

Norman Berdichevsky

McFarland & Company, Inc., Publishers
Jefferson, North Carolina, and London

ACKNOWLEDGMENTS: I owe much of my fasicination with languages to the popular works of the outstanding linguist Mario Pei. I wish to thank all those scholars who helped acquaint me with the fasicinating sagas of their own national languages, and to express my appreciation and gratitude to those individuals from many countries who answered my queries and explained aspects of the language situation in their respective countries. I express a special debt of appreciation to my wife, Raquel, for her assistance, encouragement, proofreading and computer skills.

LIBRARY OF CONGRESS CATALOGUING-IN-PUBLICATION DATA
Berdichevsky, Norman, 1943–
    Nations, language and citizenship / Norman Berdichevsky.
        p.   cm.
    Includes bibliographical references and index.

    ISBN 0-7864-1710-2 (softcover : 50# alkaline paper) ∞

    1. Language and languages—Political aspects.
    2. Language policy.   3. Nationalism.
    4. Linguistic minorities.   5. Bilingualism—Political aspects.
    6. Linguistic geography—Political aspects.   I. Title.
    P119.3.B47   2004
    306.44'9—dc22   2003025422

British Library cataloguing data are available

©2004 Norman Berdichevsky. All rights reserved

No part of this book may be reproduced or transmitted in any form or by any means, electronic or mechanical, including photocopying or recording, or by any information storage and retrieval system, without permission in writing from the publisher.

Cover image ©2004 Clipart.com

Manufactured in the United States of America

McFarland & Company, Inc., Publishers
  Box 611, Jefferson, North Carolina 28640
    www.mcfarlandpub.com

Contents

Acknowledgments iv
Preface and Dedication 1
Introduction 3

Part I. *Countries with Competing Candidates for the National Language*

1. Hebrew versus Yiddish: The Case of Israel 13
2. The Attempt to Revive Irish: A Nation Once Again 44
3. Norway's Schizophrenia: New Norse (Nynorsk) versus Dano-Norwegian (Bokmål/Riksmål) 55
4. Maltese: "The Curse of the Country and Fit Only for the Kitchen" 66

Part II. *Multiethnic Countries with Bilingualism and Multilingualism*

5. Belgium: The Classic "Buffer State" 77
6. Switzerland 92
7. Spain: Five Official Languages, or Is It Only Four and Two-Thirds? 103
8. Canada 116
9. India 124
10. South Africa 129

Part III. *The Celtic "Pygmy" Revivals of Welsh and Scots*

11. Wales, Welsh and Plaid Cymru 139
12. Scotland, Scots and the Threatened Demise of Scottish Gaelic 146

Part IV. *Dialects or Languages?*

13. Italian Dialects 157
14. Scandinavian Languages: Unification Tried and Rejected . 160

Part V. *The Quarreling Cousins*

15. Serbian and Croatian (Serbo-Croatian) or "A Common Language Does Not a Nation Make" 165
16. Czech and Slovak 171
17. Romanian and Moldavian 174

Part VI. *Ethnic or Regional Minorities: Bilingual or Using the "Wrong Language"?*

18. The Romanian-Speaking Hungarians 181
19. Alsace-Lorraine: German Speakers Who Identify with France 187
20. The German-Speaking Danish Minority in South Schleswig 191
21. The Swedish-Speaking Finlanders 199
22. Israel's Hebrew-Speaking Arab Citizens 205

Part VII. *Spanish versus Portuguese in Uruguay: The Case of Determined Government Planning to Avoid Bilingualism*

23. Uruguay: The Origins of the Buffer State 215

Part VIII. *The Struggle with the Chains of the Past (Greek, Arabic and Turkish)*

24. The Greek Dilemma: Ancient (Attic) versus Demotike versus Katharevousa 225
25. Arabic: The Koran versus Modern Standard versus the Local Vernaculars 232
26. Turkish Identity Frees Itself from the Islamic/Arabic Yoke . 241

Conclusion 245

Chapter Notes 259

Bibliography 267

Index 275

Preface and Dedication

Language is both a medium of discourse and communication and an ideological tool. A failure to distinguish between the medium and the tool has often led to generalizations that are misleading or simply erroneous. It is commonly assumed that a "national language" is the most commonly spoken language of a people in its own homeland and therefore entirely "natural" for that language to be automatically embraced as an integral part of the culture and national identity of the people concerned. The thesis of this book is that a common language is neither a necessary nor a sufficient requirement in "nation-building."

For the past few centuries language has increasingly been the object of manipulation by those who would eliminate any divergence between the language spoken at home and that spoken in school, and has been used as a way to inculcate a sense of "national identity." The many case studies presented in this book demonstrate that "home" in the nearest most immediate sense is indeed "where the tongue is" but that there is a considerable commitment required as a result of education, conviction and ideology before speakers accept that the officially promulgated "national language" is either identical with the one learned at mother's knee or the "proper" substitute for it. Often, a minority, composed largely of historians, literary figures, linguists, scholars and nationalist leaders acting or posing as "spokesmen" for their people, have argued that a specific historical-literary form of the language—or what they envisioned as a "pure" version of the ancestral language free of foreign influence as they imagined it or reconstructed and then "modernized" to fit the needs of contemporary society—should be chosen as the "National Language." This has often led to divisive quarrels extending over generations and exerting a major impact on national identity, education, literacy, cultural creativity, and politics.

This reality is often obscured by the common misconception that the political map is almost identical to the linguistic map and that "nationality has become almost synonymous with language." It is precisely this view that led to diplomats' making language the principle criteria for drawing boundaries at the Versailles Peace Conference and the monumental contempt for the "non-ethnic nations" of the United States and Switzerland shown by both the Kaiser and Hitler in both world wars.

Furthermore, non–European and "third world" examples present an even stronger case for the divergence of the political and linguistic map (see especially the chapters on India, South Africa, Turkey and the so-called "Arab World"). The conclusions show how often a shared history, ideological values, religion, race, inertia, love of a common homeland or historical accident have all been more important than language in shaping a sense of nationhood and common destiny. It has often been the case that language followed these developments instead of the other way around. The subject has been one that has fascinated me since my teenage years. It is my profound hope that readers will find this book both informative and entertaining and enjoy reading it as much as I enjoyed writing it.

I dedicate this book to the memory of the many thousands of Esperantists who believed that a neutral non-ethnic international language could help reduce antagonisms between nations but who became victims of both world wars and the twin horrors of Nazism and Stalinism. I would also like to take the opportunity to affectionately recall my parents, Sadie and "Izzy," a man who, like millions of other immigrants to America, struggled to acquire American English as his own national language.

Of Further Interest

The following periodical articles of mine contain scattered fragments appropriate to the chapters on Israel, Ireland, Norway and Spain.

"Hebrew vs. Yiddish: The Worldwide Rivalry. " *Midstream.* July-August 2002, pp. 12–17. (Republished in the anthology *Best Jewish Writing* 2003. Hoboken, N. J.: John Wiley, 2003)

"The Search for a National Language—the Examples of Hebrew, Irish and Norwegian." *Midstream.* January 2002, pp. 17–21.

"Norway's Language Question: Which Norwegian Do You Speak?" *Scandinavian Review.* Winter 2001, pp. 14–21.

"Spain's Language Diversity." *Contemporary Review.* May 2001, pp. 276–282.

INTRODUCTION

A commonly accepted view of language is that it is the core of a nation's identity. Poets, patriots and philosophers have eloquently expressed their affection for the "mother tongue" as the dearest possession of a people. The great German philosopher Johann Gottfried von Herder (1744–1803) popularized the idea of *Volksgeist* ("national character"), as expressed in the language and literature of a nation, a view subscribed to by nationalist leaders of all shades in many political disputes involving the populations of border regions: "Has a nationality anything dearer than the speech of its fathers? In its speech resides its whole thought domain, its traditions, history, religion and basis of life, all its heart and soul.... With language, the heart of a people is created."[1]

The clear assumption is that "the people" have always spoken their own "national language" in their "homeland." This presumed identity between a people, their sense of nationhood, the homeland and national language is, however, far from automatic. A host of modern states have had or continue to have disputes regarding their proper national language. In multiethnic states, a variety of mechanisms has been put in place to provide a form of local autonomy guaranteeing use of a local "minority" or "regional" or "associate national language" recognized in education and administration.

The language all of us learned at our mother's knee at home and were educated in at school is not just a vehicle of expression and communication. It is a tool of integration in the society we are a part of and is inextricably linked with a distinct national experience, literature, and culture. Therefore, although the English of America, Australia and Britain, the Spanish of Spain, Mexico and Argentina, and the French of France, Canada and Haiti each share an enormous common historic origin, vocabulary and usage, they differ as a "medium of discourse," that is a system of communication between people who live within a national framework of laws, enjoy a sense of patriotism and history and share many of the same social experiences.

Each national variety of English, Spanish and French reflects a distinct societal and historical experience. Americans, Brits and Australians may all speak "the same language called English" and can communicate on sophisticated levels, yet they do not share the same discourse of national experiences, history, humor, slang, political systems, popular culture, folklore, sports, recreational pursuits and social mores, which are all fundamental ingredients in the sense of nationhood.

The Medium That Turns Citizenship into a "Flesh and Blood Community"

It is largely language—this common medium of discourse that transforms the legal abstraction of citizenship into a "flesh and blood community, a common public culture, and a unifying collective identity."[2] This common medium of discourse unifies us in relating to common shared experiences in the TV programs we watch, the books we read, the plays we see, the games and sports we play, the jokes we tell, the social life we lead and the history we revere. It allows us to relate to each other in terms of our shared experiences and is not shared even by those who speak the same language elsewhere.

About forty years ago, before the widespread acceptance of colloquial American expressions in the U.K., a popular joke based on countless true stories related how several British tourists told their American and Canadian friends that they had "knocked up Mary" earlier that morning and had to be politely corrected by their hosts that they didn't really mean they had made Mary pregnant but that they had simply knocked on her door and not found her home. Although the time is long past when British newspapers railed against such "vulgar Americanisms" as "the movies" instead of the "proper" British expression "the "cinema," many such jokes still abound and also explain why it is common folk wisdom to say; "The Americans and the English (or the Irish) don't laugh at the same jokes."

Who Are We?

A sense of nationhood, a common territory and history are so inextricably linked that there is an assumption that a "common language" must be a part of this national identity. Yet in many cases, it was a search for and active debate over precisely the issue of national identity—"Who are we?" or "Who should we be?"—that preceded and shaped the final choice of what eventually became the one (or several) "official national language(s)."

It stands to reason that nothing would be more expected than a near universal agreement to cultivate, venerate and appreciate the national language as an expression of solidarity. Yet the awkward reality is that in many independent, sovereign states, the question of national identity and its expression through language either has not been finally resolved or was, until recently, the subject of intense controversy.[3] The definition of "national self-identity" as a concept has varied considerably over time. In many states, the crucial factor playing a decisive role in determining "loyalty" changed over time from feudal lord and church to absolute monarch, to state, flag and the nation. These symbols of loyalty were often masked by self-serving economic or social interests. Only in modern times (i.e., since the end of the Napoleonic wars in Europe) has a single national language become the prescribed ideal in the self-identity of most modern states. However, the absence of one is not necessarily proof of a lack of cohesion, as witnessed by Switzerland. Close to two dozen modern states each proclaim English or Spanish or Arabic as their official national language. Clearly the fact that the peoples of these states supposedly speak the same language has not avoided conflicts and wars between them nor has it prevented civil wars in England (1642–1645), the United States (1861–1865), Finland (1917–1918), Russia (1918–1920), Spain (1936–1939), Greece (1946–1949), Korea (1950–1953), Vietnam (1954–1975), Lebanon (1957–1958, 1975–1990), and Yemen (1962–1969, 1986).

Countries such as Switzerland or the United States, in spite of their success at mobilizing the loyalty of peoples of diverse origins (and languages) into a single patriotic ideal, were held in contempt by both the Kaiser and Hitler because in spite of their successes, they lacked what appeared to be the most important old world raison d'etre—the attributes of an ethnic group or folk (a common biological descent) with the same language and predominant religion.

Richard Hartshorne[4] gives the most widely accepted definition of a coherent nation-state for political geography, one that takes into account the importance of a sense of loyalty and community: "Any state, to become well established, must present to the populations of its areal parts a distinct raison d'être, its justification for existence as an areal unit separate from the neighboring state-areas. This raison d'être must be based upon desires or values of first importance to the population of the regions included in the state.... These include, notably: religion, language and literature, historic memories and the form of government.... Since few state areas are homogeneous in all these respects, the problem is to construct a raison d'être that will enlist the loyalty of regional groups having different associations and ideals."

The Literature of Language Competition and Controversies

Most books dealing with language competition and controversy have primarily dealt with the growth, spread and predominance of major languages such as English, French and Spanish, issues of language loyalty, how the major languages have impinged upon the speakers of declining minor languages in small states or colonial possessions[5] and the mechanisms of language policy planning and implementation[6] This book, however, has a dual focus. It specifically

(1) explores and analyzes the rivalry between competing languages in states torn by controversy to bestow the official title of national language among several competitors. It draws conclusions regarding the relative success or failure of the winner to promote or weaken national cohesion, the most crucial element in political geography in determining the life and death of states. It also subjects von Herder's premise to critical scrutiny.

(2) investigates the specific historical experiences of two dozen countries and ethnic/regional minorities according to how their political leadership, intellectual elite or independence movements attempted to solve the question "Who are we?" or "Who should we be?"

Questions to Be Answered

I evaluate how important the national language was or still is in achieving a sense of national solidarity and make comparisons with other factors such as territory, religion, race, historical continuity and memory. Three specific questions are addressed by reviewing the twenty-six case studies presented:

(1) The first applies to four present day independent states: Do the people(s) of these countries consider the speech of their fathers as the most important ingredient in the determination of their sense of nationhood?

(2) The second question refers to individuals living in multiethnic states and those living as a national minority or as a regional minority in a state that was not originally the focus of their sense of nationhood: The essential question here is "Is my primary loyalty to the community with whom I share a common language (yes) (that is, "the language of my fathers?"(as van Herder put it), or (no), it is rather to those with whom I share the same citizenship and with whom I must have a common medium of discourse.

(3) The third question to be answered applies to the three groups of "quarreling cousins": Is/was a "common (or very similar or nearly identical) language" sufficient as a basis to help create a sense of solidarity in a joint political framework?

On the basis of the answers to these questions, generalizations are made on the relationship between nation building as a conscious strategy and the purported power of language to encompass "the heart and soul" of a people.

The twenty-six case studies are divided into the following categories.

Countries with Candidates Competing for the National Language Title

The collective experiences of Israel, Norway, Ireland, and Malta all illustrate how problematic the issue of choosing a national language was and demonstrates the fragility of the quest for nationhood. The vision of national destiny that produced these modern states floundered over the question of their "proper" national language. The choice in each case was between the vernacular spoken by an overwhelming majority of the people versus a historic "prestigious" language which many scholars, poets, historians, and linguists believed embodied the "soul of the nation."

Multi-ethnic Countries with Bilingualism/Multilingualism

In Belgium, Canada, Spain, India and South Africa, the different official national languages all represent ethnic groups constituting a distinctive regional majority within a single state. These differences have often led to an administrative partition of the country and to increasing rivalry over such sensitive areas as the language of instruction in universities, special distinct commands within the army, and language legislation over road signs and even the labeling of food products. Switzerland nevertheless demonstrably proves that national unity may be achieved without a single national language and that each regionally and ethnically distinctive group has an equal share to represent the nation.

The Celtic "Pygmy Revivals" in the United Kingdom

In spite of the supposed universal appeal, popularity and undoubted utility of English as the leading international language, it is not enough to guarantee one a job of any importance in the local government and many nongovernmental organizations in Scotland and Wales. Monoglot speakers of English who are British citizens in the United Kingdom residing in Wales complain that their children (in Wales) may be forced to learn a "useless minority language" spoken almost in order to get a decent job in the public sector. In Scotland, a newfound appreciation of Gaelic has made itself felt in part through the newly established Scottish parliament and lends greater weight in asserting the country's distinctive identity.

Dialects or Languages? Italy and Scandinavia

The struggle for unification and the contrasting experiences of the Scandinavian states and their failure to unite in spite of mutually intelligible forms of speech contrasts sharply with the Italian experience of national unity in the face of mutually unintelligible dialects. This chapter will clarify the issues in determining usage of the terms "dialect" and "language." A close look at the national status of the various major Scandinavian languages (Swedish, Danish and Norwegian) reveals that their speakers are often able to understand each other yet nevertheless prefer to communicate in English, whereas many Italians learn a national language in order to communicate with each other. They cannot rely on making themselves understood outside their native region by speaking the language learned in their childhood and customarily spoken at home, which is very different from the standard Italian taught in the schools and used by literate people on a national level.

The Quarreling Cousins

These three sets of almost identical languages illustrate how political factors have become inseparable from linguistic evolution. State policy and government planning have encouraged a diversification between Czech and Slovak into separate languages, whereas they were originally very closely related dialects and mutually intelligible. The political divorce and separation of the two states (the Czech republic and Slovakia) have intensified the trend to further differentiate the two speech forms into separate languages. The same applies to Serbian and Croatian following the collapse of Yugoslavia. The use of separate alphabets (the Latin for Croatian and the Cyrillic for Serbian) always distinguished the two but hid their essential common origin.

The same occurred with Romanian and Moldavian. Aspirations to unite Moldavia with Romania in a "Greater Romania" have encouraged the tendencies to engineer a convergence of the two speech forms and the replacement of the Cyrillic alphabet with the Latin one for Moldavian. Russian too is considered the parent language of the two close variants of spoken Ukrainian and Byelorussian, which the czarist authorities regarded as "peasant dialects." Under the Soviet regime, some freedom to cultivate them as official languages of the two Soviet republics was granted, but their development as more than vehicles of folklore was not encouraged. Today, as independent states, the two countries are trying to eliminate what they consider "Russification."

Ethnic or Regional Minorities Using the "Wrong Language"

Several national disputes have resulted in relatively large minorities living on the "wrong side" of the border in terms of language. This has produced an anomalous situation where citizenship and language loyalty or utility have not necessarily coincided. The cases in this section run the gamut from patriotic French but bilingual Alsatians; a largely German-speaking but Danish-minded minority in South Schleswig; and a bilingual and bicultural population that is Finnish in citizenship but Swedish in ethnicity and that is further divided into two groups—those living in Finland proper (and by necessity Finnish speaking or bilingual) and a protected Swedish-speaking group living in the Åland islands. The most anomalous case is that of many Hebrew-speaking Arabs who are Israeli citizens and are more literate in Hebrew than Arabic but feel alienated from the Jewish state. The case of bilingual Hungarians who are Romanian citizens conforms to Von Herder's classic model of an identity between national sentiment and language.

Language Planning in a Buffer State

Like Belgium, Uruguay was established as a buffer state to avoid continual confrontations between the two major South American nations of Brazil and Argentina, near the strategic mouth of the La Plata River. With Uruguay divided almost equally into two language regions, the government at Montevideo sought to encourage the spread of Spanish into the entire national territory by a planned program of establishing Spanish language schools, extending the dominance of Montevideo and creating a sense of a shared culture with Argentina founded on common economic interests and both the Tango and Gaucho folklore.

In the Chains of the Past

In Greece until quite recently and in the greater part of the Arabic-speaking world, a dichotomy has existed between the popular vernacular spoken at home and the standard literary language based on the classical forms derived from the ancient Hellenic, pre–Byzantine Greek civilization of the old city-states of Athens and Sparta and from the Koran, respectively. The latter classical languages became the only acceptable forms of serious literature, higher education and even the press, creating a sense of remoteness that elevated these linguistic forms far above the spoken language of the masses. The struggle to end this divergence is a major issue in many Arab countries and is intimately linked with the political winds of Arab nationalism that have alternately blown in the direction of "Arab unity" and a cultivation of separate national identities. In Greece, the issue was resolved in favor of a modern *demotike* (popular or democratic) Greek as a result of the fall of the military dictatorship. Turkish too has undergone a major reform, eliminating the Persian and Arabic forms favored under the Ottoman regime. Many documents and works written before 1930 are barely intelligible today. These changes reflect the transition from a multiethnic empire united by Islam to a nation-state of the Turkish people.

The twenty-six case studies presented in this book do not represent the totality of states today, where the medium of discourse for large segments of the population is not identical with the proclaimed national language. They are simply those most familiar to an American audience and have a long historical development. It is essential to understand the origin and development of the political geography in each case to explain how the national language was selected or triumphed over rivals.

To Be Continued

The languages not covered could well be the subject for another book. These include Chinese in its written Mandarin form, which is universally understood as a written language, in the context of almost one-third of the Chinese population (mostly in the south and west of the country) speaking dialects so different from Mandarin that they are not mutually intelligible. More than a score of newly independent African states have adopted as their national language, the language of the former colonial master—English, French, Portuguese, Italian and Spanish. There are certainly additional cases of "quarreling cousins" (Austria versus Germany, Russia versus the Ukraine and White Russia)—multiethnic states that have chosen a language (English) which is not the mother tongue of a majority of the population (Singapore) and examples of a standard, written language amidst a host of spoken dialects (Indonesia and the Philippines). Many states in Latin America with large native populations, such as Mexico and Bolivia, are effectively bilingual and have recently acknowledged this reality.

PART I

Countries with Competing Candidates for the National Language

1

HEBREW VERSUS YIDDISH: THE CASE OF ISRAEL

Visitors to Israel today can scarcely believe or appreciate the enormous difficulties that were involved in the restoration of Hebrew as a living language. The Hebrew conflict with Yiddish in Palestine took three generations to resolve. Hebrew's triumph, which seems such a foregone conclusion today, was a tenacious struggle. It was greatly aided by the natural process of territorial concentration and emigration to Palestine by Jews who already were sympathetic to the revival of Hebrew as part of their Zionist beliefs but faced intense skepticism from critics who labeled it as "artificial" until the first group of children unselfconsciously played in Hebrew and expressed a full range of emotions without the assistance of another language.

Israel has succeeded in "reviving" an ancient language linking it to its historic past, a goal sought by other modern national movements—in Ireland and Norway—which have fallen far short of such success in spite of five generations of concerted effort. In the state of Israel, independence was recreated along with a cultural revival in the face of great odds and massive doubts as to the viability of both state and language. Even Theodore Herzl, the founder of the Zionist vision which launched the political efforts to create a Jewish state, skeptically asked in 1897, at the time of the First Zionist Congress, "Who among us can as much as ask for a train ticket in Hebrew?" His skepticism was shared by many European Jews, who felt that reviving the ancient language was an impossible task (or a profane, even sacrilegious, one).

In Herzl's romantic and utopian novel of a future idealized Jewish state, *Altneuland*, Jews are pictured as cosmopolitan, multilingual speakers of German and other major European languages. Neither Yiddish nor Hebrew is mentioned. One hundred and twenty years ago, there were ten million Yiddish-speaking Jews but none who were habitual, primary or native Hebrew speakers who had learned the language at home from their parents. For centuries, Hebrew had been used as a liturgical language of prayer and, on occasion, as the means of communication between educated Jews traveling abroad, whose native languages were unintelligible. It was in wide use both for religious commentary and also as an eminent, "high" language for philosophical, legal and even scientific texts by learned Jews who addressed themselves largely to a Jewish but not necessarily orthodox readership. The pioneer work of Eliezer Ben-Yehuda,[1] the individual most responsible for reviving Hebrew and adapting it to modern needs, to make it a spoken language, made its initial impact in Palestine in the late nineteenth century (Figure 1). His efforts were looked on as eccentric by most educated Jews living in the country and as a profane sacrilege by the ultraorthodox, for whom the language was reserved for God's word.

Figure 1. Members of the early Hebrew language committee. Ben Yehuda is at the far right.

Today, Hebrew is the everyday, spoken language of more than five million people including non–Jews (Arabs, Druze, Circassians) in the state of Israel and understood or read by at least another million people in the Diaspora. Its revival and adaptation to modern life deserve a comprehensive look before we examine the efforts of other nations who sought to duplicate this "miracle." The case of Hebrew's revival has been the subject of intense speculation and a model for efforts to encourage the learning of Irish, Norwegian, Basque, Catalán, and modern Greek

The Jewish "Hybrid Languages"

Although Hebrew ceased to be the spoken language of the majority of Jews in their Judean homeland between the second century B.C.E. and the second century C.E., it remained as the most important language of religious commentary and heavily influenced the various "hybrid" languages that arose in the Diaspora such as Yiddish (Judeo-German), Ladino (also called *Judezmo, Sephardi, Haketia* or *Judeo-Español*), *Catalánic* (Judeo-Catalán), *Yevanic* (Judeo-Greek), *Zarphatic* (Judeo-French), *Ebri* (Judeo-Persian), several varieties of Judeo-Arabic (including a specific Jewish Baghdadi dialect) and others, all of which used the Hebrew alphabet.

It is estimated that Hebrew words compose close to 15 percent of the Yiddish vocabulary and a somewhat lesser proportion of the other hybrids. Many Hebrew words absorbed by Yiddish indicate religious beliefs and abstractions. The Yiddish word usually has the stress on the first syllable and the characteristic diphthongs "aw," "ow" and "oy."

Original Hebrew	Yiddish	English
shabbát	shabbes	"Sabbath"
Yom tov	yontif	"a good day," "a holiday"
brit	Bris	"ritual circumcision"
mikve	mikveh	"ritual bath"
talít	tális	"prayer shawl"
zikarón	zikóren	"memory"
rachmanút	rachmones	"mercy"
chatán	chásan	"bridegroom"
milchamáh	milchúma	"war"
mishpachá	mishpúchah	"family"
kó-ach	koiych	"power"
mazál	mázal	"luck"

These Yiddish words are just a few of the most important of several hundred words of Hebrew origin that are used in modern Hebrew with a slightly different stress and the pronunciation of several sounds. Moreover, a parallel vocabulary developed in which words of Hebrew origin were used to specifically designate a concept, occupation, ceremony or item with specific Jewish content as opposed to a parallel word of German and Slavic origin in Yiddish to designate the same object or concept in use among non–Jews. Examples are *luakh* versus kalender ("calendar"), *katsef* versus fleysh-haker ("butcher"), *seyfer* versus bukh ("book"), *levaye* versus bagrebnis ("funeral"), *emes* versus Warheit ("truth") and *khokhme* versus Weisheit ("wisdom").

The Hebrew-Yiddish Rivalry

For a time, a lively rivalry existed between Hebrew and Yiddish and vied for the loyalty of several generations of literary figures, writers, playwrights and philosophers. In 1908, supporters boldly proclaimed Yiddish as "a Jewish national language" at a famous conference in

Czernowitz (Austria-Hungary) because they could always point to the fact that Yiddish was spoken by millions of Jews, whereas Hebrew was not a spoken vernacular but more of an experiment to breathe life into a moribund language incapable of meeting the demands of twentieth-century life.

Hebraists, on the other hand, laid claim to Hebrew as the Jewish national language in their congress in 1913 in Vienna, pointing out the superiority of its historical continuity, the immense prestige of the Bible, its influence upon much of European literature and its venerable age. By contrast, Yiddish was essentially regarded as a jargon or dialect. Early in the twentieth century, Yiddish speakers in Europe and among recent East European immigrants to the New World constituted a vast majority of the world's Jewish population. The largest Jewish socialist party in Poland, the Bund, cultivated an independent Yiddish culture and most Jewish emigrants to Palestine until the 1930s were native Yiddish speakers.

Many individuals who possessed a love for both languages experienced a soul-wrenching dilemma over the necessity of choosing sides in the increasingly polarized atmosphere of the new society being built in "Eretz-Yisrael" (Palestine). "I realized the revolutionary nature of Hebrew literature as opposed to Yiddish.... We had to betray Yiddish, even though we paid for this as for any betrayal," wrote Rachel Katznelson, wife of Israel's future President Zalman Ben-Shazar.

For many committed Zionists, even those who grew up with Yiddish as their first language, there was a conscious identification of the language as a mode of ghetto Diaspora existence that Zionism sought to eradicate. The choice of the Sephardi (descendants of the Spanish-Portuguese exiles) pronunciation, with its stress on the final syllable and its avoidance of the vowel combinations of "aw" and "oy," so prevalent in Yiddish pronunciation, was regarded as part of this rejection of European Jewish folkways. Ze'ev Jabotinsky was not atypical in his categorical rejection of Yiddish bordering on hatred when he attacked the very intonation of Yiddish with its "sing-song melody." He proclaimed, "Do not sing while you speak. This ugliness is infinitely worse than every other defect ... and regrettably, it is taking root in our life. Both the school and the stage are guilty; the first, out of sloppiness, the latter out of an intention to 'revive' for us the ghetto and its whining. The tune of the ghetto is ugly not only because of its weeping tone which stirs unpleasant memories in us: it is also ugly objectively, ugly in the scientific sense—ugly as all superfluous or exaggerated efforts.... That sick frenzy, which we also suffer from in our social life, is also the result of the Diaspora—an abundance of forces with no field and no outlet for the repressed storm except to explode in a bowl of soup."[2]

The Yiddish Counterattack

Detractors of Hebrew who ridiculed "modern Hebrew" also mocked the halting Hebrew speech of native Yiddish speakers who were unable to converse freely and the obviously stilted character of Hebrew novels that attempted to portray real conversations in a language that was not yet the vernacular of a community outside the struggling Zionist colonies in remote, backward Palestine. Several Yiddish spokesmen who were critical of Hebrew compared it to the artificial character of Esperanto[3] when both languages were still in their infancy. Ahad Ha-Am (the Hebrew pen name meaning "one of the people" adopted by Asher Ginsberg), an accomplished writer in Hebrew, was one of the leading figures to argue for a "spiritual Zionism" designed to bring about a modern, cultural renaissance of the Jewish people and an accommodation with modern civilization as a necessary preparation for large-scale settlement in Palestine.

His objective evaluation of the difficulties involved in turning Hebrew into a spoken language was repeated by many other visitors to Palestine before its acceptance by the British mandatory authorities in 1921 as one of the country's three official languages (along with Arabic and English) and the founding of the Hebrew University in 1922, which immediately made the world aware that Hebrew indeed had reached a level of maturity as a modern tongue and could function as a language of research and scientific investigation. In 1893, he wrote: "He who hears how the teachers and the students stammer, for lack of words and expressions, will immediately realize that such 'speech' cannot evoke in the speaker's or the listener's heart any respect or love for the limited language, and the child's young mind feels even stronger the artificial chains imposed on it by the Hebrew speech."[4]

Yiddish as the Authentic "Mame Loshen" (Mother Tongue)

Supporters of Yiddish seized on these inevitable shortcomings in the early days of Hebrew's rebirth to argue that only Yiddish reflected a distinctly Jewish social environment that could be recreated in Palestine. In fact, one segment of the Zionist political movement—the leftwing socialist "Poalei Zion" (Workers of Zion)—maintained an active stance in favor of using Yiddish alongside Hebrew during a long interval during which the new Hebrew could slowly mature. Non- or anti–Zionists and the ultraorthodox throughout the world were hostile to the notion that Hebrew could be successfully transformed into a vehicle of modern communication and cultural creativity.

The argument repeated by fervent Yiddishists was that Yiddish was the natural vehicle of expression for millions of Jews who had learned it at home, were fluent in it and had already elevated it into a literary language capable of fully expressing all the needs and desires of an entire people. It was in their view a true "mother tongue "(Mama Loshen) and capable of a warmth of expression and intimacy which Hebrew could not hope to achieve, being an imposed, "devised" language learned by most people as adults rather than as children. Moreover, several generations of Yiddish authors had raised the status of the language in the eyes of the world. At the First Yiddish Language Conference in Czernovitz (or Tshernovitz) in Galicia in Austrian-ruled Poland in 1908, Nathan Birnbaum[5] in the opening address had this to say:

> Think for example of the movement for the Yiddish language. It began decades ago. At that time, there awoke the question in certain minds: why is it that when other nations jumble several languages together and derive from this melange a separate tongue with its unique soul, it is accorded the legitimacy of a separate language and the due respect of the nations?... The nationalist intellectual must not only be bound closely by ties of the heart and will to his people but must, first of all, live in their midst. He must breathe the same cultural atmosphere, and his spiritual life must grow out of the folk-soil. Furthermore, he must be able to infuse into it the simple and unpretentious strength of the people. It never entered his mind that to speak any language other than his very own—the language of his people, the language of their innermost thoughts and feelings of joys and sorrow, of tears and of laughter—is tantamount to leaving his people and going off into the desert-wilderness without a friend or mentor, to follow the winding road into a chaotic world, to turn oneself into a rambler, a lost wanderer, torn from home and nationality.
> ...Slowly there blossomed forth intellectuals who viewed Yiddish with a brighter and newer vision than their predecessors. They were seized by the powerful feeling that this language is the very soul of our people—its very heart, the very center of our life.... Let us shed the garments of shame in which our language is swaddled—with which our weak and sickly Yiddishkeit [Jewishness] has permitted it to be clothed—and our people will once more shine forth and bask in the warm glow of a long neglected self-respect.

This was not only a spirited defense of Yiddish, an attack on assimilation and Jewish self-hate but also a dismissal of Hebrew and its supporters as "lost wanderers" turning themselves into "ramblers," "torn from home and nationality" and going off to the desert wilderness. Cartoons in the Jewish press in Europe and America frequently portrayed Yiddish as a modern, fashion-conscious, up-to-date "flapper" with the latest hairstyle and short skirt and Hebrew as a distinguished dowdy, plump, remote and somewhat eccentric, elegant dowager. Remarkably the images today are the reverse.

"Turning the Clock Backward"

Critics of Zionism pointed to the apparent absurdity of "trying to turn back the clock" to an eccentric recreation of an extinct culture thousands of years old. The same claim was often made against attempts to save and then revive the extinct Baltic languages in Lithuania, Latvia and Estonia. It was considered nonsense to struggle to learn an ancient language and try to make up for the loss of two thousand years of development. These arguments were partially correct but ignored the reality of the multilingual Palestinian society with its substantial Sephardi, or Middle Eastern, Jewish population. Not only were Turkish and Arabic of prime importance in the revived Jewish homeland, but competing Zionist agencies encouraged the use of French, Russian and German. Moreover, the enormous and continually growing American Jewish population was in the process of rapidly giving up Yiddish and fully embracing English.

Yiddish progressively lost strength through assimilation in Europe and America with continued Jewish emigration from Poland and Russia, while Hebrew grew in power and prestige due to territorial concentration through migration (*aliya*) to mandatory Palestine and then Israel. Yiddish reflected the folkways and religious life of the mass of European Jews, but Zionists correctly foresaw that Yiddish could never achieve the status of a national language linked to a specific territory or independent state anywhere and would suffer an inevitable decline even though it had brilliantly met the requirements of sophisticated urban life and modern literature. As late as 1978, Yiddish could boast a Nobel Prize winner in the field of literature (Isaac Bashevis Singer, whose works have been translated into dozens of languages), but the Holocaust and assimilation have dealt it a mortal blow.

In Palestine the rivalry of the languages reached a fever pitch in the late twenties and early thirties. The arrival of tens of thousands of German-speaking Jews from Germany and Austria following the Nazi assumption of power radically changed the balance of the language controversy in Palestine. The new emigrants who had been proud of their fluency in German and had always looked down upon Yiddish as the jargon of east European Jews became enthusiastic converts to identifying with the Zionist cause and the Hebrew language.

It also became increasingly clear that most Jewish immigrants from all backgrounds had at least a basic, reading knowledge of Hebrew as the result of their early religious training. For speakers of Arabic, the transition was even easier, as the two languages have many structural similarities and many almost identical words for the members of the family, organs and parts of the body, the numbers and natural phenomena. In the first few years of Israel's independence, the Jewish population tripled, and it is likely that no other language could have functioned so well as both a means to cultivate a sense of national solidarity and elicit a basic recognition among all Jews. The great diversity of languages spoken by new immigrants made the need for a lingua franca greater than anywhere else.

Hebrew's Struggle as a Minor Language, in Jabotinsky's View

One of the greatest difficulties in persuading secular Jews to adopt the Zionist view of Jewish nationalism was the call for a return to the historical language, along with land, the two crucial elements missing in other varieties of Jewish nationalism. Both were provincial backwaters, removed from the mainstream of modern European civilization in the mid-nineteenth century. By the latter part of the nineteenth century, many Jews in Western Europe and the United States had already abandoned Yiddish and learned the national language of their adopted homelands. Yiddish, Hebrew or any of the minor languages, such as Hungarian, Polish, Czech, Slovenian, Latvian, Lithuanian, and Romanian among many others that began to undergo a cultural renaissance tied to modern nationalist movements within the great German, Austrian and Russian empires, were initially regarded by many intellectuals as "peasant languages." They had been continually declining and unable to compete with the great cosmopolitan tongues of Europe. The same was true in the British Isles with respect to Welsh and Irish-Gaelic, in France in the case of Breton and Corsican, in Spain vis-à-vis Catalán, Basque and Galician and in Belgium regarding Flemish.

Ze'ev Jabotinsky, one of the most significant figures in the Zionist movement, was a brilliant Hebrew and Russian poet, a great orator in Yiddish, Hebrew and Russian, essayist and translator from Russian, Italian, Yiddish and English as well as the intellectual founder of the revisionist movement, which opposed the approach of labor/socialist Zionists to create a Jewish state. He was a far-sighted, eloquent spokesman for the need to merge a Hebrew nationality with Hebrew culture. Jabotinsky had observed first hand the renaissance of Latvian and its successful transformation into the language of the new Latvian republic following World War I. He described Latvia as "an oasis," rejecting narrow provincial nationalism, open to the great heritage of European culture which had reshaped its language to become more expressive of the modern world without deviating from its own unique characteristics.

In November, 1930, the Hebrew newspaper *Doar ha Yom* ("Post of the day") published an account of his travels under the title *Prakim meSe-*

fer HaNisiyot—"Chapters from the Book of Travels." During a trip to Belgium in July, 1932, Jabotinsky spoke in Flemish to a large audience in Antwerp on the subject of "The Flemish Language and Jewish Nationalism," which amazed his Jewish followers in that country, who, even in Flanders, regarded French as the natural, preferred language of "higher culture." Jabotinsky had this to say about "minor languages" and "small states."

> The world does not like small states. From time to time when one of the large European newspapers recalls one of the small states, especially those which were created after the World War, ... the writer frowns with disapproval as if to say.... "Why has the world become Balkanized?" Or else the writer takes on a stern cast and demonstrates that the small states "cannot exist." Reference is made to the fact that when these states were previously regions within one of the large states, they had a natural hinterland which is now lacking.
>
> I guess I have a different disposition: I love the small states. If I were to create the world, I would turn the large kingdoms into independent tiny states. In all probability if I live to see a Hebrew state created in my lifetime, I would immediately create a separatist movement in Upper Galilee. I would myself settle in Safed and pronounce the letter bet with a distinctive sound ... "tob" (instead of the Hebrew word for good—"tov")....
>
> My faith in the small states has something to do with this philosophy: The more capitals—the more culture. Make any place into a capital and it will actually turn into a capital from a psychological point of view. I remember Kovna, Riga and Reval (modern Tallin)[6] before the war. Their inhabitants complained of the boredom ... but an objective tourist can see the difference. Before there was nothing to explore in these towns, there was nothing to inquire about. Today, each one of them is a laboratory of innumerable creative experiments. They are creating one of God's great miracles—the nationalities.

The Jewish Predilection for the "Great Cultural Languages"

Jabotinsky was regarded by many even within the Zionist movement as an eccentric, but no other Jewish leader was more aware of the real threat of the approaching Holocaust and the urgent need to bring massive Jewish immigration to Palestine in a rescue operation. He was also a great Hebrew literary figure who rendered into the language some of the greatest masterpieces of world literature,[7] and his views on the close association of nationality and language made him much more sympathetic to the nationalism of the small nations, which Jews had traditionally looked on with suspicion and disapproval.

Very few Jews had Jabotinsky's insight. Ignorance of each other's languages was in itself regrettable, but the lack of a Jewish homeland and an indigenous modern culture encouraged many Jews to seek out the cosmopolitan "great cultures" of Europe through French, Russian and German as avenues for enlightenment, education and career progress for themselves and their children. Jews, Balts and Poles, attempting to penetrate the urban middle class, adopted Russian and German in the hope of personal advancement and assimilation to the great cultures. Although Zionism and Hebrew culture became popular, the overwhelming majority of Jews in the Baltic region were unable to sympathize with the growing movements for Lithuanian, Latvian and Estonian independence and the cultural reawakening of the Baltic peoples in spite of the similarities in their national movements.

As little as 3 percent of Jewish elementary school students in interwar Latvia studied in Latvian language schools, compared to 12 percent in German language schools, over 50 percent in Russian ones and only 33 percent in Yiddish or Hebrew schools as part of an autonomous, Jewish educational system.[8] These developments were ironic. The reborn Lithuanian government, in need of Jewish support during the negotiations leading to the Versailles treaty, provided a measure of national autonomy for the Jewish minority which even guaranteed it its own educational system in Hebrew and/or Yiddish. The Jewish community was recognized as a legal institution with the right to legislate binding ordinances, and all Jews were subject to the decisions of the Jewish National Council (*Va'ad Ha'Aretz*).

The Zionist minister of Jewish affairs in the Lithuanian government, Max Soloveichik, expressed the view that Jewish national autonomy was a form of rehearsal for a Jewish state. This measure of recognition of the Jews as a "national minority" (rather than a religious one) was a major step on the road to achieve eventual recognition of a Jewish state. The ministry of Jewish affairs was abolished in 1924. The ostensible reason given was internal bickering between supporters of Hebrew and Yiddish, but a more fundamental cause was the dissatisfaction of Lithuanian nationalists, who regarded such minority rights as divisive. Although Jews were initially viewed in a more favorable light than the powerful minorities of Russians, Poles and Germans, backed by large hostile powers, Jewish economic preeminence, especially in commerce and retail trade, aggravated tensions.

The following quote from an anthology in Hebrew of Lithuanian literature used in Lithuanian Jewish schools[9] summarizes Jewish cultural achievement, piety and attachment to a common homeland but laments the lack of Jewish appreciation and understanding for the rebirth of the local Baltic cultures:

> There is a small nation in the North of the world which has distinguished itself by hospitality and an honest human relationship with the remote

People of the Diaspora during centuries—the Lithuanian Nation. Its land has served us for generations as a storage place for the Torah, for wisdom and for the spirit of Israel. Here, we have lived for hundreds of years, here we have created an original Hebrew culture, here our essence struck deep roots in the soil and here we adapted a second Mother Jerusalem—"Yerushalayim d'Lita" [Jerusalem of Lithuania—Vilnius]. Here the study of the Torah flourished, here Yeshivot prospered and bloomed, here lived the "Gaon"[10] and our great rabbis. Here the cradle of our new literature stood, here lived our writers, here arose the new leaders of a renewed nation and here at the same time the living Hebrew language found a home and a network of schools brought forth a healthy living youth whose example one can only find in the Land of Israel. But behold, in spite of this, the literature of this people [Lithuania] is locked for us with seven seals and entirely unknown to the Hebrew People."

The Hebrew Link between Ancient Israel and Modern Nationalism

In Israel, an extreme form of a new Hebrew nationalism ultimately rejected a continuing link with Judaism and the dispersed Jewish people. It rejected Yiddish and regarded the two-thousand-year-old history of the Diaspora as an endless tragedy. It strove to develop modern forms of a national culture based on Hebrew—music, song, dance, literature, all distinctively and nationally "Hebrew" rather than religiously "Jewish."

As dissatisfaction with the British mandate grew, a clandestine underground emerged and began to contest the official Zionist leadership. The so-called dissident movements made more and more use of the term "Hebrew" (*Ivri*) as an adjective to characterize a native-born attachment to the soil and disaffection with the traditionally Jewish traits of seeking compromise and avoiding violence. Through the American-based "Hebrew Committee for National Liberation," active but clandestine support was provided to the uprising in Palestine of the Jewish underground dissident groups in Palestine—the *Irgun* and *Lehi* (Stern Gang)."[11]

The noted Israeli author Amos Kenan gave poetic expression to this link between Hebrew and ancient Israel. In an article titled "Envy Tyre" in the Israeli Hebrew daily *Yediot Ah'ronot* (June 18, 1982), he wrote:

> I always had an attraction to this wonderful phenomenon called Tyre and Sidon, and as one who was born on the sands of the coastal lowland, I feel a closeness to all that was, is and will be on the Eastern shore of the Mediterranean which I am a part of, and which is a part of me. The Hebrew language which is my language today was 4,000 and 3,000 and 2,500 years ago the language spoken in Jerusalem and Tyre, in Shchem [modern Nablus] and Sidon, in Jaffa and Ugarit ... and in

Carthage. Tyre and Sidon and Jerusalem were two axes of one culture ... the spiritual one in Jerusalem and the material one of Carthage. In those days when the prophets of Israel tried to create a universal code of morality, the seamen of Tyre established their colonies.... Why shouldn't we feel a sense of pride in our proximity to that ancient contemporary of ours who stamped his image on the area, gave to the world writing, and once sent his elephants across the Alps under Hannibal's leadership and momentarily brought mighty Rome itself in danger of destruction.

The Creation of a Base Society of Hebrew Speakers

Hebrew's amazing success has been paralleled on a smaller scale only by the relative success of Esperanto, the only devised language to emerge within a generation of its appearance as the idiom of a dispersed, nonethnic, nonterritorial but functioning community able to use the language in many walks of life and with its own literature. When Eliezer Ben-Yehuda began his work, Hebrew lacked much of the simplest vocabulary necessary to deal with many domains and the needs of modern society and technology.

The problems were not simply those of a lack of new words but also of modes of speech to express spontaneous emotions or reflective thoughts and moods. There is one essential requirement that Hebrew (and Esperanto) needed to grow and survive and without which their fate would have been similar to those of thousands of other intellectual designs of invented languages that never got beyond the laboratory stage. This requirement is what Benjamin Harshav[12] calls "a base society" or "the social existence of the language"—that is, a community of a sufficient number of speakers for whom the language is the essential tool of communication and information in all areas of human experience, throughout every social and institutional situation—"the bureaucracy, the universities, the slums and the hospitals, the highways and the cinemas, the tanks and the airplanes."[13]

Through continued territorial concentration in Palestine and their dispersal throughout every sector of the economy and society, Hebrew speakers were able to create and mutually agree upon the vocabulary, pronunciation and, to a lesser degree, spelling forms[14] appropriate for a modern spoken and written Hebrew as the language of all its informational networks. Only when children who were educated in Hebrew schools began to hear Hebrew spoken by adults in such roles as policemen, shopkeepers, soldiers, lifeguards, government clerks, and postal workers rather than only by their own parents or their formal teachers in school could they begin to imitate and even invent Hebrew words and expressions that seemed natural to them.

The proof of this can be seen in the way almost all children of new immigrants begin to learn their new language. In early Jewish Palestine, children could not initially imitate native peers since other children were also speakers of non–Hebrew languages, but they could aspire to imitate desirable authority figures and role models in adult society.

Harshav recounts an anecdotal incident showing how difficult the transition was for the first generation of Hebrew-speaking children to adopt a natural unstilted Hebrew to mirror their world. The American Yiddish poet Yoash visited one of the early Zionist settlements in 1913 and was impressed to hear teenage girls playing and making use only of Hebrew, yet when one was asked the name of flowers in her own garden, she replied, "Flowers don't have names."[15] It would take another generation and the achievement of Israeli independence for Hebrew to catch up on the backlog of essential vocabulary in all the diverse fields of flora, fauna, medical, technical, artistic and scientific terminology and be part of the lexicon of educated speakers.

The Importance of the Hebrew Schools, Radio and Press

Perhaps the most critical early achievement that enabled Hebrew speakers to surmount a major obstacle was the ability of Hebrew highschool graduates in Palestine, for whom Hebrew had become their second language (the language predominantly used outside the home), to marry and then raise their children in an all–Hebrew-speaking environment. This began to happen sometime between 1905 and 1915. This served to establish a new Hebrew-reading and -speaking base society."[16]

Even before Eliezer Ben-Yehuda arrived in Palestine, a Hebrew language press had begun as a weekly journal of information in Jerusalem. *Halevanon* ("The Lebanon") and *Hahavatzelet* ("The Lily") began publication just a few months apart in 1863 in Jerusalem. Both employed a very stilted form of Hebrew with countless new words invented by the editors, who imitated French, German, or Russian words for modern concepts. Both competed for a limited readership and were not averse to maligning their opponent before the Turkish authorities, who eventually closed both of them down.

Although originally established to serve as a mouthpiece for the devout hassidic movement, *Hahavatzelet* reappeared under a more worldly and progressive editor, Israel Dov Frumkin, who launched a campaign against the system of religious philanthropy from abroad, on which most Jewish residents of Jerusalem depended, and also defended the interests of poor Jewish immigrants from Yemen, who were badly treated by the established Ashkenazi (European) community.

Ben-Yehuda had contributed articles to *Hahavatzelet* from Paris and joined the staff of the newspaper in 1882. He remained with it until able to establish his own weekly *HaZvi* ("The Deer"), which propounded his linguistic innovations and took a secular view of world affairs. The paper reached Jews throughout Palestine, who began to see that it was indeed possible to use Hebrew as a modern vehicle of communications.

In 1904, Ben-Yehuda began a biweekly paper, *Hashkafah* ("Outlook"), which posed a challenge to the newly arrived and committed socialist–Zionists, for whom Ben-Yehuda and the financial support he received from Baron Edmond de Rothschild represented their ideological enemy. Several new weeklies were established during the wave of new socialist–Zionist immigrants from Russia, and by 1910, Hebrew readership had expanded enough to justify a Hebrew daily—*Ha'Or* ("The Light"), edited by Ben-Yehuda's son, Itamar Ben-Avi.

Immediately after World War I, due to official recognition of Hebrew as the language of the Jewish community and Zionist institutions, renewed immigration, a stability and prosperity fostered by more secure British rule, the basis was laid for several new newspapers in Tel-Aviv, which rapidly overtook Jerusalem as the center of the more secular Hebrew reading public. This period saw the founding of several of Israel's most popular newspapers, which have continued to the present day, including *HaAretz* ("The Land"), a non–party-affiliated newspaper in 1923. The much increased immigration, especially from Germany in the 1930s, and the establishment of the state of Israel in 1948 encouraged more than a dozen new political and independent Hebrew newspapers,[17] making Israel one of the most journalistically competitive countries in the world with a free, dynamic press. New immigrants often relied on a foreign language press in a variety of European languages, especially Yiddish, Polish, Hungarian, German and Romanian, but these have barely eked out an existence and are all on the verge of folding.

Some new immigrants made the transition to full literacy by first reading *HaMatĥil* ("The Beginner"), a fully vowelled (*nikud*) newspaper encouraged by teachers during the period of government and kibbutz-sponsored intensive Hebrew courses in live-in facilities (*ulpanim*). Israelis have always been fond of saying that Hebrew is the only language that "the children teach their parents," and this theme became a popular motif in many propaganda posters (Figure 2). Radio broadcasts in the new spoken standard modeling proper pronunciation became a feature of the Hebrew language broadcasts avidly listened to during the Mandatory period (Figure 3).

Figure 2. Poster encouraging parents to lean Hebrew from their children.

Hebrew's Powerful Word-Derivation Mechanisms

The inherent mechanisms for word formation in the Hebrew language have played a brilliant role in enabling linguists to draw upon indigenous sources for the necessary vocabulary to adapt the language to meet modern needs, This has been done in such a clever and convincing way that it would be no exaggeration to say that if we could resurrect some of the Biblical prophets and give them today's Hebrew newspapers, they would be able to discern the root concept and make a good guess at the meanings of many words which they had never seen before and indeed had not existed until modern times.

Figure 3. Israeli stamp honoring Kol Yisrael (Israel Broadcast Authority).

Hebrew and other Semitic languages have a vocabulary "skeleton," represented by three (originally two) consonantal, root letters from which words of related meaning are formed. This means that words with similar meanings look alike—a factor which makes the acquisition of a large vocabulary relatively easy in Hebrew and which has been copied as the basic principle of word formation in Esperanto. For example, the root letters S (*samech*), P or F (*peh* or *feh*; the exact pronunciation depends on the preceding vowel[18]), and R (*resh*) mean "to count or tell a story, to relate." The change between the letters F and P is related to euphony but is not critical since the letters are identical in the unvowelled Hebrew alphabet. This S-F-R (or S-P-R) combination is readily apparent in such words as these:

SeFeR = book
SiPuR = story
SoFeR = one who writes or tells a story
SiFRiyah = library (collection of books)
SiFRut = literature (i.e. collection of the finest stories)

The ability of Ben-Yehuda and other linguists to coin new words from the scant vocabulary stock of the Bible and the Talmud derives from

1. Hebrew versus Yiddish

this skeleton basis and the use of prefixes, suffixes and infixes that still retain the original, consonantal root letters. For example, how was the modern word for "train" derived? The word is "rakevet," and the root letters R-K-V are found in the ancient verb "to ride" (RoCHeV) or the ancient word for chariot (meRKaVa). Here, too, the rules of euphony and the preceding vowel determine whether the middle letter is sounded as K or a guttural CH. The ending "-et" is found in many ancient Hebrew words indicating an object.

Other modern languages, including French and German, were also used as models for new words. For example the modern Hebrew word for newspaper follows the German construction of *zeitung*—drawn from *zeit* ("time"). The new Hebrew vocabulary constructed *iton* from the root for time (et) and the common ending "-on," used to indicate "a thing comprising the concept rendered in the noun." For example, from the word *millah* ("word"), Ben-Yehuda derived *millon*. This is the modern Hebrew word for "dictionary" instead of the previous *sefer-millim* (literally, "book of words"), an earlier attempt to create a compound word similar to the German *Wörterbuch*. Likewise *sha'on* ("watch") was coined from the root for the word meaning "hour" or "time"—*sha'ah*—that appears in the Bible and *aviron* ("airplane") from the Biblical word for "air" (*avir*). Other words were coined by the prefix indicated by the Hebrew letter *mem* (M), which has a causative function in grammar. For the modern word for "camera," the Hebrew root TZ-L-M was chosen, meaning "image," and thus we take photos (TZiLuMim) with a *maT-ZLeMa*; *liTZaLeM* is the verb "to photograph."

Many compound words were copied directly from French (*pommes de terre*) "apples of the earth," duplicated in Hebrew by *tapuchei-adamah* and German *Gan-Yeladim* ("kindergarten"), literally, "Garden of the Children" and many similar constructs provided the format which Hebrew copied. Ben-Yehuda knew Arabic and Persian well, languages that had coexisted with Hebrew and Aramaic and sometimes provided an essential root which could be transferred to Hebrew and then serve as the basis for newly derived words. In modern Hebrew, close contact with Palestinian Arabic and the English of the mandatory regime provide Hebrew with a fertile source of slang and swear words.[19]

The trend to "Hebraize" new words was carried to an extreme by linguists and the official Academy of the Hebrew Language imitating Ben-Yehuda, who proposed constructs derived from Hebrew roots for such widely accepted international words as "radio" and "telephone." These never took hold and were removed from dictionaries after a decade or two, but a surprising number have been accepted, even if the essential, consonantal root letters had to be expanded to four. In the end, it was always popular usage as determined by the majority of speakers, not

30   I. Countries with Competing Candidates

decisions of the academy, that became integrated into the modern language. One of the few survivors of this early period of Hebraization is the Hebrew word for cinema (or movies). It began as *rieh-noa* ("moving sight") and subsequently changed to *kolnoa* ("moving sound") after the introduction of the "talkies."

The same occurred with the Hebrew word for "computer." Israel was one of the first countries to make use of computers in the 1960s, when the word had not yet acquired international acceptance. It was named *maĤSHeV*, based on the root Ĥ-SH-V, "to think." Recently, however, a reverse trend has become evident.

The Twin Sources: Native and "Loazi"

Israel's national language is in danger. Internationally based words, immediately recognizable to a foreign audience, are edging out long-established Hebrew equivalents that were in common use before independence and generally contain the recognizable three-letter, consonantal roots. The following list is by no means exhaustive. It appears that this trend is increasing. "Sociolects" (words characteristically employed by a distinct, socioeconomic level of society) with reverse snob appeal are gaining ground. This is exactly the opposite of the situation that prevailed during the Hebrew renaissance, when new words of Hebrew (or Arabic or Persian, as indigenous to the Middle East) origin were coined and the public was encouraged to use them instead of the internationally recognized words that have German or Russian suffixes. An English, German, Russian or Yiddish speaker without any knowledge of Hebrew can easily make out the "loazi" words in the left-hand column.[20]

Modern words of loazi origin (foreign origin, or "loazi")	Words based on indigenous Hebrew roots
aggresivi	tokpani
addict	mimukar
adminsitratzia	minhal
adeptazia	histaglut
alternativa	ḥalufa
breksim	blamim
illuzia	ashlaya
illustratzia	iyur
immunizatzia	ḥisun
impulsivi	ḥapizut
improvizatzia	iltur
introvert	mufnam
infekzia	zihum
ekskluzivi	yiḥudi
baby sitter	shomer taf
blondinit	tsahavonit

1. Hebrew versus Yiddish 31

Modern words of loazi origin (foreign origin, or "loazi")	*Words based on indigenous Hebrew roots*
dokumentaztiya	tiud
dinami	nimratz
diagnozis	avĥana
defektivi	lakui
helikopter	masok
tolerantzia	sovlanut
terminal	masof
model	degem
mikrob	ĥaydak
stock	milai
standard	teken
sindrome	tismonet
selektziya	biĥira
funktzia	tifkud
piston	buchna
progressivi	mitkadem
proyekt	mivtza
komunikatziya	tikshoret
koordinatzia	tiyum
kompressor	madĥase
kontekts	heksher
radiator	makren
retsept	matkon
situatzia	matzav

Better Hebrew Usage, a standard text by Dr. Reuben Silvan, published in 1969, lists well over 700 such pairs of words. Today, the number has grown substantially, to at least twice that. A generation ago, the Hebrew press catered to a veteran, Hebrew-speaking and literate population, familiar with the root structure of the language and its mechanisms for word derivation. This made it easy for those with a firm grasp of the language to recognize the new words based on the Hebrew letters forming the basic root concept, and they could often venture a correct guess as to the exact meaning of the new word.

Today, many readers who have a minimal grasp of the language and are not familiar with the written language can much more easily relate to the words of foreign origin. This explains their growing usage not only in the popular press, comic books and cheap novels but also among politicians who cater to the "lowest common denominator" in their speeches. Probably a reader without any previous knowledge of Hebrew can guess the meaning of the words in the left-hand column. An ironic concomitant of this situation is the growing difficulty of educated, native Hebrew speakers who frequently come across new coinages in newspaper headlines that are totally unrecognizable at first glance. This is because these readers are still "programmed" to recognize the Hebrew root letters forming the basic meanings of words until it dawns on them that the new word is simply the writer's attempt to spell an English word with Hebrew letters. For example, when Israel adopted various aspects of the American electoral system such as primaries, no attempt was made to Hebraize the term.

The words most subject to this loazi trend are within the areas of technology, medicine, automobiles, teenage culture and computers, where there is already a substantial similarity in the vocabulary of most European languages. Many of them are spelled with a variety of weak consonant letters (*aleph, he* and *yod*) functioning as vowels, as in Yiddish. Their ungainly appearance is immediately recognized by an educated Hebrew readership as foreign in origin.

The Soviet Zion in Birobidzhan and the Role of Yiddish as a Jewish National Language

Due to the fact that Israel served as the focal point of Zionist efforts to "ingather the exiles" to create a Jewish homeland, it is also necessary to examine the competition between Hebrew and Yiddish, its major competitor on a global scale. According to Marxist theory on the "national question," small peripheral and marginal ethnic groups were simply anachronistic remnants of the previous, precapitalist economic system. They are thus destined to be completely assimilated within the integration of a worldwide proletariat linked by class solidarity and absorbed within the larger nations. The "backward or "quaint" peoples in remote areas would, according to the Marxist theory, soon lose their distinctiveness in speech and dress and be brought into a much closer relationship with the national capitals of the states they lived in. Each mile of railroad track and telegraph wire was destined to integrate these groups into larger frameworks and encourage the rapid adoption of the national languages, standards of speech, literacy, dress and folkways.

The peoples then considered on the way to complete assimilation include the very same nationalities that have witnessed a rebirth of intense national consciousness and territorial loyalty, such as the Jews, Basques, Welsh, Slovaks, Croats, Slovenians, Catalonians, Galicians, Corsicans, Lithuanians, Latvians, Estonians, Moldavians, Ukrainians, White Russians, Georgians and French Canadians. The Jews, because of their "fossil-like" existence (a nonterritorial historical remnant of the ancient world that had lost the identifying characteristics of a common territory and language), particularly vexed both Marx and Lenin. In fact, their theories about the disappearance of minor provincial ethnic groups could be put to a litmus test.

The Jews, lacking a territory, more literate and urban dwelling and more ready, willing and able to participate in the new capitalist economy than the other minorities should "wither away" first according to those theories. The fact that they did not so antagonized Marx that he wrote a vicious attack on the persistence of Jewish identity—*World without Jews*. The new regime, however, was uncertain what policy to adopt with regard to the Jewish minority, among whom many had emigrated from czarist Russia in record numbers to escape persecution, discrimination and religious intolerance. Although many Jews initially welcomed the fall of the czarist regime, their place in the new society was subject to contradictions. The great majority of Jews in the rural areas of the Ukraine and White Russia were still speakers of Yiddish[21] and included many skilled craftsmen, simple unskilled workers and farmers, petty merchants and shopkeepers. As late as 1937, the USSR issued postage stamps representing the flags, nationalities and their respective languages of all of the Soviet republics. The stamp representing Byelorussia (White Russia) bears the slogan "Workers of the World, Unite" in Byelorussian, Russian, Polish and Yiddish (Figure 4). This set of stamps with the motif was reissued in 1948, but the Yiddish inscription was then omitted.

Figure 4. Soviet postage stamps featuring the coat of arms of the Byelorussian Republic with the inscription "Workers of the World, Unite!" In the 1937 stamp on the left, the slogan appears in the republic's four official languages of Byelorussian, Russian, Polish and Yiddish (at the lower left). On the right, the 1948 stamp has omitted the Yiddish and Polish inscriptions to reflect the changing party line.

The appeal of Zionism in its secular and even socialist form exercised an immense appeal on the popular consciousness of the Jewish masses, and by 1928 the regime decided to confront this challenge to the loyalty and integration of the Jewish minority by fully recognizing a Jewish national identity based on Yiddish. It was located in a strategic area of Soviet interest in the Far East. At that time over 70 percent of Soviet Jews indicated Yiddish as their mother tongue. The chosen area of the Amur River valley near Manchuria would also prevent Japanese expansion. The Jewish autonomous *Oblast* ("district") was officially inaugurated in 1934, and Soviet President Kalinin stated that it would achieve recognition as a Soviet republic when it reached a population of 100,000.

From the Soviet point of view, the remote location of the intended Jewish autonomous republic would provide a new society for Jews, moving them far away from their earlier environment with its traditional religious influences, garner sympathy from secular Yiddish-speaking Jews throughout the Diaspora and aid in the movement to make the Jewish economic profile more productive in areas such as agriculture and industry. As late as 1939, more than 125,000 Jews were still engaged in agriculture in the USSR, but only a tiny minority of these were motivated to settle in Birobidzhan, an extremely inhospitable, subarctic region with a severe climate and poor soils. Soviet propaganda even duplicated much of the Zionist argument about the need to make the Jews a normal nation in terms of their employment and skills.

All this would, of course, be achieved without the reliance on British imperialism for which the Soviet regime criticized the Zionist movement. It is noteworthy that even a small group of disillusioned Zionist pioneers who left Palestine in 1932, following several years of economic depression, chose to settle in the much more productive Crimea rather than go to the "New Zion" in Birobidzhan, which had been their original choice. They had formed a left-wing faction known as "the labor brigade" (also known as the Elkind group, after its leader) and even evoked consternation upon the inspection of their new settlement by Soviet communist officials from the Jewish section (*Yevsektzia*), who discovered that the children were speaking Hebrew. The number of Jewish farmers in the region even at its high point, did not amount to a fraction of the number of Jews in agricultural production in Argentina or the United States.

The debate over the language loyalty of Jews was a worldwide competition. Many Jews, while sympathetic to Zionist efforts in Palestine, were still emotionally tied to Yiddish or were skeptical that Hebrew could really be turned into a vernacular, modern language of discourse or the vehicle of a new culture and scientific endeavor. Most Jews embraced the language of the majority culture and people wherever they happened to live, but the struggle to forge a Jewish national language was eventually decided by the successful achievement of Israeli independence and the terrible tragedy of the Holocaust.

In their "open letter to the public of Jewish toilers and workers in Palestine" in August, 1932, the Elkind group explained that "Zionism included nonproletarian forces willing to serve in the interests of imperialism, which was opposed to the legitimate aspirations of the toiling Arab masses" and that the country "was far too small to provide a realistic solution for the Jewish masses in Eastern Europe." In 1935, the Jewish population in Birobidzhan reached 14,000, composing 23 percent of the total population, its highpoint. Yiddish schools that had begun with great initial hopes were closed down in 1948, even though the Jewish population had increased to almost 30,000. Since then, there has been a continuous decline, and the Jewish population today accounts for approximately only 5 percent of the total, although now both Yiddish and Hebrew are taught, there is little hope that the Jewish identity of the region will survive.

The Brief Soviet-Israeli Honeymoon

Soviet policy toward the district was always contradictory. During World War II, a Jewish, anti-fascist committee was formed to win sympathy for the USSR. Nevertheless, a long-term ban on the teaching of Hebrew remained in force, and even Yiddish was suppressed. A relaxation during the Kruschev era allowed the Jewish auotonomous district capital to publish the Yiddish language newspaper *Birobidzhaner Shtern* ("Birobidzhan Star") and the monthly literary review *Sovietish Heymland* ("Soviet Homeland"). Both were heavily subsidized by the Soviet regime and primarily designed for consumption abroad as a way of still influencing Yiddish-speaking and sympathetic, left-wing Jews in the Diaspora, a group which has by now almost totally disappeared. The region has however produced no major literary, musical or other Jewish artistic work of any note. Further emigration from the region to Israel has reduced the Jewish population to a tiny proportion of the total, very few of whom continue to speak Yiddish.

The ironic outcome of continual Soviet opposition to Zionism as a reactionary tool of British imperialism was the complete turnabout of the entire Eastern block from 1947 to 1949 as a result of the Zionist underground's successful opposition to British rule. In spite of the myth that America was primarily responsible for Israel's birth, the United States imposed an embargo on all weapons shipments to and purchases by both sides. It was Czech-equipped Zionist forces that defeated the British-trained and -equipped Egyptian, Iraqi and Jordanian armies. Dramatic confirmation of this occurred on January 7, 1949, when Israeli aircraft shot down five British-piloted Spitfires on patrol over the Sinai Desert. The Israeli fighters were former, German Luftwaffe Messerschmidts provided by Czechoslovakia to the nascent Israeli Airforce. The British aircraft had been ordered to patrol Egyptian- and Jordanian-controlled territory to make sure that Israeli forces had not made incursions and caused a diplomatic crisis. It provoked the British parliament to call for normalization of relations with the new state and de facto recognition of Israel after the failure of Britain's diplomatic maneuvering and military intervention on behalf of the invading Arab states.

The Soviet press, which had always maligned Zionism and praised the "Soviet patriotism" of Russian Jews, portraying Jewish heroism in terms of Yiddish-speaking proletarians, now lauded the new Hebrew-speaking fighters for independence and socialism against the reactionary, invading Arab armies backed by British imperialism. The turnabout was breathtaking. Dolores Ibarruri ("La Pasionaria"), the noted Spanish Communist Party leader in exile, issued a statement in support of Israel against the reactionary Arab leaders, whom she compared to the Spanish fascists. In 1948 and 1949, two other events stimulated Russian-Jewish identification with the new state—the arrival of Israel's new ambassador in Moscow, Golda Meir, and the performance in Moscow of the great American Negro singer, Paul Robeson, who unexpectedly electrified a sell-out crowd with his rendition in Yiddish of the "Song of the Jewish Partisans." The Communist Party quickly recognized it had made a colossal error in stimulating emotions of Jewish patriotic identification with the new heroic state of Israel and quickly made another about-face, intensifying its ban on Hebrew teaching and even closing down Yiddish schools, executing the leaders of the Jewish antifascist committee and launching the "doctors' plot," accusing Jewish doctors of trying to murder Stalin.

The Hebrew Spelling Dilemma

Although Hebrew won the dual battle of transformation into a modern spoken language and recognition as the official language of the state of Israel, a serious problem remains which has resisted modernization and constitutes a growing barrier to literacy and comprehension. The transformation of biblical Hebrew into a modern idiom remains unfinished as long as the language continues to use the traditional "holy" square Babylonian letters introduced in the fifth century BC, which replaced the original Hebrew-Phoenician alphabet. The retention of the archaic Hebrew alphabet has made necessary the use of three different spelling methods. The letters used in all three are the same and represent consonants but differ in the representation of the vowel sounds.

The first system used in older dictionaries shows the grammatical spelling of the original consonants. This is the bare bones, representing the "skeleton" of the word. In the second, vowels, as in Arabic, are represented by a separate system of signs (*nikud*) above, below or within certain letters. A third system (*plene*, or "full") employs the weak consonants *aleph* (a), *vav* (o) and *yod* (y) to function as vowels as does Yiddish.

One can imagine the difficulties involved in any modern language that employed different spellings for words. Nikud is used in the Bible and in children's works as well as in poetry, where meter is important. "Full spelling," known in Hebrew as *HaKtiv HaMaleh* or by the Latin term "plene," is now the standard in most dictionaries. A recent Hebrew-English dictionary, *Milon Megiddo Hadish* (Megiddo Publishing Company, Ltd., Tel Aviv, 1990 edition), explains that plene spelling is now in use in literature, science, the press and general correspondence. The use of the vowel letters aleph, vav and yod has the function of lengthening the preceding vowel to enable the reader to properly pronounce the word with "full vocalization" (sounding every syllable correctly). The lack of vowels creates considerable uncertainty regarding the identity of the word to be read. There are in Hebrew many groups of words of two, three, and four letters—which even in plene spelling appear identical and can only be distinguished by full nikud. For example the word *mDBR* may be *miDBaR* ("desert"), *miDaBeR* ("is speaking") or *mehDaVaR* ("from a thing"). Only with nikud, can the reader instantaneously read (correctly) the word.

The alphabet poses difficulties of legibility due to the square shape of most letters, with none extending below or above the line. Tests have shown that, whereas most readers can correctly read an English sentence that has been partially hidden by blocking out the top or bottom half of the line, this is impossible in Hebrew.[22] The speed of reading also appears to be slower in a right-to-left than a left to right direction, based on tests with Israelis fluent in a foreign language.[23] The difficulties the alphabet poses for literacy extend beyond the new immigrant population and explain why many veteran residents in Israel, who get along quite well in spoken Hebrew, are unable to read a daily newspaper, let alone enjoy a work of serious literature.

The claims that Israelis are still "the people of the book" and read more books per capita than anyone else[24] are misleading. Finland, with approximately the same population as Israel can boast of a recent best seller, *The Unknown Soldier* by Väinö Linna, dealing with the Russo-Finnish War of 1940, which has sold more than 500,000 copies. By comparison, the best-selling Hebrew novel in Israel, *Black Box*, by Amos Oz, and Meir Shalev's *The Blue Mountain* have sold only about 80,000 each.

When an English reader comes across the word "read," for example, there may be an initial doubt whether this verb is in the present or past tense, but by the time the reader approaches the end of the sentence, the context will make it clear which tense is intended. The Hebrew reader is faced by hundreds, if not thousands, of choices over such multiple possibilities in the course of reading a book. The difficulties are increased by the practice of tacking on prepositions and conjunctions (the words for "and," "by," "from," "to," "at," etc., all represented by a single letter) to the beginning of the next word. Since Hebrew has no uppercase or lowercase letters, these orthographic peculiarities make it difficult even for the fluent, native-born speaker to immediately identify the word to be read. Printing everything in nikud is very expensive and slows down reading considerably. There is no escape from this dilemma except a major reform of the orthography such as latinization or the addition of new, true vowel letters.

There have been well over a hundred reform proposals for new alphabets and new letters.[25] These have even included *Deror*, a latinized Hebrew newspaper begun in 1933 and edited by Itamar Ben-Avi, the son of Eliezer Ben-Yehuda. All such proposals ran into the determined and rabid opposition of traditionalists and the ultraorthodox, who view it as further tampering with the "holy tongue" and an abomination.

To give the English reader an idea of the nature of the problem, try to make sense of the following sentence, in which the vowels have been omitted and the prepositions are attached to the following word.

        thwnd nhs sl ws d tthbttr trp

Does this mean...?
a. The wind in his soul was due to the bitter trip.
b. The wound in his seal was due to the better trap.
c. The wand in his soil was due to the butter troop.

The purists argue that any distortion of the alphabet would obscure the word-building skeletal structure of the language that enables readers to recognize the essential root letters. As the modern Hebrew vocabulary has grown in complexity with maturity, this antiquated alphabet and its ambiguities create occasional uncertainty and slow down reading comprehension.

The Hebrew-Yiddish Reconciliation in Israel Today

For two generations, the language debate in Israel was marked by a polarized controversy that reached the level of street brawls, social ostracism, picket lines against Yiddish theater, a polemical literature and self-proclaimed boycotts by rival groups of the "other language." Although Hebrew emerged the winner and has increased its legitimate authority as the official language and bearer of the majority culture in Israel, elements in the Jewish population, especially among the ultraorthodox of east European origin maintain a hostile attitude toward its modern role as a secular language and insist that its use be proscribed only as the *Loyshen Kodesh*—holy language of the scriptures.

Extremist wings of the ultraorthodox (notably in Jerusalem and Bnei-Brak) study the Talmud and Bible using Yiddish for commentary and debate. They may also occasionally use it as a language of instruction in their own schools (with public subsidies). They represent a rival Jewish society that does not accept the legitimate authority of the state and many of its institutions. For them, the Hebrew language in its modern form represents a sacrilegious and blasphemous transgression. On numerous occasions, demonstrators have defaced the house of Eliezer Ben-Yehuda and monuments in his memory. One can well understand the reaction of those for whom the tabloid press, cheap detective and cowboy novels, pornographic magazines, books on sexual matters, the football lottery and a thousand and one other secular concerns are printed in a language made holy by God's written word.

Nevertheless, the authorities and a large segment of the Hebrew-speaking public have regained a sympathetic attitude toward honoring the language of many of their parents and grandparents[26] (Figure 5). Estimates denote Yiddish as the language of origin of 80 percent of the world's Jewish population and nearly 50 percent of Israel's Jewish population. Israel's broadcasting system, "Kol Yisrael" (The Voice of Israel), maintains a full range of Yiddish programs. The Yiddish theater and Yiddish singers have a devoted audience, and there is a host of degree-granting programs offered by Israeli universities in Yiddish linguistics, language and literature. Today, Yiddish is an optional subject in Israeli secondary schools, and all segments of the Israeli cultural establishment, including the famous *Habimah* Hebrew theater, now offer plays in Yiddish.

Subsidies for cultural and

Figure 5. Israeli stamp copied from poster that originally appeared in Poland showing young pioneers with inscription in Yiddish "Let Us Settle the Valley."

scholastic endeavors in the language have been made available by the government, local municipalities and institutions abroad, notably from Germany. Countless Yiddish expressions have entered popular Israeli Hebrew speech, and it may be said to have risen from the bottom of the social ladder of languages spoken in Israel.

Language Decline and Retention: Yiddish and Hebrew in the United States

From a prewar population of more than ten million Yiddish speakers throughout the world, the number of speakers worldwide was reduced to less than half by the end of the war in 1945. Estimates of the number of speakers today vary widely.[27] Many speakers are elderly. Yiddish speakers have fallen far below the number of speakers of such languages as Norwegian or Danish. Today there are no more than one million American Jews with knowledge of the language, 200,000 in Israel and only 154,000 native language speakers in the USSR, according to the census of 1989, substantially down from the 1970 census figures of 380,000 among the more than two million Soviet citizens registered as Jewish. Almost all of these are bilingual or multilingual in Russian and several other languages, and about half of them have since emigrated to Israel.

The U.S. census has become increasingly interested in language use, loyalty, retention and attrition. The figures show a steep decline among Yiddish speakers in spite of all the recent popular attempts to maintain the language. In data on mother tongue claimants collected by the U.S. census in 1970, Yiddish still stood as the sixth most common, mother tongue foreign language in the United States with just over a million and a half claimants, behind Spanish, German, Italian, French and Polish.[28]

This is hotly contested by many third- and fourth-generation American Jews who are active in trying to popularize the language as a means of gaining an appreciation for the distinctive culture of their grandparents. The renown linguist, Joshua Fishman, an authority on minority languages, even titled his two-volume study of American Yiddish with the emotional words of the World War II, Jewish partisans' song "Never Say Die." Nevertheless the statistics of language retention and loss clearly demonstrate that Yiddish has suffered more than other immigrant languages in the United States and has declined substantially. However, only about 10 percent of Yiddish speakers in the 1970 census were the native-born children of native-born parents, a much lower proportion than for the speakers of other foreign languages such as Spanish and French (55 percent), German (about 40 percent), Polish (33 percent) and Italian (15 percent), Put another way, this means that Jews born in the United

States were much quicker to lose the ability (and/or the will) to speak the language of their parents.

Twenty years later, native Yiddish speakers in the United States had fallen to the number sixteen rank of 213,000, barely ahead of twenty-third-place Hebrew, with 144,000 speakers. Most young people study Hebrew either because of religious obligations or else as an identification with the still young, vibrant Israeli society in contrast to the image of Yiddish as a somber reminder of the Holocaust. The last Yiddish newspapers in New York, which once had a combined circulation of half a million readers, disappeared or were converted to English language weeklies or monthlies.

Hebrew's Success and Its Questionable Future: Diglossia or Worse?

Hebrew's success was a matter of unique circumstances that the Irish and Norwegians were unable to repeat. Jews migrating to Palestine had no common language, and no other argument could so successfully establish Jewish attachment to Israel. Countless everyday documents, scrolls, tombstones, and monuments from the past millennia written on wood, stone, clay and papyrus have been uncovered, all of which "speak" Hebrew, confirming the Jewish connection to the land. As Hillel Halkin so succinctly put it, "Any alternative to Hebrew would have meant the loss of Zionism's historical content, the political consequences of which would have been to degrade the movement into the mere colonizing enterprise its enemies always viewed it as being and so doom it in advance."[29]

Nevertheless, the massive intrusion of English with its real importance in world trade, diplomacy, science and technology, higher education and tourism is regarded by many Israelis as a key element in achieving success in their career. It is amazing that no Israeli statesman has ever spoken Hebrew at an international meeting or conference. In this regard, it is noteworthy that many Jews in the Diaspora are unable to read or speak modern Hebrew, whereas many of Israel's male Arab citizens are fluent and more literate in Hebrew than in Arabic.[30]

If educated Israelis (or Maltese, Irish, Norwegians, etc.) are to make a name for themselves in their chosen professions, they must know and work in English. There is a continual diet of English language films and news programs that intensify the process. Americanization has affected Israel to an extent that could not be foreseen at the dawn of independence. When David Levy, then foreign minister, was assigned to attend the Madrid peace conference in 1991, there was concern in Israeli circles that the minister would speak in Hebrew or French, and he was ultimately replaced by then Prime Minister Yitzhak Shamir, whose heavy, Yiddish-accented English was felt to be more adequate to bring Israel's view to the English-speaking Diaspora and world.

At the famous meeting on the White Hose lawn when Yitzhak Rabin and Shimon Peres shook Arafat's hand, neither felt it necessary to address their Hebrew-speaking constituency at home. Both Israeli leaders spoke English, while Arafat carefully chose his words in Arabic, knowing full well he could give events just the meaning he chose for home opinion. Hebrew has a small number of speakers and a distinctiveness that makes it very vulnerable. There is a legitimate fear in Israel that the national language is being transformed into a two-tier system (diglossia) of low-caste usage for the home and workplace and that English is increasingly acquiring the status of a high-caste language for official use in an international setting at conferences, seminars, and major entertainment events such as the Eurovision song contest.

The Growing Gap between the Diaspora and Israel

In spite of the oft-repeated view by many observers and the mistaken impression of journalists that "everyone speaks English," the informational and social gap between Israel and the Diaspora continues to grow. Seven years after the assassination of Prime Minister Yitzhak Rabin, there is now a growing body of public opinion in Israel that is very skeptical about the official version of the event. A voluminous literature in Hebrew has detailed the incredible contradictions, missing gaps, and inconsistencies in the evidence. Almost nothing of this is available in English translation. Moreover, it is largely available on the Internet only. Many Israelis now believe in a cover-up that was instigated to smear and implicate the right-wing opposition in the murder and make their rejection of the Oslo accords a damning indictment, whereas the Diaspora has almost unanimously accepted the official view of Rabin as martyr for peace.

Other Attempts to Imitate Hebrew's Success

What is most remarkable about Hebrew's success and restoration as a spoken language is that it has inspired other attempts at a language revival in general by nationalists to revive, promote and teach Irish, Norwegian, Catalán and Basque. Courses in intensive Welsh and Irish advertise for boarding school pupils using the Hebrew word ulpan. The regional governments of Catalonia and the Basque country have sent representatives to Israel to study the *ulpan* system, which they have found

1. Hebrew versus Yiddish

useful to help teach the local languages to many migrants from other parts of Spain who speak only Castillian Spanish and want to feel more socially integrated in their new homes and jobs.

Hebrew's great success was in the vital role it played to create a sense of nationhood. It differs notably, however, from attempts by national movements in Europe during the latter half of the nineteenth century. There, linguists had to find a way to transform the spoken vernacular of the people into a "high," or standardized, national literary language capable of meeting the demands of the twentieth century. For the Hebrew revival campaign, the task was largely in the opposite direction—to take a high, literary language that had remained dormant or almost frozen and revitalize it simultaneously with the introduction of a new spoken variety for use as a common vernacular.[31]

2

THE ATTEMPT TO REVIVE IRISH: A NATION ONCE AGAIN

In Ireland as well as Israel, the debate over choosing and then successfully enshrining a national language resulted in a controversy extending over several generations. Was it to be the language as spoken by most of the people when the vision of nationhood was first entertained (English in Ireland and Yiddish in Israel and among Jews worldwide), or should it be the ancestral tongue conceived by a minority as the true national language connecting them to a real or imagined golden age of nationhood in the remote past (Irish-Gaelic and Hebrew)? The Irish struggle for independence was linked with the notion of a revived ancient nation quite distinct in identity from the rest of the United Kingdom. Ireland had been part of the much larger economic and social unit of the United Kingdom for centuries and by the mid-nineteenth century had a clear, English-speaking majority. Even after the country achieved political independence, the social and linguistic fabric of the British Isles could not be torn asunder. For most Irish the ancestral language was no longer an essential part of their self-identification.

Many Irish, Welsh and Scots had moved to large cities in England or to each other's nearby territory in search of work and economic and social opportunity or for greater freedom to pursue a lifestyle free from the stifling rural traditions and the power of the church. The result was that the British Isles remained one social unit without barriers of migration or employment. Irish money could even be used in the UK. Before the European community, all gates of entry to the UK divided incoming passengers into holders of UK and Irish Passports and holders of Foreign Passports.

The Celtic Heritage, Including Language?

The emotional hold of the Irish language over the Irish people is comparable only to the great place of biblical Hebrew for Jews, the Arabic of the Koran for Arabs, the *Odyssey* and the *Iliad* for Greeks and the "Kalevala" for the Finns. The *Book of Kells* is revered as the most magnificent work of art and scholarship in medieval Europe, and Irish rivaled Latin from the eighth to the eleventh century as the greatest language of education, scholarship and piety. To foster a sense of nationhood, the Irish Republic severed all bonds with the Crown, encouraged the use and instruction of the Irish language (to little avail), cultivated the Celtic heritage of music and team sports, the values of an arch-conservative Catholic church and the lifestyle of an idealized, declining rural peasantry. This vision of Irish identity was by and large not shared by the majority of the population in northern Ireland, who nevertheless felt Irish in their own right.[1] Moreover, this nationalist vision of a distinct Irish nationhood was unable to halt the constant emigration, to America, Canada, England and Australia.

Ironically, the fundamental self-image of Irish traditional values has changed remarkably over the past thirty-five years with growing education, urbanization, new job opportunities, positive steps to end discrimination against Catholics in employment and government in northern Ireland, the weakened power of the Catholic church and integration into the European community.

The Gaeltacht

No more than 50,000 people use Irish[2] as their first language today or are thoroughly bilingual in both Irish and English. This is barely more than 1 percent of the Irish population and compares badly with the 12 percent of Wales's population that is fluent in Welsh and uses it daily. The official designation of an area known as the Gaeltacht (scattered western, largely rural, coastal areas in the counties of Donegal, Mayo and Galway), where Irish continues to be spoken routinely, has not led to any nationwide or even regional revival. Recent estimates place the population of these areas at 83,000, of whom about 30,000 use it as their first language.[3] This attractive area has become popular with many British and European community vacationers and retirees, who are further diluting the area's linguistic uniqueness, and a 1980 government white paper acknowledged the failure of Irish teaching in the schools.

The Gaeltacht is now under the authority of a special government body *Udaras na Gaeltachta*, whose prime responsibility is to maintain the integrity of the living Irish language, a task that is hard to reconcile with promoting the equally important economic vitality of the region. The native speakers of Irish in the Gaeltacht are a tiny minority, both geographically and socially isolated from the mainstream of Irish national life. Attempts by the government to promote jobs and investment in the

Figure 6. The Easter uprising in Dublin against British rule in 1916 is commemorated on an Irish stamp with traditional Gaelic script. The building is the main post office where Irish rebels established their headquarters. After severing all ties to the British Crown, the name of the country was changed to Eire (in Irish) and the Irish Republic (in English).

Gaeltacht, even when successful, have not necessarily helped the language. Much of the region's prosperity is due to tourism and investment, which brings with it managerial and technical staff from outside, who are all English speaking.

A Nation Once Again

The stirring words of a nationalistic Irish song written in 1843 encapsulate the fervent passion and hope that shed light and set the blood on fire to "outshine the stars" in the transformation of the homeland to "A Nation Once Again" (emulating the glory that was Greece and the grandeur that was Rome). Irish nationalists made good on their promises in the song to make a nation once again. The Easter uprising of 1916 in Dublin and the change in the country's name to Eire (Figure 6) or "the Irish Republic" (in English) are cherished milestones in Republican mythology. This event has created a fault line or seemingly permanent partition of Ireland and divided the people of Ireland into two camps. North of the line, a Protestant majority has created its own secular mythology of unionism and loyalty to Great Britain.

A Nation Once Again

When boyhood's fire was in my blood
I read of ancient freemen,
Of Greece and Rome
Who bravely stood
Three hundred men and three men.[4]
And then I prayed, I yet might see
Her fetters rent in twain
And Ireland long a province
Be a nation once again.

And from that time
Through wildest woe,

That hope has shown a far light
Nor could love's brightest summer glow
Outshine that solemn starlight.
It seemed to watch above my head
Through foreign field and fain
Its angel's voice sang round my bed:
A nation once again!

So as I grew from boy to man
I bent me to my bidding
My spirit of each selfish plan
And cruel passion ridding
For thus I hope someday to wait
Nor can such hope be vain
When my dear country shall be made
A nation once again.

The negative image of "the other" (the loyalist Protestant majority in northern Ireland with no subjective feelings of betrayal of their identity for speaking English) became a hallmark of Irish nationalism and succeeded only in alienating that part of Ireland which the south had always claimed was part of the same nation and grows ever more anachronistic: "The Promotion and acceptance of derogatory images of the Other greatly reinforces and supports the positive image of the self, which becomes the stereotype of all that is good, honest, desirable and superior ... identity is not given in human nature, but rather learned through social interaction and communication in a complex of social structures, set in specific and distinctive places and epochs."[5]

The continued rejection by Britain of Irish demands for home rule during the nineteenth century antagonized Irish nationalists, who at the time also included numerous Protestants. They sought to create a new vision of a republican Ireland proudly bearing its ancient Celtic culture and the ancient Irish-Gaelic language epitomized in the great ballad "A Nation Once Again." In 1893, a cultural organization for a revival of Irish identity and culture, the Gaelic League, was founded and amalgamated the previous work carried out by the Society for the Preservation of the Irish Language and the Gaelic Union. It was thus contemporary with the activities of Ben-Yehuda in Palestine to revive Hebrew and the work of similar pioneers for a national linguistic renaissance in Norway (Aasen) and Malta (Preca).[6]

Douglas Hyde, the Protestant president of the Gaelic League, unequivocally linked the language with Ireland's Celtic identity as an independent basis for Irish nationality, totally divorced from religious identification. The League constantly referred to the nonsectarian and nonpolitical character of the Celtic revival at a time when the Catholic church was largely apathetic towards the language issue: "The moment Ireland broke with her Gaelic past, she fell away hopelessly from all intellectual and artistic effort. She lost her musical instruments, she lost her music, she lost her games, she lost her language and popular literature and with her language she lost her intellectuality."[7]

Nevertheless the events of the latter half of the nineteenth century, following the repeated failure of home-rule bills and the dramatic experiences of the First World War and the Easter uprising of 1916, intensified the resentment of Catholics toward continued British rule. Most Protestants remained bitterly opposed toward partition, republicanism and the nationalist movement's infatuation with the rural, devoutly Catholic and conservative western part of the country. This rural model or "cultural reservoir" came to be regarded as the only essential hallmarks of Irish identity in the republic. The division north and south of the partition line was intensified as a result of World War II, when the loyalists in northern Ireland patriotically contributed to the British war effort as part of the United Kingdom. Belfast was an important shipbuilding center and harbor and was subject to intense German bombing.

The republic maintained a strict neutrality, and Irish president De Valera threw salt on the war wounds by officially sending his condolences to the German people on the death of their führer, Adolph Hitler, in April, 1945. This terrible error of judgment was made in spite of offers by Churchill to reconsider the partition of Ireland and eventual reunification. Nothing could more effectively have demonstrated Irish nationalism's provincial nature and total rejection of any real, all–Irish solidarity at the time.

Polite Fiction or Hypocrisy?

Irish is enshrined in the constitution of the republic, which defines it as "the first official language" of the state and in an act of the parliament which calls for it to be promoted as "a living language in daily use." Nevertheless, the Irish language is neither an essential ingredient for Irish identity today nor of any practical importance for a career. Its use remains primarily symbolic and ceremonial. The only positive development regarding the language is the growth of bilingual schools in major urban areas in the republic, which are well funded and chosen by largely middle-class or well-to-do parents who resent English and American pop culture. Until the 1970s most universities insisted on some nominal Irish for admission, and failing to pass exams or present a paper in compulsory Irish led some talented scientists to leave Ireland. This symbolic and ceremonial role requires that the president speak the language fluently and necessitated intensive relearning of the language by Mary Robinson when she took office.

Perhaps the most embarrassing incident that devastated supporters of the vain hope for a revival was reported in the *New York Times* on October 13, 1961. Peggy O'Donnel, a sixteen-year-old Irish girl from the island of Aran, off the west coast of Ireland, was in Dublin on a visit. She was a native Irish speaker with almost no knowledge of English and got lost. It took her six hours of pleading with passers-by in the streets of Ireland's largest city before being able to finally encounter someone who was able to help her by responding in Irish she could understand to direct her to an Irish-speaking policeman.

The Irish Hope to Imitate the Revival of Hebrew

As early as 1927, the president of Ireland, Eamon de Valeira, lamented to the head of the World Zionist Organization, Nahum Sokolow, that the Irish, in spite of having all of the tools available to a national government, had so far been incapable of imitating the successful revival of Hebrew, which was already apparent in Palestine. The same view was repeated more than thirty years later by Arthur Webb, the long time editor of the *Irish Times* in Dublin after a long absence in an interview with the *New York Herald Tribune*.[8]

Sean Cronin, writing in the Irish press, repeated the accusation that the entire mass media of the republic overwhelm the high school graduate in the republic with an English-language cinema, radio, and press in contrast to the Hebrew environment of Israel.[9] The lives and works of Eliezer Ben-Yehuda and Douglas Hyde, president of the Gaelic League, were directly compared and contrasted in a lecture in Irish by Shlomo Wolfson, a student at the University of Dublin, which achieved notoriety in the Irish English-language press.

Nuala Ní Dhomhnaill, the best-known and most colorful woman poet writing in Irish today, is a major cultural personality who has won wide acclaim in her native Kerry, all of Ireland and throughout the Irish Diaspora. Nevertheless, much of her work is read in English translation in spite of her claim that it loses its effectiveness. She has made direct reference to the comparison with Hebrew in expressing regret that, unlike it, Irish was not imposed, yet even she admits that it is too late to bring it back on a massive scale.[10] Many Irish nationalists, including those in the IRA leadership, have never made a fetish of the language, knowing full well that it offers nothing to attract supporters in Ulster, even among disaffected Catholics there. Scottish nationalism, which overtook the Conservative Party in the last general parliamentary elections, is much stronger than the Welsh Nationalist Party is in Wales and is proof that the absence of a distinctive national language in Scotland is not a barrier to cultivating a strong national sentiment.

The Peculiarities of the Language

There are considerable objective difficulties for adults to acquire Irish as a second language, a fact recognized by the European Union. Although the E.U. recognizes Irish as one of Ireland's two official languages, it has resisted any attempt to provide the same level of translation and interpretation services available in other, official minor languages, such as Danish and Dutch. Several studies comparing the length of time required to reach levels of adequacy in learning a foreign language undertaken by the European Community rank Irish as the most difficult by a considerable margin.

According to tests, the number of hours required by a native Spanish speaker to gain a medium level of proficiency in the European languages (shown below) gives an indication of the difficulty of Irish:

Language	Number of Hours Required to Gain Medium Proficiency
Esperanto	325
Italian	1,050
French	1,275
English	1,350
German	1,400
Irish	1,600

Source: Helmar Franck, Dept. of Experimental Pedagogy and Educational Sciences, University of Geneva; see Helmar Franck, *Kybernetische Padagogik/Klerkibernetiko. 1993.*

Even within the Irish elementary-school system, the number of qualified teachers in Irish is inadequate. The language is often written in traditional Gaelic script, a form of medieval writing much like Gothic letters, which require some training to read. Its vocabulary contains few words immediately recognizable to speakers of English, French or German, and its grammar and syntax appear unwieldy to speakers of the other major language families outside the Celtic group.

Irish Language Television

In 1996, the Irish government, responding to criticism that no serious attempt had been made to make Irish a living language, created "*Teilifís na Gaeilge,*" a full-time, bilingual channel (four hours in Irish-Gaelic and six hours in English). It is heavily subsidized. Few sponsors see any economic sense in advertising for a very small Irish viewing/listening public, and there has been considerable opposition from critics including the *Dublin Times*, which labeled its excessive cost "more than calamitous." It called the station a "true scandal" and "prohibitively expensive" as well as "failing to win sufficient viewers except occasionally for its non–Irish output which is hardly its purpose." This remark refers to the large audience attracted by showing live Spanish soccer matches with commentary in English, hardly a feature of native Irish culture.

This is all the more controversial when measured against the skimpy budgetary allocations for medical care and social security benefits. Direct annual subsidies have totaled about $15 million, and the station is able to buy programming from Irish National Television (RTE) at reduced costs. When Ireland joined the European Community, it was with the expressed understanding that Irish would not be an official language of the community—a demand which would have been impossible to meet regarding qualified translators and interpreters. Even Donnacha O hEallaithe, a member of the station's advisory council, has stated "people are not particularly interested" and "we must face the reality that there is little national demand for Irish-language programs on a separate TV station." With so few speakers there is little appeal for the Irish language television network (TV-4) at considerable cost. English-language programs capture an audience many times larger, and Irish viewers have their choice of many more hours of more varied programming on British television.

The attempt to revive and preserve Irish came much too late. Neither the church nor the early Irish nationalist movement had an interest in stemming the tide from Irish to English. The schools responded to the wishes of the parents to educate their children in English. As part of the United Kingdom and even after independence in a Republic of Ireland, millions of emigrants sought more reliable employment, social benefits, professional advancement, a more liberal life style and greater opportunity in London, the north of England and Scotland. Almost as many Irish left to settle in other parts of what was the same country for centuries (the United Kingdom) as emigrated abroad to America, Canada and Australia. The great potato famine reduced the population by half and hit the Gaeltacht hardest. Even prior to this catastrophe, it is estimated by the 1851 British census that Ireland had only 300,000 monoglot Irish speakers and more than one and a half million English or bilingual speakers. Today there are only about 3,000 monoglots.

The Great Subconscious Heart Throb of the Race

Although almost all Irish would like to see the language preserved, there are few today who foresee any possibility of its being more than a fond memory or fulfilling the role described by Seán O Faoláin in 1947: "It has gone underground. It is so to speak, being forgotten consciously.

It nevertheless beats like a great heart throb in the subconscious of the race. The Irish language is thus become the runic language of modern Ireland. Even though only a dwindling few think overtly in it, all of us can, through it, touch, however dimly, a buried part of ourselves of which we normally are unaware. Through Gaelic, we remember ancestrally."

Countless other Irish intellectuals, writers, poets, playwrights, artists and politicians have expressed similar views. A paradoxical consequence of all this is the conclusion of Irish historian Joseph Lee, who has written: "It may well be that there is an Irish emotional reality which is silenced in English but it can be argued, conversely, that if English had not become Ireland's first language, then the Irish could never have made their remarkable contribution to English literature, and would have lost the self-confidence this has brought."[11]

In spite of such noble sentiments, many secondary school headmasters (principals) admit privately that Irish is the least popular subject in the syllabus and most pupils would drop it if allowed. The "vision" of a Celtic-Irish speaking and devout Catholic nation has always been divisive even among the supporters of the nationalist cause. Irish is a declining school subject even in the Gaeltacht. Many Irish intellectuals and cultural personalities have been unhappy with Ireland's ultra-Catholic religious image as "The Pope's Last Bastion" and are aware that the loss of the "national language" has wounded the nation's distinctive identity and cannot be resurrected as a shared inheritance with the Protestant population of Ulster.

A look at the Irish case demonstrates that speaking the national language may be an accident of history. It is even conceded by many Irish nationalists that the cause of national unity embracing Ulster was seriously hampered by the unrealistic and even fictitious role given the Irish language in the republic. Ireland's greatest authors—Swift, Shaw and Joyce—all achieved worldwide fame writing in English, and modern-day speakers of Irish only (monoglots) are regarded as eccentric. After more than seventy years of Irish independence in the republic, deputies in the Dail (parliament) from the more traditional and rural conservative areas in the west outside the Gaeltacht frequently complain that there is still a lack of an appropriate infrastructure through which Irish can be used in the carrying out of people's daily business.

Music: The Eurovision, Dance and the Gaelic Athletic Association

The Irish love of distinctive music, dance and sports is universal across the island and has enabled the Irish people to take pride in numerous achievements. In no way has language functioned as a barrier in this regard. All of the great Irish artistic and athletic achievements have been made through the medium of English. The popular, annual Eurovision contest, which Ireland has won more often than any other country, took advantage of the special dispensation from the general rule in force until just a few years ago that the entry must be sung in the country's official language. Ireland never submitted an entry sung in Irish. This in no way lessened the sense of triumph, especially over the rival song entered by Great Britain. Irish dance has also scored numerous stage triumphs throughout the world, notably in the recent "River Dance" shows starring Michael Flatley, and is as popular in the north as in the republic.

Traditional Gaelic sports such as Gaelic football, field hockey, and hurling are the main events held at a kind of all–Irish olympics, and leagues in these sports cross the international border. The games are run by the state-supported Gaelic Athletic Association, with 800,000 members has long been regarded as the organization second in influence and power only to the Catholic church. Soccer and rugby, once looked upon by nationalists as "foreign" or "English" games, have since been integrated into the Irish sports pantheon and have received nationalist legitimacy.

It is undeniable that bilingual educational programs offered by private schools are increasingly popular in Dublin, much as Welsh language programs are among middle-class families in Wales, but the suspicion in both cases is that these schools do not attract pupils primarily for the language program offered but rather for their general high level of academic achievement.

Irish-Gaelic in the Diaspora

Unlike Hebrew with its attendant religious function in preparation for synagogue participation and its role for the Jewish Diaspora as a Window on modern Israel, the cultivation and teaching of Irish-Gaelic is a comparative rarity in the great Irish communities of the United States, Canada and Australia. This is hardly remarkable since many Irish immigrants to these countries originally lived in the poorer western areas of the Gaeltacht and Ulster but, by their time of emigration, were already English speaking.

The renewed prospect of a peaceful agreement renouncing the use of violence and the decommissioning of arms by the IRA has raised hopes throughout the island on both sides of the old political divide that some form of power sharing or joint sovereignty or even a unification of Ireland may take place. Without the old political animosities, it is entirely conceivable that the language issue could be amicably resolved along the lines of agreements worked out in Wales.

Instead of nationalists painting out and defacing road signs and inscriptions on government buildings, bilingual information would be provided both north and south, reinforcing the sense of the Irish language as a marker of common Irish identity and history rather than a point of contention. Whether such an interest or enthusiasm for the language can be cultivated in the north, when three generations of constant exhortations have failed to produce more than a meager result in the republic, is open to question. Proponents of teaching the language as a common, cultural heritage rather than as a symbol of nationalism and purely in opposition to the prevailing English-language popular culture are hopeful that a reduction of religious and political antagonism will inevitably have beneficial results in promoting Irish. It is not only in the republic but also in northern Ireland and among the Irish around the world that there is an enormous pride in the cultural achievements Ireland made in the Middle Ages, such as the *Book of Kells*. What is lacking is a broader campaign to familiarize the Irish abroad with the work of modern Irish-Gaelic authors. Divorcing the language from its old baggage of devout Catholicism and a mythical, rural, pastoral environment is the first step, and new textbooks for the teaching of Irish are much more in tune with the modern world. The teaching of modern Hebrew in the Diaspora followed a similar route, having initially relied on traditional religious themes and then identifying more and more with the actual spoken language and the issues and problems facing the country and the individual in modern society.

3

NORWAY'S SCHIZOPHRENIA: NEW NORSE (NYNORSK) VERSUS DANO-NORWEGIAN (BOKMÅL/RIKSMÅL)

While the Hebrew revival can be considered a great success and that of Irish a striking failure, the case of Norwegian falls somewhere in between and is practically unknown outside the country. This is largely because most foreigners are aware that Norway is a homogeneous country with no significant ethnic minority. The notion of language conflict implies a struggle between contending languages and ethnic groups, as in Canada or Belgium. In Norway, the contending languages are two varieties of Norwegian spoken only by Norwegians. Nynorsk (New Norse) was part of a general cultural-linguistic reaction by Norwegians against four hundred years of Danish rule, during which time the many Norse dialects in geographically isolated parts of the country were the spoken language of the people, who learned a standard literary language in school.[1]

This language was Danish as spoken by Norwegians, with a distinctive pronunciation (called Dano-Norwegian by linguists and later Riksmål—the "language of the realm"), and generations of educated Norwegians in the large towns came to regard it as their own language. Norway's greatest writer, Henrik Ibsen, wrote only in Dano-Norwegian, and it has always been the spoken medium of most of Norway's business community.

All education, the Bible in common use, the courts and other public institutions cultivated Danish. Some Norwegians alive today tell anecdotal stories about their grandparents, who believed that Danish was God's holy language because this was the language of the Bible. The result was a standard literary and "foreign" language used for formal occasions quite different from the Norse dialects spoken in the country a thousand years ago, when, together with Iceland, the Norwegians produced the magnificent sagas of a golden age. The people of both Iceland and Norway never experienced the same feudal traditions as the rest of Europe and later came to resent a much less democratic rule imposed on them by the Danish monarchy. It was the catastrophe of the black plague that killed more than half of the population in one year (1349–1350), weakened the country and led to the loss of political independence and Danish rule.

By 1400, Danish rulers began to introduce written Danish into Norway as the language of administration. All old laws that had been written in Old Norse were translated into Danish. The effect on the spoken Norse dialects was minimal, due to the very poor communications and widely dispersed population. By the eighteenth century, however, the urban-based middle classes, clergy and bureaucrats began to speak Danish. University education was available only in Copenhagen. By 1800, it is estimated that more than 90 percent of the people spoke numerous dialects of Norse, but a powerful, though very small, urban ruling class spoke Dano-Norwegian.

The Nationalist Movement, Independence and the Reemergence of the National Language Controversy

Following the Napoleonic wars, Norway became a Swedish possession. This development only increased the desire for independence that matured and eventually forced Sweden to relinquish control, and an independent Norway was proclaimed in 1905. Nationalist advocates were aware that the great majority of the Norwegian people had always regarded the Danes as foreign rulers and their language as an imposition. Various reform proposals to adopt a standard Norwegian based on a local dialect from one of the major fjords were rejected by representatives from other parts of the country.

The lack of any acceptable standard produced a debate on the nature of Norway's cultural identity. The issue was not resolved until an innovative linguist, Ivar Aasen, proposed a new national language in the mid-nineteenth century, based on an amalgamation of the major regional dialects, to be called "Nynorsk." His ideas were attacked by the established ruling circles, who believed that the new language would distance them from the rest of Europe and that trying to produce a neutral form of what had been Old Norse and calling it Nynorsk was absurd.

Aasen was the son of a poor farmer from the west coast of Norway and had to work on the farm of an elder brother before being able to become a teacher and continue his education. He experienced the contempt of the country's social elite, who scoffed at his origins and attempt to reform "their" language. He traveled all over Norway between 1842 and 1846 and collected information on the various dialects, from which he published grammar books and dictionaries. These works attracted attention from linguists in Europe and made Aasen a respected figure in academic circles. His great achievement was to show that the local Norse dialects were not just diverse variants but together constituted the elements of a language which would have developed into a standard national form, had independence not been snuffed out. The first newspaper in Nynorsk appeared in 1858, and by 1885 the Norwegian storting (parliament) recognized Nynorsk as a national language besides Danish.

Independence in 1905 gave the Nynorsk movement a further impetus, and in 1906 a Nynorsk theater was founded. An extremist vocal minority demanded the return of Danish possessions—Greenland, the Faeroe islands and Iceland—that had originally been settled by Viking Norsemen. They even protested the retention by Great Britain of the Hebrides and Orkney islands, off the coast of Scotland. To make it more nationalistic, a spelling reform of Dano-Norwegian was carried out in 1907, making it look quite distinct from Danish. Nynorsk encountered resistance, however, especially in Oslo, where it found it difficult to penetrate the most populous part of the country.

Too Many Reforms

To add to the confusion the government sponsored a reform of the official national languages in 1938. Riksmål was renamed Bokmål ("language of the book"), subjected to considerable spelling changes to make it appear in closer harmony with Nynorsk. This did not, however, change the social reality that most Norwegians, including an overwhelming majority in the largest towns (Oslo, Bergen and Trondhjem), continued to speak Dano-Norwegian (i.e., Danish with a distinctive Norwegian pronunciation). Before 1938, written Riksmål resembled Danish, and even to this day, many Danes, when reading a newspaper or book in Riksmål, have the impression that it is simplified Danish written by young children who don't know how to spell. The new spelling of Bokmål made the language look somewhat different, but anyone with a knowledge of Danish still had no problem in understanding it. A similar reform with Nynorsk in 1938, renamed Landsmål ("rural language" by its critics and "national language" by its supporters) was also implemented to bring it closer to the Riksmå variety of the majority. The result, as might be expected, was considerable confusion. The expressed goal followed by subsequent social democratic majority governments has been a linguistic unification into a single, national Norwegian language.

The Ideological Background: Class and Language

Although the social-democratic parties in Scandinavia have promulgated similar programs of socialism and welfare benefits, the Norwegian branch alone has linked their ideology with a linguistic program, attempting to reverse what it regards as four centuries of foreign (i.e., Danish) rule. This involved rewriting history books and changing the many place names in the country (altering maps and road signs). By 1945, conservative adherents of Dano-Norwegian rallied their forces and counterattacked. They pointed out that the great majority of Norwegian writers, artists and scientists produced their works in Riksmål-Bokmål. Industrial and shipping interests in Oslo and several other large towns had grown up with Dano-Norwegian as their spoken language and felt particularly threatened.

The Decline of Nynorsk in the Schools

School districts in Norway have always had a choice in determining the language of instruction. In the 1930s, more than one-third of all Norwegian primary pupils attended Nynorsk schools, but today it has fallen to a mere 17 percent. Its decline has been an unavoidable consequence of the closure of small rural schools and migration to Oslo and its suburbs in the more developed southeast of the country. Supporters of Nynorsk, organized in a powerful interest lobby—Noregs Mållag—still maintain they are discriminated against because the best jobs in Oslo and other large cities demand both written and spoken fluency in Bokmål, which is also the dominant language of the press and national advertising. Norway has stayed out of the European Community, aided by its new oil wealth, and has spared the public from a new debate over the language question. If Norway is admitted to the European Community, with its policy of language equality, it will have to be represented by both languages.

The Written Languages

The written forms are not very divergent and can be understood with a minimal effort, but the ability to write correctly and precisely on demand is quite taxing. A comparison of Nynorsk, Bokmål and Danish is presented here with the "Lord's Prayer" in all three languages:

> **Danish**
> Vor Fader, du som er i Himlene!
> Helliget vorde dit navn;
> Kommer dit rige;

Ske din vilje
På jorden, som den sker i Himmelen;
Giv os I dag vort daglige brød;
Og forlad os vor skyld,
Som også vi forlader vore skyldnere;
Og led os ikke ind i fristelse;
Men fri os fra det onde
Thi dit er Riget og magten or æren i evighed! Amen.

Bokmål
Fader vår, du som er i himmelen!
La ditt navn holdes hellig.
La ditt rike komme.
La din vilje skje pa jorden
Som i himmelen.
Gi oss I dag vårt daglige brød.
Forlat oss vår skyld,
Som vi og forlater våre skyldnere.
Led oss ikke inn i fristelse,
Men frels oss fra det onde.
For riket er ditt, og, makten og æren i evighet. Amen.

Nynorsk
Fader vår, du som er i himmelen!
Lat namnet dit helgast.
Lat riket ditt komma.
Lat viljen din råda på jorda
Som i himmelen.
Gjev oss i dag vårt daglege brød.
Forlat oss vår skuld,
Som vi forlet våre skuldmenn.
For oss ikkje ut i freisting,
Men frels oss frå det vonde.
For riket er ditt, og makta og æra i all æva. Amen.

An outsider might come to the conclusion, after a brief look at all three, that this is a case of "much ado about nothing," yet that would be a grave error. Language sensibility seems to be greater, the closer the alternatives resemble each other.

The Growing Opposition to Nynorsk: Tyranny by a Minority

Supporters of Bokmål who organized in Bokmålsforbundet (the "Book Language League") aggressively reject the notion that somehow the small, rural and particularly regionally concentrated population in west Norway has the right to determine the national language and claim that it is entitled to special consideration or that it is more culturally deserving. They reject the subsidies provided by the state to Noregs Mållag and other interest groups for specially edited textbooks to be used in the Nynorsk schools and bilingual road signs as well as government forms, where it is claimed there is no need for a Nynorsk version.

Opinion surveys by reliable, unbiased sources, such as the Gallup poll indicate that 87 percent of all Norwegians correspond exclusively in Bokmål/Riksmål. The decline of Nynorsk has been an unavoidable consequence of migration to Oslo and its suburbs in the South by families who have relocated there from the West coast. The groups using Nynorsk most are rural dwellers in the West, in costal fishing villages and mountainous regions.

They further reject as a historical distortion and demagoguery much of the ideological content that was linked to the Nynorsk movement during the first few decades of independence. This view held that a decidedly Danish, formal written language and an attempt to imitate Danish pronunciation were mechanisms of the ruling class that hindered the development of the peasants' mobilization and participation in commercial activity, cultural creativity, politics and religious life. Nothing similar has occurred in either Denmark or Sweden, where there are considerable regional dialects too but no ideology or political movement linked to language, as in Norway.

A movement by parents of school children, the Parents Movement against Linguistic Unification, became active in the fifties and pressured the government into another language reform act in 1958 that partly reversed the 1938 act by allowing many older Riksmål spelling varieties to be accepted as equivalent optional forms. Since 1981, a back-to-Riksmål movement has agitated for a return to the more traditional spelling and grammar of Dano-Norwegian as used a hundred years ago. Norway's largest newspaper, *Aftenposten*, is published in Riksmål without any apologies.

Higher Education

Norway has four universities—Oslo, Bergen, Trondheim and Tromsø—and a number of specialized colleges for training in agriculture (near Oslo), veterinary medicine in Oslo and business in Bergen. With the exception of the institution of agriculture, all utilize the majority Bokmål language, and students speaking local dialects who have had their formal education in Nynorsk feel disadvantaged. Scientists with this linguistic background often feel the necessity to develop new terminology in their respective fields. Apart from agriculture, philology, history and some of the social sciences, almost all scholarly papers are published in Bokmål.

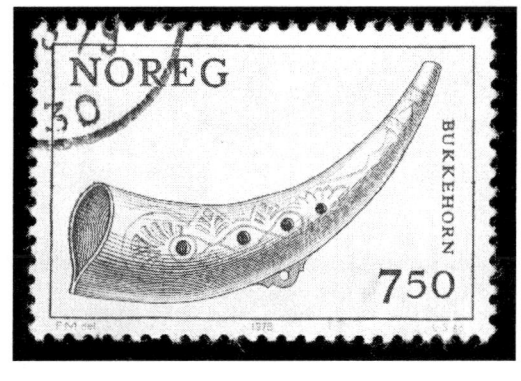

3. Norway's Schizophrenia

Figure 7. Three Norwegian postage stamps showing the various spellings of the country's names—Norge and Noreg.

The result has been considerable spelling confusion. Government regulations require that a certain percentage of official publications by the university and other institutions located in Oslo appear in Nynorsk and ensure that all nationwide public radio and television broadcasts as well as school examinations and the educational curriculum are in the approved 1938 varieties. Norway is so sensitive to the language issue that precise quota rules have been worked out for the issuance of banknotes and postage stamps, allotting a fixed percentage to the representation of the name of the country in Bokmål (Norge) and Nynorsk (Noreg) as well as in both versions on the same stamp (Figure 7).

The Debate Over New Word Derivation

Conflicts between the supporters of the two language variants have been intensified as a result of the growing influence of English and the necessity to adapt new words by finding native equivalents from a variety of fields and disciplines, where the United States has been a pacesetter.

I. Countries with Competing Candidates

A dual vocabulary has begun to emerge which has intensified the language debate in Norway. The following compound words are typical of hundreds of such pair forms:

English and Danish	Riksmål	Nynorsk
Braindrain	hjerneflugt	hjerneflukt
Knowhow	fagkundskab	fagkunnskap
Handout	handout	støtteark

Whereas Danish and, to a slightly lesser degree, Swedish have often simply incorporated new compound words untouched from their original English format, duplicating the spelling, the two Norwegian variants have struggled with an adaptation that runs the gamut from a local, Norwegianized spelling to a literal translation of the compound words.[2] Some supporters of Nynorsk have been tempted to model the introduction of new words based on native roots after Icelandic and Faeroese practice, the two very minor national languages that derived from old Norse and are spoken by very small populations (250,000 and 50,000 respectively).

Whereas the following are all spelled in Danish as in English, their adaptation by Nynorsk speakers renders them unrecognizable to English speakers.

seils promåsjen	sales promotion	saiens fiksen	science fiction
vaid skrin	wide screen	skriptgørl	scriptgirl
selfmeid	self-made	sjørtsliste	to short list
slovv måsjen	slow motion	bisnissvumæn	businesswoman
vikend	week-end		

Nynorsk purists prefer entirely native renditions of many compound words such as matmølle ("food" and "mill") for the Danish or Riksmål terms "madprosessor" (a literal rendition of the English "food processor"). When the term is essentially of Nordic origin, such as for various winter Olympic sports and equipment, the Norwegians are adamant in refusing to accept English words. A complete unanimity exists in Norway on preferring "snøbrett" to snowboard.

A famous anecdotal illustration of the continued deep divide between the two groups of Norwegian speakers is the case of the English "milk shake." Opponents of Nynorsk have ridiculed the Nynorsk rendition of this, "skakamjølk," (the root "skak" means "to shake"), a form that many speakers of Bokmål/Riksmål thought looked so strange, they put it on t-shirts and pretended to be supporters of Nynorsk as a demonstrative display of their view that such spellings are ridiculous. The official Norwegian body for Nynorsk usage, Språkrådet, is constantly alert to prevent the wholesale degeneration of Nynorsk from following Danish and Riksmål forms that threaten what they regard as the continued Anglicization of the national language.

The Political Struggle Over Language, the Environment and Globalism

The fear that globalism carries with it enormous economic, political and social pressures to conform to the needs of a world economy portend the end of small societies' ability to maintain their cultural distinctiveness. Young people are attracted or forced to migrate to economically more active areas paying higher wages. Their interest in maintaining their parents' folk costumes, dancing, handicrafts, cooking and distinctive speech (whether we call it a dialect or a language) becomes a very low priority. What is preserved is not a living culture but a tactic engineered to increase the appeal of "quaint" customs to attract tourists. In turn, demands upon local resources have the power to change the entire economic life of a community. Will the community use its local resources to maintain a traditional way of life or become a tourist resort? This is the question that is posed most often in Noregs Mållag's literature. They claim that their fight to strengthen Nynorsk is part of the struggle to preserve local communities, their way of life, cultural identity and near democracy.

Many of the same issues provide political support for other small nations—Catalonia and the Basque country in Spain—or regions that have a considerable antagonism toward the central government, such as northern Italy. Many people in these areas fear both a gradual diluting of their regional and linguistic distinctiveness from foreign immigrants and the powerful economic trends of a global economy symbolized by Coca-Cola and McDonalds.

The very choice of the names to replace Riksmål (Bokmål) and Nynorsk (Landsmål) stimulated a political debate that had not been intended. Supporters of Nynorsk were adamant that Riksmål conveyed a sense of official recognition that was apparent in other parallel uses of the term "Riket" (the "realm"). Bokmål, however, was not simply a written language but the manner of speech of a large proportion of urban-dwelling Norwegians.

Most linguists by this time had agreed on the definition of a standard language as a spoken and written form recognized as official by the national government. By contrast, a dialect was regarded as a linguist variant peculiar to a given locality or social group and a variant that did not enjoy official national backing. Nynorsk was not a dialect of Danish or

Dano-Norwegian, nor was it similar to modern Hebrew. The Norwegian rural varieties spoken by 90 percent of the population were a living language but lack a standardized written form. Nynorsk was devised as the neutral written form of this speech and was a direct continuation of Old Norse—the original language of the country—in spite of meaning "New Norwegian," subsequently changed to Landsmål.

The term Landsmål has two connotations. The first is that of embracing the entire national territory, but the other that came to mind first among most Norwegians was linked to the concept of "rural." Aasen had rejected the Danish-influenced speech of the towns as too distant from the ancient character of the Norwegian language, but he had not tried to assert that his Nynorsk project was more fit for the rural countryside or less fit for literature and scholarship. He argued that this speech form and its written version were simply a more authentic expression of their common, Old Norse origin.

Nevertheless, because the dispute in Norway has been emotionally burdened by the political assumptions that Nynorsk-Landsmål was the language to be cultivated by all those who valued the rural environment, old folk costumes, folk music, folk tales and superstitions, whereas Riksmål represented foreign influence, urban life, literacy, higher education, and so on. Much of this emotional baggage has been carried forward due to present political controversies, in which supporters of Nynorsk-Landmål inevitably see their position set on other issues such as opposition to Norway's entry in the European Community and NATO and support of the "green" environmental movement and the political left.[3]

The Challenge Ahead

In Israel's unique case, Hebrew played a major role in establishing a sense of national unity and identity for millions of immigrants from diverse cultural backgrounds. Moreover, the success of Hebrew has been a role model for proponents of Irish and Nynorsk, and their spokespersons never tire of pointing to what can be achieved with enough effort, willpower, economic resources, dedication and patriotism, arguments that seem increasingly to fall upon deaf ears as the decline of Nynorsk as a language of choice for elementary education and the criticism of Irish television attest.

Nevertheless, all three nations are facing a challenge to maintain this sense of national identity in a global world dominated by English. The hard facts of life support an approach to learning languages that values the practical benefits of communication, travel, and career. For the Irish, English is the vehicle of their national identity today, but it does not make them any more English than the Americans. It is all the more remarkable that the three nations were convinced to make enormous efforts and sacrifices to become "a nation once again."

For many Norwegians, however, the search for their national language was considered a costly and unnecessary luxury that has only introduced a serious measure of division and has effectively socially and politically partitioned the country. Norwegians who speak Dano-Norwegian are not Danes, nor are they any less Norwegian than those who cultivate Nynorsk and speak in their local dialects. Each new government has to reconcile the contending demands of two language communities on how both can equally express their sense of nationhood. This is sometimes a daunting task. Lars S. Vikør, author of *The New Norse Language Movement*, has summarized the extent to which many Norwegians constantly have to think before opening their mouth:

> In theory, everybody is free to speak his own dialect in every situation, with some special exceptions. For instance, actors on the stage and those employed in broadcasting must use one of the official languages, in the case of broadcasting, also the pronunciation defined in the official spelling.... Prejudices about "good" and "bad, "correct" and "incorrect," "vulgar" and "dignified," "beautiful" and "ugly" language usage flourish beneath and often above the surface. Especially urban lower class dialects are targets of much discrimination: in school, where they are branded as "ugly" and persecuted (despite the law that the instruction shall be based on the children's speech); at work, prestige and promotion often depend upon the extent to which a person masters conservative DN (Dano-Norwegian); in broadcasting, urban dialects are often ridiculed in entertainment programs—and in many other ways.
> (*The New Norse Language Movement*,
> Forlaget Novus, Oslo, 1975, p. 113–114)

4

Maltese: "The Curse of the Country and Fit Only for the Kitchen"

In a fourth case, Malta, the spoken language of the entire people was ignored by self-styled nationalist spokesmen, who preferred the "high-cultured language—Italian" for all public and official use and even referred to Maltese as "the curse of the country" and a language "fit only for the kitchen." Maltese, like Hebrew, is a small, insular, remnant language spoken only in its homeland and a far-flung Diaspora. Both languages are living testimony to the ancient world and staged modern revivals from opposite directions. Maltese was the everyday spoken language of all Maltese in the home and workshop and on board the many fishing vessels of the island but never used for any serious purpose in education, the church, the courts, or literature. Today, Maltese shares the distinction with Iceland of having the smallest number of speakers of any independent European state (approximately 300,000).

The survival and flourishing of Maltese is unfamiliar to most tourists who have even visited Malta without knowing that the entire population speaks a Semitic language written in Latin characters. Moyra Mintoff, the wife of the former, long-time prime minister of Malta, wrote in an introductory Maltese phrase book for English residents that "English people can literally spend a lifetime in Malta without finding it necessary to speak in the language of the people to whom God has given this tiny group of islands."

Origins of a Semitic Language in Europe

It has been estimated that the proportion of Romance to Semitic entries in a Maltese dictionary is about one to two, but the Romance/English origin of technical and abstract words is much higher. Maltese may have some underlying Phoenician elements that were superceded by a North African Arabic dialect brought to the island by Muslim invaders in the early Middle Ages. The Normans conquered Malta in 1090, and the last Muslims were expelled in 1249. Massive Italian influence followed during the long period when Malta was ruled by the Knights of St. John, a Crusader order that took control of the island after being forced from the Holy Land.

An Embarrassing Reminder of Arab Rule and Black Africa

A majority of educated Maltese felt that culturally they were Italian and shared a Catholic-Mediterranean-Latin heritage. Even when nationalist and independence sentiments developed later, they were primarily in Italian, and one Italian-speaking, upper-class nationalist spokesman, Fortunato Mizzi, a politician and intellectual, viewed the vernacular spoken by the poor people as an embarrassing reminder of Arab rule and Black Africa.[1] Much like Herzl with respect to Hebrew, Mizzi believed that the price of converting Maltese into a modern national language would be the country's total isolation from the rest of the world. In Malta, the debate centered on whether it would be possible to use Maltese—the spoken vernacular of the entire population—for any higher purpose, such as administration, education, the legal system and the sciences, rather than a "high" literary European language—first Italian and then English. Unlike in the various Italian regions, educated Maltese did not evolve a specific regional dialect but spoke the standard literary Italian, which had been taught by Italian teachers in private classes. During the entire nineteenth century, however, Italian remained the literary, written and socially cultured language of a tiny minority. At least 95 percent of the Maltese people, mostly illiterate, spoke only Maltese. For them Italian was regarded as an instrument of class oppression.

A Canaanite/Hebrew/Phoenician Speaking World

In both Malta and mandatory Palestine under British rule, a nationalism developed based on an affinity for the pre–Roman, pre–Christian past of the Canaanite/Hebrew/Phoenician-speaking world that at one time (ca. 500 B.C.E.) embraced much of southeastern Spain, Tunisia, the Balearic islands, Malta, Corsica, Sardinia, southern Spain and Phoenicia and Judea to the east. Had Hannibal managed to get a few more elephants over the Alps and conquered Rome, then all of the Mediterranean world might have inherited a Semitic tradition of Phoenicia-Judea-Carthage, having nothing at all to do with Arabs and Islam or with Greece and Rome.

Of course, subsequent historiography with its Hellenic and Roman bias as well as traditional Jewish and Christian theology sought to minimize the achievements of the early Hebrew-Phoenician-Punic-speaking civilization. However, even the conservative *Encyclopedia Judaica*[2] cites a number of scholars who maintain that the expansion of the Phoenicians involved the collaboration of the Hebrews and that Jewish proselytizing was common in those North African regions and Mediterranean islands that had been settled by the Phoenicians. After the fall of Carthage, the descendants of some of these Phoenician settlers converted to Judaism to preserve their Semitic identity and avoid assimilation to the Roman-Hellenistic culture they so hated.

The movement for an independent Israel drew in part upon the Jewish plight of homelessness and in part on a radical, cultural-historical-linguistic thesis linking the ancient Hebrew past to the present. A similar but largely nonviolent movement occurred in Malta. A new Maltese nationalism looked upon Hannibal—the great leader of Carthage, which had been founded by Phoenician emigrants—as the father of the nation, and the language of Carthage derived from Phoenician (known as Punic) as the source of Maltese. Instead of a tiny, provincial Italian island, the new radical Maltese nationalists saw Malta as the remnant of the great maritime empire that had started as the alliance mentioned in the Bible between King Hiram of Tyre and King Solomon. This ideological and historical justification, known as the "Punic build-up,"[3] was utilized to demand the use of Maltese as the main language of primary and secondary education and for all legal purposes. This view was useful in promoting support for independence and rejecting the overtures of pan–Italian nationalists. It was favored by the Labour Party and later by the British government, which saw it as a means to weaken the pro–Italian elements.

It was in the 1850s that scholars finally adapted Maltese to a standard written form in the Latin alphabet, which greatly increased literacy. This was also conclusive proof to would-be reformers of Hebrew and Arabic that it was entirely possible to covert these languages to the Latin alphabet. The Bible was translated into Maltese, further increasing the prestige of the language and resulting in a remarkable rise in the rate of literacy (Figure 8). This success had already elevated the status of the language, but it was the publication of a book in Italian that enabled the cause for Maltese to finally make headway among the island's elite, who had previously spurned the language. In his book, *Saggio intorno alla lingua Maltese come affine all'Ebraico* (The internal wisdom of the Maltese language and its affinity with Hebrew; Valettta, Malta; Micallef

IL-KTIEB TAL-ĠENESI

IL-KTIEB TAL-ĠENESI (nisel, oriġni) jirrakkonta l-istorja tal-bniedem primittiv u l-istorja tal-Patrijarki: Abraham, Iżakk, Ġakobb u wliedu. L-ewwel parti tiddeskrivilna b'mod addattat għal dak iż-żmien, l-istat reliġjuż tal-bniedem midneb imbiegħed minn Alla, li ħalaq l-univers u l-bniedem fi stat ta' perfezzjoni; minkejja l-ħniena ta' Alla u l-inizjattiva tiegħu biex isalvah il-bniedem dineb u webbes rasu. Ghalhekk kien hemm bżonn li Alla jaqbad triq oħra billi jsejjaħ lil Abraham, ibierku u jwegħdiu li permezz ta' nislu jbierek il-ġnus. Dan il-kwadru jservi biex jgħaqqad f'ordni wieħed u direzzjoni waħda, it-tliet tradizzjonijiet J.E.P. li jiffurmaw il-Ktieb.

Il-Ktieb tal-Ġenesi għandu valur kbir għax jittratta l-problemi fondamentali tal-bniedem fir-relazzjonijiet tiegħu ma' Alla u r-relazzjonijiet tal-bnedmin ma' xulxin. Bih tibda l-istorja tas-Salvazzjoni li għadha sejra sallum. Għalhekk insibuh imsemmi bosta drabi fil-bqija tal-Bibbja sa l-Apokalissi.

Il-ħolqien tas-sema u l-art*

1 ¹Fil-bidu Alla ħalaq is-sema u l-art; ²u kienet l-art taħwid baħħ; u d-dlam kien fuq wiċċ l-abissi u fuq wiċċ l-ibħra kien jittajjar riħ ta' Alla.

L-ewwel jum: ³U qal Alla: "Ha jkun id-dawl." U d-dawl sar. ⁴U ra Alla d-dawl li kien tajjeb. U Alla fired id-dawl mid-dlam. ⁵U d-dawl Alla semmieh jum, u d-dlam sejjaħlu lejl. U dalam u sebaħ - L-ewwel jum.

It-tieni jum: ⁶U qal Alla: "Ha jkun hemm medda f'nofs l-ilmijiet u tifred ilma minn ilma." ⁷U Alla għamel il-medda u fired l-ilma ta' taħt il-medda mill-ilma ta' fuq il-medda. U

hekk sar. ⁸U l-medda Alla semmiha sema. U dalam u sebaħ - It-tieni jum.

It-tielet jum: ⁹U qal Alla: "Ha jinġemgħu nahal waħda l-ilmijiet ta' taħt is-sema u jidher l-inxif." U hekk sar. ¹⁰U sejjaħ Alla l-inxif art; u l-ġemgħa ta' l-ilma sejħilha baħar. U Alla ra li kollox kien tajjeb. ¹¹U qal Alla: "Ha tnibbet l-art il-ħaxix, ħaxix li jagħmel iż-żerriegħa, siġar li jagħmlu l-frott biż-żerriegħa ġo fih skond għamlithom, fuq l-art." U hekk sar. ¹²U nibbtet l-art il-ħaxix, ħaxix li jagħmel iż-żerriegħa skond għamlietu u s-siġar jagħmlu l-frott biż-żerriegħa skond għamlictu; u ra Alla li kien tajjeb. ¹³U dalam u sebaħ - It-tielet jum.

Ir-raba' jum: ¹⁴U qal Alla: "Ha jkun hemm

Figure 8. First page of a Maltese Bible.

Publishers, 1880), Annibale Preca argues for the close association of Maltese to Hebrew and Aramaic, the languages of Jesus and the Biblical prophets and disciples).

A handful of local scholars in the 1870s, believing that Maltese primarily derived from Punic (the language of ancient Carthage) rather than Arabic, sought to convince the common people of Malta that their language deserved to be respected instead of held in contempt. Why should it be denied as the language of instruction in the schools, of the courts, and of a great literature when a similar language had already produced the Bible?

Change of Alphabet

These scholars were vindicated in their lifetime by having the opportunity to observe the enormous increase in literacy achieved by the new alphabet. They adapted the language to twentieth century needs and strove to create a "Malti Safi" ("pure Maltese language"). This new orthography made use of the letters q, w, and k, which are absent from Italian, and differed from the one originally adopted, that had a slight Italianate appearance and was more appropriate to portray words of Latin and Italian origin. However in Malti safi, many new terms were derived from a Semitic-Arabic root to replace the great number of Italian and English terms that had been in common use in the spoken vernacular.

The Lure of Italian Culture and Italia Irredenta

Until Mussolini's assumption of power, Italian governments were wary of lending any support to Maltese proponents of union with Italy. The cynical Italian view that prevailed was that the Maltese were only rank opportunists who wanted the religion of Rome, the language of Dante and the English pound. Under the conservative Italian monarchy, the government was at pains to distance itself from a tiny but disruptive group of Maltese who demanded incorporation into the new united Italy. In the 1930s, this pro–Italian circle was attracted to Mussolini's dynamic leadership and dreamed of integrating Malta in his new empire extending across the Mediterranean to Ethiopia, Somaliland and Libya. Italian publications had always enjoyed a wide circulation in Malta, especially in the literary, legal and scientific fields. For the educated Maltese, Italian had always been "a symbol of moral and civil progress and imaginative thought."[4]

Malta's strategic importance to Britain increased following the opening of the Suez Canal in 1869 and led to a gradual reduction in the privileged position of Italian in the schools and courts. Although most Maltese were reluctant to embrace fascism, the events leading up to Italian participation in the war in 1940 created a crisis for the old, ruling, Italian-speaking elite. In June, 1940, immediately after entry into the war, the Italian government erected a monument to Fortunato Mizzi, the old Maltese politician who had been the leading spokesman on the island for Italian culture. This was a vain gesture. Most Italian-speaking Maltese realized that the British government had not been prejudiced against Italian on cultural grounds or favored Maltese out of spite but were motivated by defending British interests.

After Italy's aggression against Abyssinia (Ethiopia) in 1936 and

1937, the British government and Maltese authorities abolished Italian as one of Malta's official legal languages, and great strain was placed on British-Italian relations due to Malta's inclusion in a list of Mussolini's territorial demands. When Italy entered the war in May, 1940, crowds in the streets chanted for the "return of Corsica, Savoy, Tunis and Malta!" (the last two had never been part of Italy).

Affection for and veneration of literary Italian was not, however, simply a political expression of a desire by a small minority for annexation by Italy. Many conservative and devoutly Catholic Maltese saw in Italian their link with European civilization and a truer expression of historic Maltese identity with its links to the church and Latin than English. Many Italian politicians and literary figures had sought temporary asylum in Malta, and most aspiring Maltese writers and poets wrote in Italian. Even after the success of the rival Labour Party to establish Maltese as an official language and the language of all primary and secondary education, more conservative Maltese preferred the more Italianate orthography and rejected many of the newly coined words of Malti Safi.

A new appreciation of Italian since World War II has become apparent with the growth of the Italian economy, its participation in the European Community and the popularity of Italian television and films. It is no longer restricted to the middle and upper classes. The Maltese people have demonstrated they are no longer divided by the old controversies over language and the pro- or anti-Italian and British sympathies that were so divisive in the interwar period.

Postindependence Orientation to the East and the Arab World

The leading political movement in Malta during the postindependence period has been the Labour/Socialist Party, which had always taken a negative stance toward Italian as the language of the upper classes and linked to the church hierarchy, with its high regard for Latin and Italian. The Labour Party, even after independence, was committed to Maltese at home and English as the primary second language. Under the leadership of Dom Mintoff, the Labour Party even strove to bring about Malta's integration within the United Kingdom in 1957. These efforts were rebuffed by the conservatives and the Catholic church, which feared the influence of Protestantism, British secularism and American materialism. A referendum on this proposal won 43 percent of the popular vote, with only 13 percent opposed and 42 percent abstentions.[5]

The use of language as a political football marked the Labour Party's long term in office following independence in 1974. After its earlier efforts to promote Maltese as the national language and its support of English rather than Italian, the party embarked on a policy of drawing closer to neutrality and cooperation with both the eastern Bloc and Libya's mercurial leader, Colonel Omar Khaddafi. The old debates on language were renewed, and scholarly treatises rejected Preca's theory of a remote connection with Carthage and ancient Phoenician.[6]

Maltese's debt to Arabic was fully recognized, and the Libyan cultural center and embassy were upgraded to become the most visible foreign presence on the island. Arabic was made a compulsory subject in state secondary schools, and scores of Libyan teachers were imported to fulfill the new academic requirements. The result was predictable. The Maltese people are renowned for their continued devotion to the Catholic faith, as shown by attendance at masses and confession, yet they share a linguistic kinship with the Arabic- (and Hebrew-) speaking world. This is only a remote kinship, however. They never felt a contradiction in referring to God the Father as Allah, an example that substantiates the old saying that the Maltese vernacular is "Semitic material in a Roman mouth." Enzo Rossini summed up this remarkable attempt to mix language, culture and politics: "The Catholic Maltese abhor the Muslim Libyans, and though they stand to gain economically by co-operating with their richer neighbours to the south, the political and military aspects of the Libyan connection are unpopular and an electoral handicap for the Socialist Party."[7]

This did not prevent Mintoff from proclaiming that the Maltese and Libyans were "blood brothers" and the new socialist prime minister, Dr. Carmelo Mifsud Bonnici, who succeeded Mintoff, went on to say in an interview with an Algerian newspaper that "The Maltese people cannot forget their Arab ethnic origin." In 1987, the Libyan-Maltese honeymoon ended, and the socialists were thrown out of power in the elections that returned a conservative majority and abolished Arabic as a compulsory subject.

Maltese: The Accomplishments of the Last Hundred and Twenty Years

Malta's heroic stance during World War II resulted in the awarding of the George Cross medal to the entire island for the bravery of its people under fire (a greater tonnage of bombs fell on Malta than on London during the "Blitz"). The postwar period has greatly strengthened the position of Maltese first and foremost and then English, which most Maltese use daily. As for Maltese, it was the primary language at home and understood by the islands' entire population. Linguists realized, however, that it was in constant need of "artificial respiration" in the way of invented or adapted new words from Italian and English to provide the vocabulary necessary for twentieth century life.

It has been a remarkable success, second only to that of Hebrew in answering the essential question, "Who are we?" Almost all Maltese today do not regard themselves as anything but Maltese, although they may speak fluent English or Italian. Like Israel, the even smaller state of Malta has been transformed from a peripheral province or colony, subject to the rivalry of contending outside great powers, to the homeland of a distinctive people who no longer see any contradiction between their language, culture, and religion. Only one hundred years ago, the choice of an official language in a future independent state was in doubt in all four countries. Ireland was part of the UK; Malta, a British colony; Palestine, a province of the Ottoman Turkish Empire; and Norway, a part of Sweden. Language planning by government and official institutions during the period of national independence has played a large role in the development of the official national language. It has achieved its widest success in Israel and Malta. In Norway and Ireland, attempts were frustrated by the prevalence of a more widely useful major language which in no way was perceived as foreign any longer.

The Uncertain Future

Almost all Maltese speakers are thoroughly bilingual and even switch to English to count, use common everyday expressions, interjections and greetings when speaking Maltese (okay, sorry, thank you). The massive intrusion of English with its real and supposed importance in world trade, diplomacy, science and technology, higher education and tourism are regarded by many Maltese as a passport to a wider world beyond the tiny area of Malta and is a cause of concern. Sensitive and proud people, whatever their political views, are aware that there is a potential danger of reaching the state of partial denationalization, as has occurred in Ireland. In modern Maltese, many English words or terms derived from English are readily apparent in such areas as traffic summons where "handlebars," "windscreen" and "arrest" are immediately recognizable. English speakers have the right to request all proceedings in English.

Some Maltese have publicly expressed their regret at the loss of Italian and the overwhelming penetration of mass Anglo-American culture, including even the popularity of country-and-western music. Assimilated Italian words have frequently been replaced wholesale by their English equivalents. Like Ireland, Malta was allowed to enter their song for the Eurovision song contest in English. No one imagined that a song sung in Maltese could possibly have a chance. More than one authority feared that "the very survival of Maltese as a linguistic species lies in the balance."[8] Moreover, among the most important and immediate effects of globalization is the worldwide impact and growing importance of the English language. In Israel, Malta and Ireland, the need and popularity of English as the language of common discourse are so great in all walks of life that there is a serious concern for the protected status and cultural creativity of the national language.

Part II

Multiethnic Countries with Bilingualism and Multilingualism

The countries in this chapter are all multiethnic states where the formal equality of citizenship masks substantial differences among the component population groups. To a large degree, these peoples constitute separate societies, each speaking its own language. Several languages are thus held to be the country's national languages. Belgium, the first in this group, is often singled out as the state with the most contentious language problem in Europe. Many Belgians automatically add the descriptive designation of "Fleming" and "Walloon" (Figure 9) as a prefix to their ethnicity.

Figure 9. Belgium divided between Flemings and Walloons (courtesy of Lee Ebner, Louisville Courier-Journal).

5

BELGIUM: THE CLASSIC "BUFFER STATE"

In spite of tensions over language, there is no imminent threat to Belgian stability, prosperity and the people's common loyalty (or apathy) to the ruling house. Nevertheless, the country lacks a national identity based on shared aspirations of its component regions, peoples and languages. Belgium became an independent state through the mutual interests of the major, nineteenth-century European powers—France and Germany—to create a buffer state between them with considered British approval. Unlike Switzerland, where the motivation for unifying diverse regions was resistance to tyranny, Belgium lacked any single ideal or source of common loyalty to create a nation.

Its people were not able to draw upon the common memory of a heroic struggle for independence and a pantheon of national heroes. The artificiality of this new political creation was evident from the very beginning, with a foreign prince chosen to inaugurate the royal house and the intervention of the rival powers of Britain, France and Germany to forcibly join the Walloon French and Dutch Flemish speakers. The country must now work out a precise formula to ensure that there is no feeling of one language dominating. Stamps and currency are bilingual. Belgians know that the song entered in the popular Eurovision song contest must vary in alternate years with Flemish and French lyrics.

In the ensuing 170 years, Belgium has sought to enshrine a sense of national identity through preservation of much of its medieval architectural heritage (Bruges, Ghent, Brussels), attempts to become a major European colonial power by retention of the Congo, cultivation of its cuisine (its magnificent brewed beers and delicious steamed mussels with fried potatoes have become a trademark of gourmet tastes), the popular appeal of bilingual singer Jacques Brel, the invention of fictional heroic characters such as the boyhood hero Tin-Tin and the great detective Hercule Poirot, who has to repeatedly correct new acquaintances that he is not French, he is Belgian! Although not a nation, the Belgian state has at least become a permanent feature of the European map. Many observers are convinced that what holds Belgium together is the lack of any viable alternative, and the Belgians are so prosperous and naturally staid, placid and conservative that both Walloons and Flemings fear that any radical change is liable to place their vaunted prosperity in jeopardy.

The most paradoxical and ironic characteristic of Belgian identity is that this contentiously divided state has become the very symbol of European unity with aspirations to embrace the entire continent—a dream that Caesar, Charlemagne, the Holy Roman Emperors and Hitler all aspired to. The world press is almost daily full of articles referring to Belgium or Brussels as a great economic and political power. Of course what is meant is not the ministate of Belgium but the aspirations of a powerful, European superstate.

The personal attachment and sense of loyalty to the Belgian monarch as ruler has cut across ethnic and linguistic lines. A remnant of this premodern characteristic can still be seen in the title of Belgium's ruling house. As a result of dynastic marriages and common economic and religious interests, Dutch-speaking and Catholic Flanders and French-speaking and Catholic Wallonia have been united under a ruler whose title is "King of the Belgians" (i.e., his subjects rather than as king of a distinct national territory).

Historic Origins of Belgian Identity: Flanders, the Ardennes and Wallonia

The more-than-one-thousand-year-old boundary between the Romance and Germanic languages runs through the lowlands from west to east, just skirting Brussels, which lies just to the North. The region has had a role in European affairs since Roman times, when Julius Caesar defeated the Gauls and Celtic Belgae tribes. The language dividing line has hardly moved since the creation of the Belgian state in 1830. In the Middle Ages, the Belgian heartland of Flanders and the rolling hills covered in forests to the south (Ardennes), as well as adjoining Burgundy, with its capital in Dijon, comprised a powerful vassal state of France with ambitions to remain outside of royal control.

This feudal remnant was the heritage of Charlemagne's son Lothar, whose kingdom was a narrow band of territory straddling the Germanic-Romance linguistic divide and sandwiched in between the west and the east Frankish kingdoms. It continues to dissect modern Belgium, although the capital city of Brussels has enjoyed a special status, with formal equality granted to both languages. The city and its environs form an enclave island with the Flemish area.

One of Europe's greatest historians, Henri Pirenne,[1] deals extensively with what he termed the "Belgian question," arguing that this territory, by whatever name, was the inevitable outcome of medieval history. Its origin in the aftermath of Charlemage's empire under hereditary dukes was an essential ingredient in maintaining the stability between the two arch-rival kingdoms of the West Franks (France) and the East Franks (Germany), along the great river systems of the Scheldt and Meuse. From its first appearance, this entity embraced Frisians, Flemings, Walloons, French, Alsatians, Germans, the Provencaux and North Italians.

The Medieval Legacy and the Shibboleth Tactic

Visitors to Brugge (Bruges) are made aware of the historic nature of the language struggle by an impressive monument in the main square of the beautiful medieval city to Jan Breydek and Pieter de Coninc, Flemish-speaking butcher and weaver respectively, who led a peasant revolt (that ended in the "battle of the golden spurs") in 1302 against the Francophile city council. Taking a page from the Bible, the Flemings were able to distinguish French speakers disguised as peasants by their faulty pronunciation of the "unpronounceable" *sch* sound in the Flemish word for "shield." The Flemings insisted that any suspect pronounce the Flemish slogan "Schild en Vriend" ("shield and friend"), which invariably gave away the French imposters.

The Biblical story is the source of the word "shibboleth." On February 22, 1995, Prime Minister John Major spoke to the House of Commons about the initiative to reach a settlement in northern Ireland acceptable to Catholics and Protestants. He appealed to both sides to "avoid the shibboleths of the past." He used the Hebrew word for an "ear of corn" (shibboleth) because he was aware that most of the members of the house were familiar with the Bible. The figurative sense of a shibboleth would thus immediately be appreciated. The similarities of the tragic situation in Ireland, with the story of the two warring tribes in the Book of Judges (Judges 12:5–6), are truly remarkable. The Ephraimites, unlike the Gileadites, were unable to pronounce the *sh* sound at the beginning of the word. Shibboleth has thus come to mean any outward sign— accent in speech, dress, flags, songs, religious symbols—that distinguishes "friend from foe."

Is this just ancient history? No. Shibboleths have figured dramatically in decisive events as recently as World War II, when German agents in Holland could be detected by Dutch resistance fighters by being asked to pronounce the name of the resort town Scheveningen. Although German and Dutch are closely related the *sch* sound exists only in Dutch (and, of course, Flemish). It is by no means an accident that the most vivid modern-day recurrences of the shibboleth tactic occurred in Belgium and the Netherlands.

The unveiling of the monument in Antwerp in 1887 to Breydek and de Coninc and their victory in the battle of the golden spurs was accompanied by controversy and a political crisis. For years, the campaigning and fund raising for the statue were sources of Flemish pride. The first unveiling was sponsored by the organizing committee. At the second ceremony, attended by the king and the mayor, both dignitaries spoke in French, provoking a storm of protest.

Differential Demographic and Economic Development

The Walloons have gone from a majority at the state's inception to a minority, comprising only about one-third (less than four million) of the present Belgian population (ten million). The economic heartland of Wallonia, concentrated in the coal-rich, Sambre-Meuse valleys, extending from Mons through Charleroi and Namur to Liège, became a European powerhouse in the nineteenth century and, with the help of British capital, helped drive the industrial revolution. It was this early industrialization that led to such a pronounced gap in standards of living between Wallony and the rest of the low countries. The French-speaking and Catholic Walloons saw no reason to continue being part of the largely Protestant, Dutch-speaking, great merchant families in the Netherlands who had overseas interests. The Catholic Flemings (or Flamands) had little love for the same, distant Dutch rule over their beloved Flanders, and the two regions were coupled together to form Belgium—a not too unreasonable solution for that time.

The Belgium of Today: A Historic Reversal of Roles

Belgian industry turned out a considerable production of railroads, rolling stock and arms. Even today the Belgian arms industry, "F.N.," is a major producer of hand weapons. The area experienced a major recession, however, when the coal seams were exhausted. High unemployment has plagued the region, although this has declined somewhat over the past two decades with the development of biotechnology and the aerospace industry. Nevertheless, the core of modern, Belgian high-tech and light industry has clearly shifted to Flanders. The reversal of economic, social and political roles among the two component regions and nationalities in Belgium has been remarkable. For a century and a half the Flemings struggled to overcome a sense of being the inferior, repressed or decidedly junior partner shut out of the Francophone establishment.

Today, Flanders is the prime economic region of the country, and devolution has proceeded to such an extent that Flanders operates almost without passing reference to Belgium. Flemish self-confidence continues to manifest itself at every level. The prime motivator of this assertiveness has been the struggle for linguistic equality at the national level and predominance within Flanders. Although French is taught in Flanders and the German-speaking region, increasing demands are being made to make it optional and allow pupils to elect English instead.

Flemish Separatism

At the very beginning of the state, Dutch speakers were a majority, but practically no recognition was given to this fact. This was true even in Brussels. A French-speaking elite dominated the state and the capital, Brussels, and embraced the wealthier and more educated Flemings as well. It was not until 1881 that secondary education in Flanders was made available in Dutch. All higher education until 1898 was in French. It was not until this same year that all the laws of the country were promulgated in Dutch as well as French. The first university using Dutch as the language of instruction at Ghent was not established until 1930. Francophones, most of whom spoke no Flemish, dominated the army and colonial service. Dutch became an official language within the armed forces only in 1938. Thus, anti–French propaganda made serious inroads among Flemish speakers, who gave considerable support to the pro–German, Flemish nationalist party and were feared by many French-speaking Belgians as a potential "fifth column."

Although often referred to as a dialect, the language spoken in Flanders—Flemish—is basically standard Dutch, with minor variations in vocabulary and spelling, a few minor regional variations in the pronouns and the prevalence of directly transferred, literally translated Gallicisms. The two forms of Dutch are almost identical and would not rank at being defined as either a dialect or a distinct written language (as Nynorsk and Dano-Norwegian are). Nevertheless, in reaction to the continuing demands of the Flemings for a binational state and equal status for the two languages, some Franco-Belgian writers founded a Societé de Littérature Wallonne in Liège in 1856, thereby attempting to cultivate a specific Belgian literature. Nevertheless, the most prominent, French-speaking Belgian authors and artists eventually moved to Paris, abandoning their nativist Belgian colleagues.

The Conflicting Legacy of World War I

Even before the outbreak of World War I, Belgium had begun to experience greater tension between its French and Flemish speakers. The two groups were oriented toward France and Germany respectively. By 1910 Germany had replaced France as Belgium's major trading partner, and much of the Flemish Catholic population admired conservative German society, with its remarkable achievements in the area of industrial progress and were suspicious of French anti-clericalism in the wake of the Dreyfuss affair.

In World War I, the Belgians rallied behind Albert, a popular king, to defend their homeland against German attack. The country felt confident enough after the war to even demand territorial concessions from Germany and was awarded the districts of Eupen and Malmedy. Nevertheless, the rift between the Flemish-speaking community in Flanders and the French speakers in Wallonia was never healed. The Flemish population considered itself to be the very junior partner in a state where French culture and language were the keys to personal advancement within the administration, education and the professions until after the First World War.

During World War I, almost the entire country was occupied, but a large part of the Belgian army was able to retreat, reorganize and continue fighting. Although the army conducted itself well, there was some resentment among Flemish-speaking troops, who claimed that they were often led by arrogant, monolingual, French-speaking officers. Nevertheless, the Belgian army's continued presence on the battlefields of northern France and on a small sliver of unoccupied Belgian territory for most of the war remained a source of pride for the civilian population. German attempts to sow dissension among Flemish speakers by claims to racial brotherhood were not as successful, as during the Second World War.

German administrators had to work together with the German military to decide on a policy to follow in occupied Belgium. The military were especially concerned about the coastal region and the major port city of Antwerp and nearby Ghent. Their first preoccupation was with the British naval blockade and how best to ensure the continued free flow of raw materials and food. In order to keep their jobs, Belgian civil servants were forced to take an oath of loyalty not to commit sabotage. Although much Allied propaganda exaggerated claims of atrocities, the Belgian population was spared from the far-reaching plans initially contemplated to make massive use of forced deportations to work in Germany.

The German general governor von Moltke and General Friedrich Wilhelm Freiherr von Bissing were aware that a policy of total economic exploitation would deprive Germany of a possible political ally among the Flemings. Although anxious to display some favorable treatment of the Flemings, the occupation authorities were able to take only some symbolic but ineffectual steps in the cultural field. This policy received the name *Flamenpolitik*. German Chancellor Bethmann-Hollweg spoke in April, 1916, of Germany not abandoning the Flemish people to Latin influence: "We will secure for them a sound development, according to their resources, founded on the Flemish language and character." The German high command envisioned some sort of eventual protectorate status, but nothing came of these plans. In March, 1917, the country was administratively separated into Flemish and French regions. A council of Flanders was appointed to act as an advisory body and as a collaborator in the building of Flemish political life and Flemish officialdom. Belgian prisoners were thereafter to be separated in German camps according to nationality (Flemish or French), yet in a manifestation of loyalty, few Flemish prisoners so identified themselves. Street signs bearing French names were removed and replaced with Flemish-sounding equivalents but were generally the butt of jokes and mocked by most of the local population. The official language of instruction at the University of Ghent was changed from French to Flemish, but most of the Flemish-speaking faculty refused to accept positions there. Clearly, the effect of the occupation and the heroic resistance of the Belgian forces and King Albert inspired a sense of patriotism. Unfortunately, this patriotism was not to be repeated in World War II.

All Belgians alike suffered from German requisitions of food, accommodations, clothing and equipment. The British and the French won valuable sympathy from most Belgians by relaxing their economic blockade so that American food aid and supplies from other neutral ships could reach Belgium through the Belgian ports. Belgium's success as an Ally was rewarded at the peace conference, which further strengthened and expanded the country's African empire, and in Europe it was awarded with a small area of former German territory. Belgium was so taken up by its role as a victorious ally of France that the Belgian army participated with French troops in the two short-lived occupations of the Rhineland in 1919 and 1923.

The 1930s: Whither the State?

In a free election in 1936, fascist and or far-right candidates received 20 percent of the vote—a European high in a democratic state. One must, however, carefully distinguish support for the fascist-leaning Vlaamsch Nationaal Verbond (VNV, Flemish National League) whose primary objective was equality and the cause of autonomy for Flanders. It disassociated itself from all foreign models and did not claim to seek the abolition of free elections, parliament and the freedom of association. Moreover, it was antimilitarist.[2] Other fascist parties like Rex drew support from extremely conservative Catholics. The name is derived from the Latin *Christus Rex*—Christ the King. The Légion Nationale (a veterans' lobby) had no basis of ethnic support. Verdinaso, (an anagram of the Dutch words meaning league of the national solidarists of the Dutch tongue) was another far-right movement that agitated for national solidarity among all Dutch speakers. This meant incorporating a future state embracing the Netherlands, Flanders and Luxembourg under a regime of law and order. This idea had already emerged in 1897, when a group of Dutch-speaking intellectuals founded the Pan-Netherlandish League to safeguard the unity of all Dutch speakers in the Netherlands, Flanders, French Flanders and South Africa.

Rex moved so far from Catholic consensus, however, that the church eventually openly distanced itself from the party and its demagogic and controversial leader, Léon Dagrelle. By April, 1937, the church openly condemned the Rexist leader, an extremely handsome and gifted orator whose personality was particularly appealing to women and said to exude "Rex appeal." Although Rex's program did not advocate dictatorship, most observers agree that potentially it was the most dangerous of all the far-right parties in Belgium and was directly financed by both Italy and Germany.

All these movements received the support of disaffected and especially unemployed Belgians. Many of them were already antagonistic to traditional democratic values and easy prey to the draw of an authoritarian and anti–Semitic, mass-appeal party. They feared that any close association with France would again drag Belgium into another world war, and so Belgium's surrender was viewed by many as a blessing in disguise, sparing the country the experiences of being at the center of the European battlefields for four years. The Flemish nationalists were also convinced that the French elite had not made good on its promises of more equitable treatment after the sacrifices of World War I. However, not all these groups then proved to be so easily manipulated between 1940 and 1945 by the Germans.

The Stain of Flemish Collaboration in World War II

After a great ideal of initial confusion, both Légion Nationale and Verdinaso joined the Resistance, while both Rex and the VNV members collaborated and were appointed by the Nazis to important posts. As the war progressed, Rex dwindled and lost all influence in future Belgian politics. Its leader lost all credibility and popularity. The VNV, however, increased its membership and stained a part of the Flemish nationalists with the taint of disloyalty. The close association and admiration of the Walloons for everything French received a severe blow following France's overwhelming defeat. This also severely damaged the prestige of the army and especially its officer class which had been French oriented. German propaganda under the Nazis envisioned the Flemings as part of a Nordic-Germanic commonwealth of nations to be fostered as a means to throw off French tutelage, which had been cultivated by the francophone Belgian elite since the creation of the new state in 1830.

The King Who Failed

Why was this solidarity not repeated in 1940? The quick defeat of allied forces in June, 1940, imposed multiple strains on Belgian society. Many people were convinced that the Belgian army had borne the brunt of the fighting. The immediate occupation of the entire country within a few days left only the few units that had been evacuated at Dunkirk. During the depression, fascism had exercised a strong attraction for many Belgians, but democratic traditions and institutions were strong. The Catholic church exercised a stabilizing and moderating force in society, and the prestige of the monarchy—inherited from the heroic resistance of World War I—was still strong. This was to receive a fatal blow from which Belgian society has never recovered.

King Leopold III sought to pacify German designs on the country by pulling it out of the alliance with Britain and France, which had gone to war in 1914 to "save Belgium from aggression." Following the German occupation of the Rhineland in 1935, which went unanswered by Britain and France and enabled Germany once again to station troops on Belgium's border, the king withdrew Belgium from the alliance. He looked passively on in 1939, when the war began, although aware that a German attack on France would likely try to repeat the maneuver by striking across the Flanders lowland or the Ardennes. He then had to call upon his former allies, again only to desert them by unilaterally surrendering on May 27, 1940, after heroic Dutch resistance had temporarily slowed the German advance.

He did so against his constitutional authority and against the expressed wishes of his government. He decided not to follow the example of the Dutch queen and Norwegian king, who had gone into exile. His decision to surrender was denounced by Churchill, French Premier Reynaud and Belgian Premier Pierlot. In his defense, a certain segment of Belgian opinion agreed that the king had acted to avoid further devastating casualties, as the Belgian forces were under more sustained attack than either the French or British troops, but his decision made a route inevitable, and only due to German indecision were most of the Allied forces able to be evacuated on the beaches of Dunkirk.

During the occupation, the Flamenpolitik was repeated by the Germans with greater success and with the establishment of Het Vrijwilligerslegionen Vlaanderen (the Voluntary Flanders Legion). The underground Belgian press was largely written in French initially, and most appeals for support to the allied cause began with the exclamation "Walloons!," strengthening the impression that Belgium had divided along ethnic lines in support of the Allies and Germans. Many Flemings feel that this view of the Second World War is biased and ignores the Flemish contribution to the resistance.

The controversial king refused, however, to serve as a puppet and was held in custody by the Germans. During the occupation, German attempts to cultivate Flemish separatism were better received than during the First World War. When the king was freed and Belgium liberated, his brother Charles agreed to a request of the parliament to serve as a regent following a referendum depriving Leopold of the throne. There was still considerable hostility against the king for his wartime decision in 1940, and, even when a Catholic majority parliament allowed for his return from exile in Switzerland in 1950, violent street demonstrations threatened to plunge the country into chaos or civil war. Leopold wisely abdicated then in favor of his son Badouin.

The Belgian Constitution and Internal Partition: A Fractured Society

Agitation by the Flemish nationalist party Vlaams Blok continues to erode a sense of national unity among Flemish speakers. The memory of the fight to preserve the country's independence during World War I has faded. In that conflict, over 90 percent of the national territory was occupied by German forces, and the fighting took a toll of 40,000 killed in action (approximately 10 percent of the total Belgian forces mobilized). Each anniversary of Armistice Day, commemorating the war fatalities and casualties is marked by fewer and fewer Belgian flags, indicating a disregard for what used to be a sacred symbol of national honor and unity. Growing economic, demographic and political power has not lessened Flemish resentment but only served to increase it, and the evident lack of national solidarity everywhere in Belgium today is symptomatic of the country's instability.

A number of constitutional amendments and political reforms have effectively partitioned the country into four zones, all defined by language. The line separating the two language communities, enshrined in their respective territories of Flanders and Wallonia, was drawn and recognized in 1963, and no deviation of the line for administrative purposes is possible in spite of any local demographic change. This is official recognition of the principle that language is synonymous with nationhood, ethnicity and territory. These areas are Flemish-speaking Flanders, French-speaking Wallonia (located north of the linguistic divide stretching from Lille across the country to Maastricht), and bilingual Brussels, forming an island surrounded by a Flemish-speaking hinterland and a small, German minority district with local autonomy.

A measure of reciprocity does exist, however, in the requirement that students in the Flemish zone study French as a required foreign language starting in their third year in elementary school, and the reverse applies for French-speaking students in Wallonia, who are required to learn Flemish. Whatever the school of choice in the Brussels region, the students must study the "second Belgian language," and many opt for an additional foreign language, that is, either German or English.

Three regional assemblies have the most responsibility rather than the central government. They have the primary responsibility on matters of housing, education, culture, the environment, transportation and public works. The central government has been left to oversee foreign policy, defense, justice, taxation and monetary policy. There are no real national political parties. Instead, each major party has a linguistically labeled regional affiliate in each of the regions. The language controversy split the historic and world-famous Catholic University of Louvain, so that French-speaking students were required to transfer to a new college, called Louvain-la-Neuve, just beyond the language boundary in the French zone, while the Flemings remained in the town they call Leuven (Louvain). The Belgian Catholic church has always played an important role in Belgium's history and tried to prevent the split but was powerless to stop it.

The Flemish authority refers to itself as a government and acts more as a quasi-independent state than a federal region. Prominent Flemish personalities in the worlds of sports and culture and in the media have been accorded the title of "cultural ambassador of Flanders." Under the administration of Luc Van Den Brande (1992–1995), a Christian Democrat in coalition with socialists and Flemish nationalists (Vlaams Blok), a ten-year plan called Vlaanderen-Europa 2002 was implemented to publicize Flemish culture abroad.[3]

Belgium's Foreign Worker Population: Forced to Choose

The continuation of a separate administrative region of Brussels is a bone in the throat of Flemish nationalists, who regard it as an anomaly created by centuries of a French-speaking elite. Although the present composition of the city is roughly divided into a large French majority (75 percent), a small Flemish minority (15 percent) and a large, foreign worker population (10 percent), Flemish nationalists regard this situation as a violation of the territorial integrity of Flanders. Their proposals range from increased subsidies for the Flemish minority for schools, cultural centers, museums and theaters and envision a future arrangement in which the francophone majority will be granted linguistic facilities only, that is, the right to maintain limited administrative services. This cavalier treatment of the francophone population in Brussels, which is nothing less than the largest, French-speaking city in the world after Paris, is a measure of the degree to which Flemish nationalists have assumed the psychological status as the majority in the whole country.

Although recent Gallup polls still show a majority of the population in favor of a continued Belgian state, there is little enthusiasm anywhere for returning any devolved powers to the central government.[4] Political parties are primarily ethnic, no matter what their formal position on major economic issues. Competency tests in the dominant regional language are a precondition to holding political office. Prime victims of these policies are immigrant groups (largely Moroccan and Turkish), who cannot move freely from one part of the country to another to take advantage of jobs and other opportunities without having to learn another language.

The German-Speaking Region of Eupen-Malmedy

Belgian gains in World War I amounted to 282 square miles of territory and the right to use a railroad running through the towns of Eupen, Malmedy and St. Vith. There was no ethnic factor involved. Belgium's demands were restricted to the historical claim that the area had been Belgian (i.e., at that time "Dutch territory") until 1815, when it was awarded to Prussia for help in defeating the French at Waterloo. There were also economic benefits. Germany reannexed the territory in 1940 and then had to return it to Belgium in 1945. Belgium had been "thrown a bone" after World War I to make up for its suffering, and its French allies rearranged some of the borders in Germany's lost African colonies as well to the advantage of the Belgian Congo, but many Belgians were disappointed that so little had been won at such a great cost.

The Source of Nationality: Territory or Language?

Sentiment to reattach Flanders to the Netherlands in a greater Dutch-speaking state and leaving Wallonia to establish some form of integration within France is growing, and, although violence has largely been absent, no one is ruling it out as a future possibility. As in Canada, the Basque country and the former Yugoslavia, separatism is a threat to the stability of the state. The separatist Vlaams Blok has an overall support within the Flemish community of 12 percent and decisive power in Antwerp, the second largest city.

Even among the most radical separatist group, however, there is a difference of opinion. It revolves around the critical question, is Flemish nationality identical with language or territory? If it is language, then indeed, the revolt of Belgium from the Netherlands and its creation as a separate state in 1830 was a fundamental error. At the time, the religious Catholic population of Flanders felt that their identity and well-being were threatened by the dominant Protestant majority in the Netherlands. The supporters of a language-based sense of national identity have begun to refer to their language as Nederlands (Dutch) rather than Flemish.

They are eager to eliminate all traces of French influence, such as Gallicisms—literal translations of French expressions used by all Flemish-speaking Belgians—and insist upon the use of standard written and spoken Dutch. This is the same program espoused by the prewar Verdinaso movement. The eventual political goal of this group is unification with the Netherlands in a greater Dutch-speaking state. Proponents of this anti–Belgian view even envision a world community to include speakers of Afrikaans and those individuals in Indonesia and Surinam who have retained a knowledge of the language or use it for business and cultural purposes. There is little support in the Netherlands for absorption of Flanders, but there is growing sympathy for mobilizing support in Europe to advance the prestige of Dutch.

Even those in the Netherlands who are suspicious of and opposed to any unification with Flanders are convinced that the Flemish nationalists in Vlaams Blok have alerted the Dutch public to the danger of losing a sense of identity in the European Community primarily due to the dominance of the "big three" languages (English, German and French). For those Flemings to whom the basis of their identity is the territory of Flanders and its distinctive history—including the successful revolt against the ruling Dutch House of Orange in 1830s—the language, with its shades of different usage, pronunciation and grammatical peculiarities, is simply an expression of their distinctive identity: Flemish and not Dutch.

They are also motivated by what they believe to be the justice of their cause and that "two wrongs make a right." This is the best way to describe their anti–French sentiments and belief that a great historic wrong was perpetrated against French Flanders, the narrow strip of still

Flemish- speaking rural territory adjacent to the Belgian border, whose population has been assimilated to French culture and language. This region has been French territory for more than two and a half centuries, and only a remnant of between 50,000 and 100,000 Flemish speakers remain who are wholly integrated within French society.

Whither Flanders?

Should Flanders be merged again with the Netherlands? It remains to be seen how such a new state would be integrated economically, socially and politically. Historically, this idea has been proposed several times and never attracted significant support. The Belgian case is entirely different from the language disputes in Ireland, Israel, Norway and Malta. Within each of the two constituent groups comprising Flemish and French speakers, there is a considerable doubt and question as to their own identity. Fewer and fewer people find the answer "We are Belgians" satisfying to either themselves or their neighbors.[5] Having visited Belgium several times, I have made it a habit to look at the most popular songs on the Belgian hit parade, featuring the patriotic theme of the country's beauty. Dozens of songs mention Mooi Vlaanderen (beautiful Flanders), Vlaanderen mijn land (Flanders—My Country), Mijn Vlaanderen (My Flanders), Ik Ben Een Vlaamse Jongen (I am a young man from Flanders), Terug In Vlanderen (Back to Flanders). Not one mentions België, the name of the country in Flemish.

Flemish speakers may ascribe their identity to their homeland of Flanders or alternatively regard themselves as part of a greater Netherlands homeland, which was partitioned in the past. Walloons who previously did not question their separation by history and tradition from France must ponder the possibility of playing some role other than French speakers in the great, historic capital city of Brussels. How such an integration into a new, peripheral region of France surrounded by parts of Flanders could possibly be accomplished is still only a subject of speculation. Geography works against such a project. Brussels cannot be converted into an exclave of France, and no Flemish nationalist will surrender any part of Flanders.

The Future Outlook

With the growth of the European Community and increased economic integration and the introduction of the common Euro currency, all of the old nationalist concerns over territory and language seem to many Europeans to belong to the Dark Ages. Nevertheless, they are still a very considerable element of irritation. The historical experience of

Belgium illustrates that national identity has not been a consistent factor and at various times was closely aligned with religion, territory, and loyalty to a king. Neither of these factors nor the troubled and contentious past have been potent enough to serve as a rallying point with which to unite the Belgians of today. Language has only added to the divisions and made all Belgians aware of their links to a language community outside the country.

A Look at the Bright Side

Many Flemings and especially the separatist Vlaams Blok are opposed to Belgium's participation in the EU and the choice of Brussels as its capital. This is due to the migration of French-speaking foreigners (many of them from North Africa) to Brussels. Nevertheless, there is also the bright side that many Belgians are authentically bilingual. Even in Flanders and Brussels there are many parents who choose a French secondary school for their children. They are confident and proud of their Flemish heritage but choose a French higher education to enable their children to look out through a larger window on the world.

They will often admit in private that they are no less Flemish than the separatists and charge that much of the language controversy has been exacerbated to gain political sympathy. Although many fewer in number, there are francophones in Wallonia who also choose a Flemish secondary-school education for their children so that they will not feel themselves a minority in their own country.

Many Belgians, whatever their ethnic-linguistic origin, prefer to call successful countrypersons who win honors abroad—whether in the Olympics, a chess championship or the Nobel prize—simply Belgians without any qualifying adjective. This certainly gives ground for hope and warns observers not to single out Belgium as an example of the worst in human behavior or proof that Europe will never unite. Many bilingual Belgians are better placed for prestigious jobs in the growing EU bureaucracy and can take full advantage of what a united Europe has to offer.

6

SWITZERLAND

Belgium's failure to overcome the language divide is due in part to constant political agitation and has often been used as a convincing argument in favor of the benefits of a single national language. It is argued that only a single national language can act as a decisive stabilizing element in the development of common loyalty to a state and its institutions: "In those cases in which a state has had to recognize more than one language the resulting situation is often fraught with danger."[1]

Nevertheless, Switzerland's four official national languages have not hindered a strong sense of cohesion and national unity. In the face of Hitler's ravings about the destiny of one German-speaking nation, all segments of Swiss society stood firmly behind a policy of a strong defense. German-speaking Swiss were no less patriotic than their French- and Italian-speaking fellow citizens. No segment of Swiss society feels it is more authentically Swiss than any other, and the answer to the "Who are we?" question, so unsatisfactory for most Belgians, is never asked in Switzerland. Rivalries, conflicts of interest and even war plagued the early history of the country, but it was never based primarily on the cultural-linguistic cleavage between German, French and Italian speakers. Other issues such as urban or rural interests and religion cut across the ethnic divisions, but for a century, more than any other multilingual country, the Swiss have evolved a loyalty to a shared sense of nationhood.

The stability won, through centuries of peace, an ability to militarily defend the country against any aggressor and the integrity of an incorruptible banking system, and its uninterrupted democratic institutions have resulted in the stability of Swiss currency and a reputation as a world-renowned safe heaven for foreign investments and private assets. These very reasons made Switzerland the natural choice for the headquarters of the former League of Nations and the International Red Cross. The country has nevertheless continued to reject membership in the European Union and by a very narrow referendum approved membership in the United Nations in March 2002.[2] The long-standing opposition was

92

the result of its disappointments due to the experience of the League of Nations after World War I.

To many foreign observers, Switzerland has more than a slight reputation as eccentric. It is hard to merge the idyllic Alps, picturesque folk legends of Wilhelm Tell and Heidi with the world's most efficient citizen-army, the luxury hotels of the world's premier tourist industry or the world's most famous watches and clocks. Among other things, its eccentricity[3] manifested itself in rejecting women's suffrage for almost a century after its adoption everywhere else in western Europe. How could a country located in a hostile alpine environment with almost no natural resources achieve the world's highest standard of living? However, the question which has fascinated the rest of the world even more than the economic one is the how such a country, whose people are "divided" by four official languages and two major religions, could maintain a strong sense of cohesion and solidarity.

Origins and Expansion of an Antifeudal Defense League

The three original, entirely German-speaking forest cantons of Schwytz (whose name, somewhat altered to Schweiz, became a common designation for the entire country), Uri and Unterwalden, around the eastern shore of Lake Lucerne, entered into a defensive alliance in 1291 to protect their rights. The Swiss remained free from the interference of feudal lords and maintained their oath to the Holy Roman Emperor to protect the St. Gotthard Pass through the Alps between Italy and Germany in feudal times. When the Hapsburg dynasty first began to abuse its obligations, the forest cantons rose in rebellion and established a confederation celebrated in Swiss folklore by the Wilhelm Tell legend.

Attempts by the Austrians and the Holy Roman Emperor of the German nation to crush Swiss independence were defeated, and the success of the forest cantons inspired neighboring city-states to join the confederation. Bern, Zurich, Zug and Lucerne brought with them considerable resources and urban sophistication. The trade of these cities was linked to the passageways through the Alps and across the Rhine River. Gradually Swiss successes in war and its policy of religious tolerance between Catholics and Protestants enabled it to escape almost unscathed from the devastating Thirty Years War (1618–1648). This further acted as a magnet to later draw in the Italian-speaking Ticino and French-speaking Vaud regions.

Other new candidates for membership were attracted by Switzerland's republican form of representative democracy, and several of them deposed a bishop or prince in order to join the Swiss confederation.

Switzerland's triumphs obscure what was a long, painful, formative period of development. The loosely organized confederation of autonomous cantons did not encourage a common sense of Swiss nationality until 1848, when, following a civil war instigated on a religious basis, a new constitution was adopted. It copied the American federal system of government. Until then, the country lacked a permanent site for its federal parliament (the Diet). Switzerland was not a fact determined by destiny but the outcome of choice and chance. It was not inevitable and certainly not the natural outgrowth of a common, cherished remote past in spite of the fact that many prehistoric Celtic sites have been excavated in Switzerland, and it is generally acknowledged that much of today's German-speaking population were not originally Germanic in origin.[4]

Several times in its history, Catholic-Protestant rivalries exploded in war, and the 1848 constitution banned the Jesuits from residing in Switzerland. Until the new federal constitution of 1848, the country was internally divided by hundreds of toll barriers and had no common currency or even system of weights and measures. As late as 1798, when France invaded the country, there was no federal army available to oppose them. Nothing approaching a unified national consciousness beyond the cantonal level existed until 1848, and yet by 1939, a Swiss national consciousness and patriotism had reached such a peak level that Nazi Germany was forced to shelve any aggressive intention to conquer and absorb the country.

Was Switzerland Inevitable?

The idea of a Swiss state embraces diverse peoples who differ in various cultural attributes, including the language spoken at home in intimate surroundings. The Swiss are not German or French or Italian speakers who happen to live in the Alps. Swiss history is the saga of devotion to representative democracy and honest government and opposition to feudal privilege. It also demonstrates that many observers of the relationship between language and nationalism have put the cart before the horse. Political geography and not language or ethnic origin is the key to understanding Switzerland's origin and development into the most stable state in a continent torn by controversy and war. The German-speaking Swiss were originally no more distinct in their variety of a spoken German dialect than other German speakers in such regions as Schleswig-Holstein, Bavaria, or Silesia, all of which later were united with Prussia to become one country. The peoples of these regions adopted the official high German language as their patriotic duty and molded their local speech to more closely match the written standard.

One cannot speak of a "typical Swiss" and his or her tastes in music, food, art, leisure and hobby activities, folk customs or even superstitions. These have been mapped and shown to overlap to a considerable degree across the borders with France, Germany and Italy. One such notable example is how parents explain to children where babies come from[5] (Figure 10). Most French-speaking parents prefer the explanation of the cabbage and pumpkin story, Italian-speaking Swiss children learn that they have been purchased at a store, while German-Swiss parents repeat the familiar stork-delivery story. In the region south of the great alpine watershed, the most popular tale is that babies are found by monks and hermits.

At home in their respective cantons, each segment of the Swiss population feels entirely free to cultivate their own way of life, yet all have

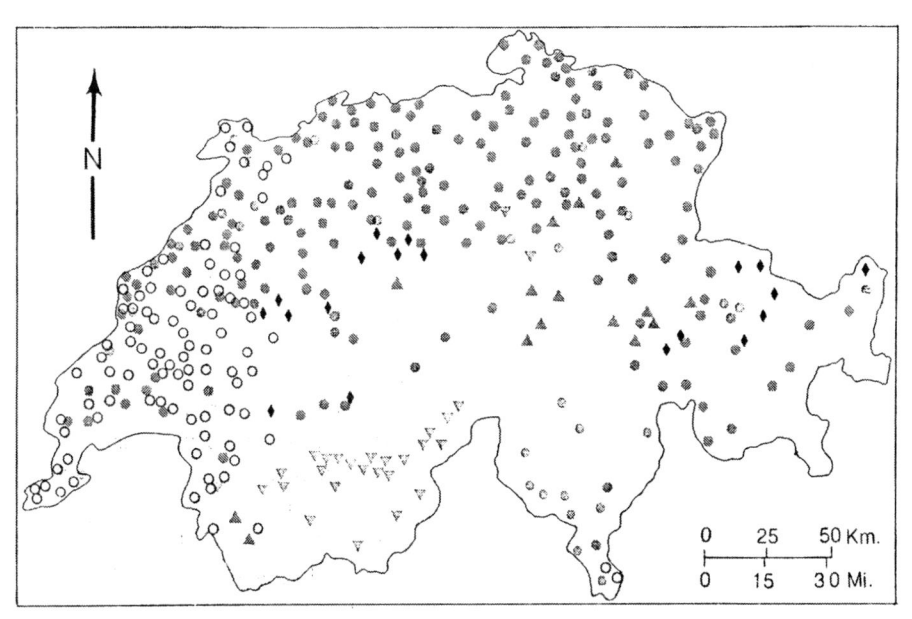

- Purchased at store
- Monks of the forest or hermits
- Church, chapel, or monastery
- Cabbage or pumpkin
- Hollow tree or log
- Stork

Figure 10. "Where Children Come From." Map illustrating folklore explanations in Switzerland. Diverse stories reflect language areas. Source: After Elsbeth Liebl, "Herkunft der Kinder" in Paul Geiger et. al. Atlas der Schweizerischen Volkskunde, Basel; Schweizerische Gesellschaft für Volkskunde, Vol. 2, plates 202–205. Map in *The Human Mosaic; A Thematic Introduction to Cultural Geography* by Terry G. Jordan and Lester Rowntree, 2nd edition, Harper and Row, 1979, p. 233.

become united by a common loyalty, democratic institutions, a shared history and sense of destiny. This has been achieved over 700 years of a painful common past, not by an original common language or culture. The Swiss, like the Jews, the Greeks or Japanese are convinced as they sing in their national anthem that they have been chosen by God to be a free nation in His most favored land[6]:

> When the morning skies grow red
> and over us their radiance shed
> Thou, O Lord, appeareth in their light
> when the Alps glow bright with splendor,
> pray to God, to Him surrender
> for you feel and understand
> that He dwelleth in this land.
>
> In the sunset Thou art nigh
> and beyond the starry sky
> Thou, O loving Father, ever near,
> when to Heaven we are departing
> joy and bliss Thou will be imparting
> for we feel and understand
> that Thou dwellest in this land.
>
> When dark clouds enshroud the hills
> and gray mist the valley fills
> yet Thou art not hidden from thy sons.
> Pierce the gloom in which we cower
> with Thy sunshine's cleansing power
> then we'll feel and understand
> That God dwelleth in this land.

Swiss Federalism and Nation Building (Confederatio Helvetica)

Although the Swiss system of federalism owes much to the model copied from the United States, there is an additional element called "consociation" that involves a "constitutionalized distribution of power among presumably permanent (inter-generational) groupings—religious, ideological or linguistic—within a polity so as to guarantee all their ability to maintain their particular ways of life while having a share in the governance of the whole polity. They differ from ordinary pluralism in that the polity recognizes the existence of permanent groups, provides them with resources for their self-maintenance, and guarantees them an equal place in the constitutional system that can only be changed through constitutional means. By and large, such arrangements are designed to guarantee religious, ideological and cultural differences and autonomy in the spheres that relate to the maintenance of those differences (e.g. education, mass communications, religious services, etc.)."[7]

This means, for example, that recognized religious institutions such as hospitals, orphanages, and health insurance societies receive government assistance in providing services to their members, and translation services are available practically everywhere to deal with cantonal or federal matters and the courts.

The problem with all attempts to use the Swiss system of autonomous cantons as a model for interethnic disputes elsewhere in the world (such as in Bosnia or Israel) is that the Swiss did not invent the system first to solve interethnic disputes. It evolved over centuries and eventually came to integrate diverse peoples, all of whom freely chose the model as preferable to other alternatives. The first cantons were all thoroughly German speaking. The powerful attraction of the confederation for other areas was the result of its rejection of feudal overlords and serfdom. It ensured mutually beneficial economic ties to manage the transalpine trade and the military preparedness. The original confederation expanded as the best means to ensure its defense and to avoid the bloody interreligious wars that followed the Reformation.

The subsequently annexed, French-speaking areas in the Vaud and Aargau and in the Italian Ticino were originally rotated among the more powerful German speaking cantons as joint dominions but given the opportunity to become equally sovereign cantons in time. This political status as outlying but equal members of the confederation proved much more attractive to the people of these areas than the alternative of annexation to the centralized nation-states of France or Italy based on language and ethnic homogeneity."[8] Few of the cantons of modern Switzerland are entirely homogeneous in both language and religion. Minorities of whatever kind within each canton can seek redress of grievances without causing an ethnic or religious conflict with other cantons. The name of the country on international driving plate emblems is abbreviated "CH," for the Latin "Confederatio Heveltica." On postage stamps, the neutral shorter Latin form "Helvetia" is used; otherwise, Switzerland might have to crowd their stamps with four different names (Figure 11).

Switzerland's Great Test

In spite of almost a decade of hostile propaganda, Swiss opinion was united behind the government's total rejection of Nazi Germany's attempts to absorb its fellow Germans in a new Reich. The Swiss were not and are not Germans. The country built an enormous military structure to resist invasion and was fully mobilized at the outbreak of World War II within forty hours, even before the formal British and French

II. Multiethnic Countries

Figure 11. Swiss stamp honoring the annual World Esperanto Congress with neutral Latin name "Helvetia," thereby avoiding the necessity of using the country's four names in the oflcial national languages.

declarations of war, following the invasion of Poland. The government had refused to extradite the Jewish medical student at the University of Bern who had shot and killed the head of the Swiss Nazi Party in 1936. The federal police force and secret service assiduously kept watch on German agents and Swiss Nazi sympathizers.

The Swiss air force shot down ten German fighters and bombers crossing Swiss air space by the first week of June, 1940, and during the war executed seventeen Swiss citizens convicted of spying for the Germans. What sympathy there was for the Nazi cause among Swiss citizens was very often linked to close family ties across the border. In November, 1940, the Swiss government banned both the Nazi and Communist parties. Hitler called the Swiss "German renegades," and the Hitler youth choir sang "We'll get you too, Swiss porcupine!" but all attempts to appeal to a sense of a common German nation fell on deaf ears. Moreover, the Nazis were readily aware that Swiss counterespionage was among the best in Europe.

Swiss policy underwent a change in mid-1942 and reached an understanding with Germany regarding economic cooperation, allowing the transit of trade between the two Axis allies, Italy and Germany. It even permitted the sale of Swiss-made arms to Germany. The Swiss air force desisted from aggressively challenging German incursions of Swiss air space, and the border police turned back thousands of French Jewish refugees. These pro-Axis policies also allowed a partial demobilization of Swiss military forces. In spite of such measures, however, it should be borne in mind that no other neutral country openly resisted and defied Axis propaganda and the attempt to blackmail it into submission. This happened in spite of the fact that close to 80 percent of the Swiss spoke the same languages as the Germans and Italians, thus proving that language is not synonymous with nationality, no matter how convinced the Nazis were to follow this dictate: "Greater Germany," annexed or reannexed Austria, Alsace-Lorraine and Luxembourg—but they never got the chance in Switzerland.

The Cantons, Alpine Valleys and Language

French Switzerland (La Suisse Romande)

The highly decentralized cantonal structure of the Swiss government was organized to reflect the population geography of the country with its many narrow, isolated alpine valleys, a feature of the landscape which operated to differentiate language into many spoken dialect varieties. The only exception to this feature of the human landscape is the western, French-speaking region of Switzerland (Romandia), whose population comprises a little more than 19 percent of the total and is predominantly urban. The cities of Geneva and Neuchatel were centers of literary creativity and often served as a refuge for progressive French writers and philosophers such as Rousseau and Voltaire. This area never developed a specific Swiss form of French. French Swiss writers have been able to take advantage of the great French metropolitan and world market for their works.

Schwyzerdütsch: German-Speaking Switzerland (Alemania)

Schwyzerdütsch, spoken by close to two-thirds of the Swiss as their mother tongue, is immediately recognizable even to foreigners with no knowledge of standard German.[9] It is not a single language but is differentiated into a number of dialects as numerous as "there are valleys in the Alps."[10] It is certainly incomprehensible to most Germans on a visit to Switzerland. Although all speakers of Schwyzerdütsch are educated in standard high German and are able to read and write in it and most can speak it when called for, they prefer to speak the local variety at home and in comfortable social surroundings. Efforts were made by Swiss nationalists, especially on the eve of World War II, to try and codify, standardize and develop a written Schwyzerdütsch beyond the level of a dialectal folktale type of literature, but it never got off the ground due to a recognition that it was not needed and that most Swiss could ill afford to turn their back on a medium of discourse with their powerful neighbor in a postwar world.

Nevertheless, the local dialect has increased in use and moved higher up the register, being used more and more on radio and in television programs, religious worship, political debate and even higher education. Politicians or other public figures who speak in standard high German are likely to give the impression of being snobs or even making themselves sound foolish by their unfamiliarity with a language many of them rarely speak in private. Swiss writers have, however, always written for the much larger German language market, encompassing Germany and Austria. Several of Italy's and Germany's most notable authors such as Ignazio Silone, Erich Maria Remarque and Herman Hesse even fled to Switzerland to continue their writing following the Nazi takeover.

As German is the majority language, most affairs handled in the federal government capital of Bern, including the parliament, originate in this language. As in Belgium, some high schools are provided in the other language, that is, French-language schools for French-speaking civil servants in Bern.

The Italian-Swiss Ticino

The lovely Italian lake district at the southern foothills of the Alps, with its picturesque hamlets and colorful churches perched above narrow valleys, has long been a holiday resort for Europe's wealthiest vacationers. Queen Victoria spent her honeymoon here. The food, architecture, outdoor living style and driving habits of the population are decidedly Italian. Italian has increased its share of the Swiss language pie, rising from about 5 percent after World War II to 7.5 percent today, in part because of a higher birth rate and migration from Italy. Italian speakers in Ticino are divided by the main range of the Alps.

Those to the north have traditionally spoken a rural dialect, whereas to the south the native speech of the region is close to standard Italian, also spoken by most Italian emigrants to Switzerland. Much closer to Milan and Turin than to the major cities of German-speaking Switzerland, the Ticino folk nevertheless sought to ally themselves with the Swiss confederation as early as 1440. Although ruled by the original, German-speaking cantons of Uri, Schwyz and Unterwalden for centuries, Ticino resisted incorporation by Napoleon in a new puppet Cis-Alpine state and successfully demanded equality as an independent canton within Switzerland under the banner of "Liberi e Svizzerri!" (Free and Swiss!) in 1803. The long-awaited unification of Italy (1858–1860) came much too late for the inhabitants of Ticino, many of whom were anticlerical and antimonarchist. For both these political reasons, even dedicated Italian nationalists saw no point in a quarrel with neutral Switzerland to try and absorb the Ticino. Instead, they devoted their energies to completing Italian unification by annexation of the Austrian-ruled Italian-speaking areas in the Tirol, Dalmatia and the Istrian peninsula in the northeast and French-ruled Savoy, Nice and Corsica in the west.

The Ticino region has always had a higher standard of living than adjoining areas of Italy, and neutrality in both world wars presented an attractive alternative for political refugees, pacifists and opponents of fascism. Even Mussolini sought refuge there when, as an anarchist, he was hounded by the Italian police in 1901.

Although almost all residents of Ticino are proud to have remained Swiss and look down on Italian migrant workers, who flock to the region to work in the tourist hotels during the busy summer season, there is still a general discontent at not being within the European Union. For generations, Ticino residents faced high fees to study at nearby Italian universities or at the German-language, Swiss ones far from home. The Università della Svizzera Italiana was founded in Lugano only in 1996. The local residents have even invented a special term of disparagement for their fellow German-speaking Swiss: Oltre Gottardo (beyond the St. Gotthard Pass).

Romansch—Lingua Svizra

One of the most curious aspects of Switzerland's linguistic identity is that the tiny Romansch-speaking element describes its language as "Romansch, lingua svizra." It used to be a common joke that the most blatant example of geographic ignorance was the belief that the Swiss spoke "Swiss," yet in a literal as well as figurative sense this is true of roughly 50,000 people in the canton of Graubünden, comprising less than one percent of the Swiss population, who speak Romansch. In neighboring Italy, diverse dialects are referred to as Rhaeto-Romanic and are spoken by a much larger population than in Switzerland.

Although originally an oral dialect, it was made an official national language in 1938 with a standardized orthography encouraged by the Swiss government. This was a clear political act to demonstrably defy Italian claims that Romansch[11] was an Italian dialect, implying an Italian claim to the region. The Swiss move was resented by the Italian authorities, who saw in the elevation of one particular dialectal form of Rhaeto-Romansch to the status of an official Swiss national language, an attempt to tie the local speakers more closely to a sense of Swiss nationhood.

In Italian eyes, the Swiss, who already had three official languages, lost nothing by granting national status to the tiny Rhaeto-Romansch minority group in their isolated mountain valleys. The intention was viewed by the Italians as distracting their own attempts to integrate the much larger group of Rhaeto-Romansch speakers in Italy within the framework of a monolingual Italian state. Prior to 1938, the Italians had been lax in their attitude toward the Romansch speakers in the border area with Switzerland and Austria.

Difficulties and tensions have arisen over the continued influx of retirees, who are mostly German speakers, and although the canton of Graubünden is officially bilingual in German and Romansch, the balance is quite unequal. The largest city in the canton is Chur, where only about 10 percent of the population uses Romansch as their first language, and the next largest concentration of urban speakers of Romansch is in Zurich, in the heart of German-speaking Switzerland. Due to limited resources, Romansch speakers cannot expect to receive the same standard of services. Even in the home canton, secondary-school education is available only in German, and Romansch speakers cannot deal with the federal government or its courts in that language.

The Swiss Educational System and Language Choice

Each of the Swiss cantons has complete cultural autonomy and control of its own educational system. In recent times only one serious dissent over the question of language required the division of one canton (the Jura), as an exception that proves the rule. Although the working language of all–Swiss affairs was always German, this in no way interfered with internal cantonal rights. Until a few years ago, the second language studied in schools had to be one of the three, major, official Swiss languages"; the second could be English as well for those pupils who chose a program requiring a second foreign language. In Alemania (German-speaking region), the first foreign language studied had to be French, and in Romandia (French-speaking region), German. However, the growing popularity and importance of English has changed the picture. It is now the first foreign language chosen by most pupils in Ticino and threatens to overtake the traditional "other Swiss language" in both Romandia and Alemania.

Although this trend worries some Swiss educators—that in the future some Swiss may communicate with other Swiss through the medium of a non–Swiss language—others are pleased that the trend is a sign of Switzerland's integration into a larger European framework, even if not formally a member of the European Union. The Swiss genius has been to create a federal arrangement in which Swiss citizens enjoy a maximum of local self-rule that ensures their cultural identity in their own canton. For centuries, Switzerland has hung together as a kind of United Nations that acted only at the national level in the face of foreign threats. It is a model that many observers believe can show a path for others to follow for closer European integration through the European Union and eventually perhaps a world government.

7

SPAIN: FIVE OFFICIAL LANGUAGES, OR IS IT ONLY FOUR AND TWO-THIRDS?

Castillian and Spanish (Castellano y Español)

Spain has always been and remains a multilingual country—the largest in Western Europe. It is today torn by controversy over the language issue, even as the Castillian language abroad continues its rapid growth and probably has already overtaken English as the language with the greatest number of native speakers (after Mandarin Chinese). For all Castillians and many speakers abroad, the terms "Castillian" and "Spanish" are synonymous. For part of the population in the autonomous communities of Catalonia, Galicia, Valencia and the Basque country, their native language or mother tongue is not Castillian which practically all understand and speak but regard as only one of Spain's national languages.

Both Spanish and English share the distinction of being the most widely distributed languages in the world. Both have more than 350 million native speakers, and each is the official or widely spoken language in more than two dozen independent states spread across Europe, the Americas, Africa and the Far East, yet both are also not entirely sovereign in the United Kingdom and Spain. Each must recognize the aspirations of speakers of other languages who claim priority in their own regional homelands, most notably Wales in the UK and Catalonia, Galicia and the Basque Country (País Vasco) in Spain.

Many tourists and casual observers who encounter Catalán and Galician (Gallego) for the first time immediately see the close similarity with the dominant language of Spain—Castillian Spanish (Castellano, Figure 12) and leap to the conclusion that these are only regional dialects, blending it with French and Portuguese respectively. Nothing is more calculated to infuriate their speakers, who point out that these are official Spanish languages, so designated by law and on an equal footing with

Castillian. In Spain, all languages but Castillian were regarded as regional variants or even looked down on as dialects such as Catalán, Gallego and Valenciano. They have only recently been accorded an official status as regional languages in the educational systems, courts and mass media. In these areas there is still a considerable debate over whether a distinctive language is synonymous with a distinctive sense of nationhood.

Central Rule versus Autonomy

In today's Spain, the constitution grants the three autonomous regions of Catalonia, Galicia and the Basque country control over their cultural identity and education. The result is that education in those parts of Spain is today bilingual, and the minority languages are recognized by the local administration and courts as absolutely equal to Castillian. Anyone looking at Spanish-produced food items in a supermarket anywhere in Spain will find the wrappers, cans and bottles crowded with the ingredients and instructions in all four languages. Many textbooks used in the teaching of English are the same throughout Spain, and a precondition for their use is that the vocabulary lists provide translations of the English words in all four official languages. Since both Catalonia and the Basque country are developed industrial regions that have attracted a lot of migrants from other parts of Spain, there has been a growing tendency for their children to acquire the regional languages that are taught from the first year of primary school.

The Spanish example is more complicated than the Belgian or Swiss cases. Most Cataláns and Galicians would not challenge the appellation of "Spaniards." Many Basques do. Spain liberated itself from Arab-Muslim rule largely through the efforts of the kingdoms of León-Asturias, Castille and Aragón-Catalonia. Castille, in the central upland, was better situated to dominate the liberated lands and first absorbed

Figure 12. Spanish stamp honoring the one-thousand-year anniversary of Castellano.

León and then through dynastic marriage (1476) was united with Aragón. The Catholic sovereigns Ferdinand of Aragón and Isabella of Castille were joint rulers of Spain but also the separate rulers of their respective kingdoms. Not until 1707 did Spain became a totally centralized state. Before then, the honorary title king of the Spains (Rey de las Españas) was used to indicate (much like the title czar of all the Russias) the royal dominion over several associated lands. This tension between a centralized state and autonomous regions led in the past to conflicts over the degree of local autonomy permitted. The present Spanish constitution is the most liberal since the formal unification in the fifteenth century. It accords a large measure of autonomy to the local communidades ("autonomous communities") and, in the case of Catalonia, Galicia, the Basque country and Valencia, the right to use their languages in administration and education.

The Spanish Languages

Catalán and Galician lack the rough guttural *ch* sound of Castillian that is marked by the letters *j* or *x* (as in Don Quixote) derived from Arabic and by contrast share the soft *zh* sound found in French and in an English word like "plea*s*ure." Basque with its multiple *z*'s and k's looks quite unusual. The following sentences in the four languages will give the reader an idea of the similarity of the three, Latin-derived languages and the mysterious remoteness of Basque.

English: In the case of Spain, the existence of a state face on the euro offers a historic occasion to incorporate Catalán, Basque and Galician on the coin of legal tender.

Castillian: En el caso de España, la existencia de una cara estatal del euro ofrece una ocasión histórica de incorporar el catalán, el euskera y el gallego a la moneda de curso legal.

Catalán: En el cas d'Espanya, l'existència d'una cara estatal de l'euro ofereix una ocasió històrica d'incorporar el catalá, l'euskera i el gallec a la moneda de curs legal.

Galician: No caso de España, a existencia dunha cara estatal do euro ofrece unha ocasión histórica de incoporar lo catalan o eusquera e o galego á moeda de curso legal.

Basque: Espainiaren kasuan, euroak alde estatal bat edukitzeak aukera historikoa eskaintzen de katalana, euskera eta gailegoa erabilera lealeko monetaren barruan sartzeko.

Spain's Diverse Regions

Some historians and cultural anthropologists see in today's regional and social diversity the outcome of Spain's historical division among four great cultural and religious traditions. The Castillian heart of the Spanish state most accurately reflects the values of medieval Christianity and devout Catholicism—the haughty pride and exaggerated sense of honor and disdain for manual labor, exemplified by the quest of Don Quixote to achieve the status of a knight errant and create a just world but one in which everyone knows his place.

The opposite pole is represented by Catalonia, which is said to have absorbed the commercial astuteness of Spain's great Jewish community—a respect for industriousness and initiative and oriented toward finance, international trade, sobriety, literacy, and ambition. These values are often held in contempt by the wealthy, land-owning class. The Catholic church in Castille and Falangist propaganda during the Spanish Civil War regarded Catalán separatism as an indication of a "Judeo-Catalán conspiracy" to destroy Spain. The third region of the northwest, modern Galicia, reflects an older Celtic and Gothic mystical past in much the same way as Scotland and Ireland within the UK, complete with a fondness for storytelling and a Germanic love of nature and bagpipes.

Andalucia, in the south, with its great center in Granada, remained under Muslim rule the longest. Its verve, attitude toward women, the presence for centuries of a nomadic gypsy population, a fatalistic belief in one's destiny, an artistic sense with a fondness for geometrical forms, warbling music and dance (flamenco), bragging, vanity and cruelty (bullfighting) have endured and set it apart, Although Castillian Spanish is the language of Andalucia today, there is a regionally distinctive mode of speaking which some local enthusiasts would like to elevate to the status of a separate regional language, as in Catalonia and Galicia. Most Spanish Muslims are today concentrated in this region.

Catalán

In Catalonia, there is considerable tension over the issue of language and a constant struggle to ensure that Catalán receives priority in every sphere of public life, including official actions that many Castillian speakers believe threaten their identity and civil rights. Catalán was the original language of the medieval kingdom of Catalonia-Aragón, the most important rival to the supremacy of Castille. Today Catalán is the primary language of Catalonia, adjoining Valencia (where it is called Valenciano), the Balearic Islands (Las Islas Baleares), the neighboring principality of Andorra, a small section of the southeast of France (Roussillon) and several villages on the island of Sardinia. These areas recall the extent of an independent Catalonia, which was a major maritime nation controlling much of the trade of the Mediterranean and that at one time, in the fifteenth century, dominated Sardinia, Corsica and Sicily as well as gaining a temporary foothold in Greece.

Cataláns justifiably point out that more people speak Catalán as their native language (at least 6,500,000) than Danish, yet their language is not accorded the same respect and official status outside of Spain. They have had to pursue a long campaign to gain equality in their own homeland with Castillian Spanish. Catalán is more distinctly different from Spanish than is Portuguese, yet the language was derisively labeled as a dialect by supporters of a strong centralist government based in Madrid, who believed that Castillian was a major unifying force in Spain.

Catalán nationalists are convinced that Castille usurped their previous dominant position as the leading region in the Iberian peninsula as a result of Columbus's voyages and the expansion of Spain overseas in the Americas and the Philippines, shifting the center of commercial prosperity away from the Mediterranean. No other part of Spain identified so strongly with the antimonarchist and republican cause as Catalonia. The region has always had a more commercial, industrial, liberal and radical character than Castille and has been influenced by French and Italian ideas and fashions that are expressed in an appreciation of elegant styles in art and architecture.

Support for a republic, socialism and a reassertion of the Catalán language has always made relations with Madrid difficult. The language issue became a central tenant of the movement for Catalán autonomy. The language was suppressed under Franco, who prohibited its use in education, the press and theater and even encouraged campaigns to prevent people from speaking Catalán in public. These included putting stickers up in telephone booths, urging callers to conduct their conversation in Castillian. Catalonians were insulted by the exhortation of Francoist officials to "speak Christian!" (used with even more vehemence against Basque speakers), as if they were natives of an underdeveloped, remote and primitive country. The insult has been historically paid back by the public assertions of some Catalán nationalists, including an elected member of the Cortes (national parliament), that Castillian Spanish has already seen the last of its glory days and is now spoken badly, mostly by illiterates from the third world. Such views are often expressed publicly.

Catalán has made enormous strides during the last twenty-five years, and recent surveys indicate that, for the first time, most young people in Catalonia prefer to read books and newspapers in Catalán rather than Castillian. Generous subsidies by the local government promote Catalán authors and films and the teaching the language (Figure 13A). Catalán is alive and thriving. More than 93 percent of the Catalonian population understands Catalán, and more than two-thirds speak it. Yet it still sticks in the throat of many supporters of the present, dominant, nationalist-political party in Catalonia, the CiU (Convergencia i Unió) that the

108   II. Multiethnic Countries

region, especially Barcelona, continues to attract new migrants from other parts of Spain who are reluctant to educate their children in Catalán and that, due to the past suppression of the language, about 50 percent of the population in Catalonia regard Castillian as their mother tongue and use it in a greater variety of situations than Catalán. Many Catalán nationalists continue to be unhappy that, however much "we may have won the lecture hall, we have lost the street."

The law has made Catalán the language of instruction in all primary and secondary public schools. Other laws guarantee the equality of Castillian and Catalán with Catalonia but in fact favor Catalán. These have been modeled after the laws passed in Quebec that favor French in education and public places and have similarly provoked indignation, anger and protests by local Castillian speakers, who have pushed for their case to be taken up by the European Community's organs to protect human rights. Although shop windows and some public services often post bilingual signs in both Castillian and Catalán, the passerby is well advised to be able to read Catalán as it is often the only language used to warn the public of nasty fines for traffic violations, illegal parking, and smoking on the metro. The government, local authorities and public institutions as well as utilities conduct all their business in Catalán and,

Figure 13A. Poster on Mallorca urging the study of Catalán, "A Language for Everyone."

although the citizen or consumer is guaranteed the right to correspond in Castillian Spanish, this requires a special request that is sometimes honored only if written in Catalán. Delays resulting in fines are the lot of many Castillian speakers, who have tried to utilize these theoretical equal rights.

Valenciano: Language or Catalán Dialect?

The linguistic situation is even more ludicrous due to the intense jealousy of neighboring Valencia and the Balearic islands, whose citizens speak a variety of Catalán which is perhaps slightly more different from the language in Catalonia than American English is from British English, yet both these autonomous communities label their official languages as "Valenciano" and "la lengua de las Baleares" and resent any attempt to present them as dialects (the height of political incorrectness). The population of Valencia and the Balearics resent Catalán smugness and often felt left out in the past, when Catalán nationalists focused all of their activities on the region of Catalonia alone.

There is also some historical resentment that these regions were liberated from Muslim rule by the Cataláns who resettled the area with little regard for the remnant Christian population, which also included many converted Jews and Muslims. Castillian Spanish is much more widely spoken in the southernmost third of the communidad, effectively making Valencia bilingual. South of a precisely drawn language boundary just south of Alicante, Castillian remains the sole language of instruction and education, whereas north of it, teachers must qualify in Valenciano to be able to teach in the local schools, a task which some Catalán speakers find as difficult to master as Castillian. Via Digital, a commercial TV subscriber network, dubs all its films and programs or presents subtitles, giving viewers a choice between Castellano, Gallego, Catalán, Valenciano, and Mallorquín (i.e., a Catalán variant spoken on the island of Mallorca, in the Balearic islands). This situation is described by the astute writer and commentator John Hooper as "typical of a rampant localism. Many of the inhabitants of the Balearic Islands and Valencia object to their language being called Catalán at all. So as not to offend local sensibilities, attempts have been made in the past to get people to call it *bacavés* (a neologism derived from the initial letters of Balearic, Catalán and Valencian)."[1]

Many Spaniards who resented Catalán demands have gloated over the difficulties encountered by teachers, many from the region of Catalonia, who were drafted to teach in the schools of the Balearic islands or Valencia, where the regional speech forms, called Mallorquín (in Mallorca), Ibicenco (on the island of Ibiza) and Valenciano prevail. In many aspects, Spain represents a model of compromise in allowing a policy of

II. Multiethnic Countries

linguistic diversity, albeit amidst considerable grumbling. At the monastery of Lluc, on the island of Mallorca, long considered the spiritual center of the Baleares, there is a mosaic map in the courtyard displaying Catalonia, Valencia and the islands with the polemical inscription in Catalán, "uma lengua, un poble, uma cultura" ("one language, one people, one culture"; Figure 13B), yet for many of those speaking "Catalán dialects," there is a rejection of the idea of a single "greater Catalonia." The policies of both the Valencian and Balearic governments are to foster their local language, and both are loath to accept any references to their local speech as a mere dialect.

Galicia (Gallego)

At one time in the Middle Ages, Galician and Portuguese were identical and have diverged only slightly after many centuries. How and why Galicia came to be part of Spain rather than Portugal proves that the long-cherished ideal of so many poets, patriots and philosophers that "language is the heart and soul of the nation" is not necessarily so. If it were, then Galicia would have been part of Portugal, not of Spain. Galicia was liberated from Moorish rule before the independence of Portugal with the help of nearby Asturias-León. The early development of the great pilgrimage center in Santiago de Compostela tied Galicia to other parts of Spain even though the original language was basically Portuguese. A great lyrical-poetic tradition developed in Galicia and spread to other parts of Spain, including Castille, where Galician even became the accepted vehicle for court poetry.

By the fifteenth century, Galician had declined as a result of dynastic wars, in which most of the local nobility supported the losing side in the struggle for the throne of Castille. From the sixteenth to the eighteenth centuries Galicia became firmly integrated in the centralized Spanish state, and Castillian Spanish became the only language of government, literature, the church and administration. Very little literature was then written in Galician until a revival in the nineteenth century, following the French invasion under Napoleon, that stimulated local patriotism. By the middle of the nineteenth century, a renaissance of Galician took place, and competitions were held for poetry and serious literary works, modeled after the movement to revive and promote Catalán. During the last decades of the nineteenth century, a great deal of work was done to devise modern grammars and dictionaries to standardize the language. Galicia remained a poor region and suffered considerable emigration, provoking a further effort to preserve the language lest it die out.

Opposite: Figure 13B. Mosaic map at monastery of Lluc on Mallorca showing "Greater Catalonia: One Language, One People, One Culture."

By 1931, when the republic was established, Galician was proclaimed as the official language of Galicia. As Galicia fell quite early in the civil war to nationalist forces, Franco took a more relaxed attitude towards what was simply considered a dialect of the poor, semiliterate rural population, all of whom also spoke Castillian. A new revival got underway in the mid–1950s, and some progress has been made to develop a wider vocabulary to meet modern needs and literary expression. Recognition of the past achievement of medieval Gallego-Portuguese lyrical poetry has helped stimulate local pride.

Today, about 2,100,000 Galicians out of a total of 2,700,000 speak the language, along with Castillian, and are essentially bilingual, but few use Gallego for purposes outside the home. Some of the best literary work in the language has been written by exiles and emigrants to Argentina and Cuba. The original Royal Galician Language Academy was founded in Havana in 1905. Foreign viewers of Galician television who know both Portuguese and Spanish will immediately recognize the similarities to Portuguese vocabulary (the definite article *o* instead of *el*, *rua* instead of *calle* and *boa noite* instead of *buenas noches*, etc.) but without the presence of so many nasal diphthongs (the "ow" sound, spelled ão, the ending on many Portuguese abstract nouns). Galicia is envied by most Spaniards who are interested in a calm resolution of language issues. The only requirement for teachers in the state school system is to take a two-year course in Gallego, and the only enforced requirement of pupils is that they study at least two subjects in the regional language.

Basque (Euskera)

While both Catalán and Gallego are so close to Spanish that most Castillian speakers can easily read and understand texts in both minority languages, the Basque language (Euskera) presents a totally different case. It dates back to the Stone Age and is the oldest surviving language in Europe without any known relatives. Of the more than 2,000,000 Basques in Spain, all use Castillian Spanish, but no more than 40 percent speak Basque, many of them infrequently, only about 25 percent read it and no more than 10 percent write it). The language issue is emotionally tied to the demand for Basque independence. Outside observers agree that these are inflated figures. Many Basque adults have had to go to special schools (*ikastolak*) to learn the rudiments of the language that their grandparents had stopped using a century ago. This includes the present *lehendekari* (Basque prime minister). Few migrants see any point in trying to learn it.

Another major difficulty is the existence of widely diverging dialects (at least eight) and the difficulty that almost half of Basque speakers must learn how to read the standard orthography adopted for the written language. The entire population of Basque origin is fluent in Castillian Spanish and uses it on a daily basis. Resistance to the Spanish state in the past, before the violent campaigns of ETA began, focused on preserving the language. Maps and road signs were constantly subjected to mutilation (spray painting), and all Spanish place names were obliterated and replaced with their Basque equivalents—Pamplona is Iruña, San Sebastian is Donostia, Vitoria is Gasteiz, and so on. As the autonomous community (País Vasco) is controlled by the Basque Nationalist Party, these names now prevail on official maps and road signs within the region.

Basque Nationalism

Although all Basques in Spain are fluent Spanish speakers and many Basques have made notable contributions to the country's commercial, intellectual and artistic creativity, their full integration within society was postponed due to their peripheral location and involvement primarily in primary industries such as agriculture and fishing. Few Spaniards were attracted to settle in the Basque country until the development of modern industry in the nineteenth century, which posed a challenge to their self-contained existence in a cocoon-like environment. Traditionally the Basques had been allowed a degree of autonomy under their old customs and laws, known as the *fueros*, but the new liberal forces seeking to promote national unity and economic development and to limit the power of the king and the church met strong resistance from arch-conservative Basques.

Even more than Catalán, Basque and the nationalist government were brutally suppressed during the Franco era for their republican sympathies during the civil war. The Basque people have traditionally been very devout Catholics, and during the nineteenth century they supported the reactionary Carlist cause. Modern Basque nationalism, which seeks to reintegrate the entire Basque country, including the provinces under French control, into an independent state, traces its origin to a remarkable and eccentric leader, Sabino Arana. Arana provided an ideology of nationalism, a history of the Basque nation in which Basque contributions to Spain, Spanish culture and the Castillian language were reinterpreted as mistaken, misguided or the result of Spanish deception and intrigue. He designed the Basque flag and also helped modernize the language by supplying the missing vocabulary to a language that had few words for abstract concepts such as nation, homeland and patriotism. His views were colored by the awareness of Basque physical distinctiveness (type Rh negative O blood and "big ears") and the uniqueness of the language into a racist ideology.

Just as Spain had expelled the Moors and Jews to preserve the "purity of blood" and its Catholic identity in the fifteenth century, Arana and the new Basque nationalism seized upon Nazi-like racist ideas, for instance that all intermixing of Basque blood with "foreign" (i.e., Spanish or French) blood was a threat to the purity of the Basque people and anathema. Spain's defeat and loss of territory (Cuba, Puerto Rico and the Philippines) in the Spanish-American war added fuel to the fire of Basque nationalism. Arana was arrested and imprisoned as a result of his attempt to send a telegram to President Roosevelt in 1902, thanking him for the liberation of the Spanish possessions from slavery.[2]

The Basques were living proof that Franco's propaganda about an atheist, anticlerical and procommunist republican conspiracy at the very outset of the civil war was a lie. A majority of the Basques supported the republic in return for the willingness of the government to accord a maximum of local autonomy, including official recognition of the Basque language and local use of the Basque flag, both rejected by Franco, who believed strongly in a centralized, Castillian-dominated state. As early as 1957, the Israeli cultural consul in Paris, S. Levine, received a confidential letter mailed from France from a group of Basque intellectuals in Spain,[3] asking advice on how to implement a program of instruction in Basque modeled after the successful Israeli methods to teach Hebrew to new immigrants. During the brief period of republican Spain before the outbreak of the war (1931–1936), there was a flowering of Basque cultural expression through Euskera in literature, poetry, the theater, dance, singing, and traditional sports. In the postwar period, the Franco regime tried to woo traditionalist and conservative opinion in the Basque country by permitting an expression of cultural activity, but deep suspicion remained against any attempt to develop literature or make semiofficial use of the language. The central authorities in Madrid were suspicious, all the more so, due to increased migration of workers from all parts of Spain to work in industry in the Basque region.

Forced underground by Franco's oppression at the end of the civil war, the Basque language was cultivated in secret. Since the 1960s and particularly after the end of the Franco regime, folk songs, theater productions, a daily press, the celebration of traditional sports and festivals are all now a visible expression of Basque cultural creativity. The local government of the autonomous "communidad" (Figure 14) has been controlled by the Basque Nationalist Party for many years. In 1975, when Franco died, almost 40 percent of the population in the Basque provinces were migrants or their children with no Basque parent. Considerable progress has been made in the adaptation of a standard literary language to overcome the numerous regional dialects. Under the aegis of the Basque National Party, which is the dominant political force in the autonomous regional government, there is direct local control of the police and the school system. In only twenty years, a working knowledge of Basque has been acquired by 75 percent of teachers in the state sector, compared to 5 percent at the outset. New legislation is designed to eliminate teachers who have no knowledge of the language from the entire elementary school system. Basque is the language of instruction in many schools and is a required subject in schools where Spanish is the language of instruction. This has meant that, today, practically 90 percent of pupils in the elementary schools in the region study bilingually or wholly in Euskera, but the percentage drops sharply to less than 40 percent for those completing high school and studying for admission to a university.[4]

Figure 14. Stamp celebrating Basque autonomy.

The Graffiti Plague

The difficulties of this multilingualism are legion. Spanish officials, police officers, military officers, soldiers, teachers and ordinary citizens face serious problems of integration and the education of their children when contemplating a transfer to a different region in spite of the supposed "universal acceptance" of Castellano. Even tourists can judge the harsh feelings evoked by the language controversy by the frequent graffiti on thousands of official public notices as well as on road and street signs that bear the name of a locality and that were designed as bilingual with diverse spellings but that now have one variant effaced in the autonomous regions (almost always the Castellano spelling).

8

CANADA

At first glance, Canada appears to be a Belgium on a continental scale. Two communities that descended from the original two groups of European settlers, one from Britain and the other from France, thus speaking different languages, now share power in an uneasy and unequal relationship strictly defined by geography, have competed for the loyalty of new immigrants and threaten to tear the country asunder. In Belgium, French and Flemish speakers are right next door to their respective linguistic homelands—France and the Netherlands.

In North America, however, English-speaking Canadians are next door to the United States—the most powerful, the largest and most culturally creative, dominant, English-speaking society in the world. French Canadians, however, live in a country six times larger than France but with only one-eighth the population and geographically isolated in North America and have thus always felt cut off from European France and the rest of "Francophonie"—the remainder of the French-speaking world. French-speaking Canadians number only seven million, approximately one-quarter of Canada's population of thirty million, but, as they are fond of pointing out, they would, if independent, be larger in population than more than half the member states in the United Nations and one of the ten largest countries in the world in area.

Unlike the Flemings in Belgium, the Quebecois (French speakers in Quebec) have no memory of common loyalty to a joint sovereign. The British monarchs have always been an anathema imposed on them. There is no memory of a common loyalty, heroism and a shared burden in the two world wars. Quite the opposite is the case. Quebecois opposition to the draft and service in the Canadian armed forces in both world wars is mostly remembered with anger, disdain and contempt by Anglo-Canadians, who recall that latent fascist sentiments and anti–British feelings surfaced with a vengeance after the fall of France in 1940. The Vichy regime of Marshal Pétain in unoccupied France was hostile to Britain and particularly to Churchill's efforts to rally support for a continuation of the Allied war effort. These views found a strong echo in Quebec, when it seemed for a while (1940–1943) that Vichy France and Germany were allied against Great Britain. In Belgium, the two major ethnic-linguistic groups are roughly equal, whereas new immigrants to Canada from a diversity of ethnic backgrounds joined the already preponderant English-speaking majority and intensified the sense of the inevitable decline of the French-Catholic minority. In the past the Quebecois birth rate was among the highest of European-descended peoples. Today it is among the lowest. In Canada, the two peoples were sharply divided by religion. The Catholic church in Quebec served as a focus for the Quebec sense of grievance and alienation from the Anglo-Protestant majority that dominated the rest of the country. In the case of Belgium, religion, at least, served for a time to shape a national identity and forge some links of common loyalty between Flemish and French speakers. The bitter intra–Canadian antagonisms of language, national origin, political outlook and geographical situation have all been intensified by religion.

The Maple Leaf Forever

For almost a century, until 1965, when Canada adopted its present maple leaf tricolor flag, the Canadian flag included the Union Jack (as do the Australian and New Zealand flags to this very day) on a bright field of red, with a shield displaying a variety of symbols representing the flora and fauna of the country. There was no hint of French representation in the Canadian pantheon of symbols. The tiny fleur-de-lis smbol of French origin representing Quebec was scarcely visible on only one of the many versions of the Canadian flag (Figure 15). The most patriotic" song, still beloved by practically all Canadians (outside of Quebec), and a second national anthem speaks of the history of Canada in terms devoid of affection for the Quebecois:

> In days of yore from Britain's shore,
> The dauntless hero came
> And planted firm Britannia's flag on Canada's fair domain.
> Here may it wave.
> Our hopes, our pride are joined in love together,
> The thistle, shamrock, rose entwined[1]
> The maple leaf forever!
>
> The maple leaf, our emblem dear
> The maple leaf forever
> God save our queen
> And Heaven bless our maple leaf forever!
>
> Our fair domain now extends from Cape Grace to meet the sun
> and peace forever be our lot
> and plenteous store above,

And may those ties of love be ours
Which discord cannot sever.

The song may have been unintentionally prophetic—who, after all, threatened "discord" to sever the "ties of love"? The answer was obvious. The title of a 1971 book describing the Quebecois as "The White Niggers of America"[2] left no doubt. Is it any wonder that the last thirty years have been marked by a resurgence of ethnic sensitivity associated primarily with language, increasing instability and threats of French Canadian separatism? Two narrowly defeated referenda promising the creation of a separate society in Quebec have only postponed the inevitable divorce foreseen by many.[3] The two founding peoples, the English and French, had been at war with each other for centuries in Europe and brought this hostility with them to the New World in North America, where Britain finally won a decisive victory in 1759 with the conquest of Quebec and Nova Scotia.

Figure 15. The official Canadian flag (1922–1957) above with its familiar Union Jack symbol of British origin and rule. The shield at the right just manages to squeeze in the fleur-de-lis symbol of the French Quebecois next to the Irish harp, English and Scottish lions and stylized maple leaves. Many Québécois are unhappy with the current maple leaf flag (center) and regard their own blue-and-white cross and fleur de lis (below) as the only proper national symbol. Some wear a pin with the slogan "Demain Nous Appartient" (Tomorrow belongs to us).

Bilingualism: Remedy or Illusion?

Some observers of the Canadian scene, who are prone to believe in the advantages of a multicultural society, inevitably suggest that a universal dose of bilingualism would offer a partial remedy to the increasing acrimony among Canadians. Is language the cause or the effect of this antagonism? This certainly must be the first question asked. Canadians have come to accept an enormous expenditure on bilingual programs of education and public services designed to ensure a reduction in tensions without proof that it is feasible or would be an acceptable solution to separatist viewpoints. These now abound among many Anglo-Canadians as well as the Quebecois.

Clearly the experience to date, in view of the many billions of dollars spent on teaching foreign languages, translating documents, bilingual labeling and packaging, special training programs in the armed forces, and training a staff of bilingual bureaucrats, is not encouraging. Much money has been spent (or misspent) to train civil servants to become bilingual for positions where the second language is in use by a small fraction of the population. This is due to the concentration of French speakers in Quebec (91 percent), an historical fact. Each year in Canada a number of available, bilingual, civil service positions are unfilled. Much more significant is the simple fact that the majority of French speakers in Quebec neither know English nor desire to learn it, and the same is true with respect to the lack of knowledge of French among most English-speaking Canadians outside of Quebec.

What is often neglected by proponents of bilingualism is the marked inequality among language users. The same antagonism exists and has existed for centuries among speakers of the less prestigious language (e.g., the Dutch [Flemish] speakers in Belgium, the Catalán speakers in Spain and the French speakers in Canada). Whatever the local importance of the less prestigious language or its number of speakers, the number of effectively bilingual speakers is always much greater among the speakers of the less prestigious language. In Quebec, the local variety of French was even looked down upon by French visitors, thus depriving the Quebecois of even the consolation of having the support and prestige of a powerful France behind them.

Many French Canadians even preferred emigration to nearby Maine, Massachusetts, Vermont and New Hampshire rather than be accorded the second- or third-class treatment they encountered in Canada. The resentment of francophones toward the speakers of the more prestigious English language, who feel they have little incentive to become bilingual, is the most serious irritant, confirming a status of inferiority and superiority.

This of course was all said in relation to minor variations of regional dialects and class accents of speakers of the same mutually intelligible language. The same but even stronger sentiments apply to those people who speak languages we cannot understand. In Canada the constitution of 1867, which joined lower (Quebec) and upper (English-speaking Ontario) Canada provided a measure of equal rights among unequal groups. French speakers outside of Quebec constantly faced the harassment of local officials, who denied their right (on paper) to maintain French-language schools. The same fictitious rights to utilize French in the prairie and west coast provinces, where French speakers were few and far between, made Quebecois reluctant to leave their native province.

Even at the federal level, monoglot French speakers in the parliament at Ottawa and appearing before federal courts spoke to a "deaf" audience of English monoglots. The language barrier was also a class barrier. Advancement in a professional career and business was limited even in Quebec, where Anglos constituted an overwhelming majority of those in high office, the universities and big business. Language is intensely personal. Only those who have attempted to learn and utilize a foreign language in important social situations know the disadvantage they face. For many, it means being reduced to a level of expression equivalent to that of a small child.

The Canadian government's efforts are laudatory, and official literature always takes the optimistic view that the grievances of the past can be eradicated. One major claim heralded near and far is that the bilingualism rate among anglophones aged 15 to 19 is more than double that of their parents. The 1996 census shows that 17 percent of the Canadian population could speak both English and French, compared with 13 percent in 1971, a change that can largely be attributed to the learning of French by native English speakers. It is a clear sign that the French presence is leaving a growing mark on the Canadian linguistic landscape. Overall, the number of bilingual Canadians almost tripled between 1951 and 1996, increasing from 1.7 million to 4.8 million. This is still less than one-sixth of the total population.

The conclusion reached by the government is that "A generation of bilingual Canadians is now emerging."[4] Even if correct, this achievement may prove to be too little, too late. The government too recognizes that much of the progress has been achieved with what it calls "restrictive laws," another term for coercion. Canada is unique in that it is the only country that is simultaneously a member of the commonwealth and the Association of French-speaking states (Le Francophonie). The government not only supports the learning of the two languages, but it also encourages their use in various ways. It makes concrete efforts to achieve these broad objectives. It provides financial support to nonprofit organizations that seek to promote bilingualism by encouraging dialogue, mutual respect and understanding among communities.

In spite of these positive signs, Quebecois nationalists point out that the optimistic picture often does not provide a geographic breakdown and that the progress made by French is essentially limited to Quebec. According to statistics, the number of francophones outside Quebec dropped by 0.6 percent between 1991 and 1996, to a total of 970,000. There is also the reality not captured by the statistics. Learning another language, even to the point of being bilingual, does not necessarily result in acquiring a strong belief in tolerance, nor do the many statistics measure the extent of hostility on the part of the monolingual population after years of forced and ineffective language training. Many Canadians, including not a few bilingual Anglos and Quebecois, believe that the bilingual programs primarily serve a self-serving bureaucracy that is encouraged to roll out reams of paper in both languages which are of little use or study in intensive, language-learning programs that have cost taxpayers in the range of $20 billion since their inception following passage of the Official Languages Act in 1969.[5] Costs associated with the act have since been integrated into various departments' operating costs, and the annual reports set out only the costs of certain specific items, such as language training for that year. Today, all government publications are produced in both English and French, regardless of how many speakers of the lesser-used language live in any area.

People who give up their first language for another, the low birth rate, and immigration have all considerably altered Canada's linguistic makeup in the last thirty years. In 1971, 60.1 percent of Canada's population recorded English as their first language, while 26.9 percent cited French. About 13 percent of the population spoke a nonofficial language. The 1996 census shows that the proportion of Canadians whose first language is English had dropped below 60 percent, while those whose first language is French had fallen to 23.5 percent. People whose first language is neither English nor French represented 16.6 percent of the population. The two traditional communities declined proportionally, but francophones suffered the greater loss. There is little doubt that the great majority of this third ethnic group learns English first almost everywhere in Canada—and struggles with French only in Quebec.

The Social Barrier of Language: Canada as a Prime Example

The language barrier can and has been precisely measured in a variety of situations. Geographers have long used a gravity model, which records the decrease in interaction between two places as a function of their size and the distance between them when all other factors are equal. Of course, in the real world, "all other things" are not equal. Political boundaries or differences in language exert a major distortion and are the equivalent of much greater physical distances. One famous study undertaken in Canada is particularly relevant. In 1968, Ross McKay[6] measured telephone traffic between Montreal (largely French-speaking) with (1) other cities in French speaking Quebec, (2) other Canadian cities in predominantly English-speaking Canada and (3) the United States.

For cities of roughly the same size and located at the same distance from the target city, the number of calls within French-speaking Quebec and Montreal was ten times more than the number of calls made to cities outside of Quebec in English-speaking Canada and almost fifty times more than to similar size and distant U.S., English-speaking cities. Graphs and charts demonstrate the statistics borne out by many real-life anglophones and francophones willing to admit they have no friends in the other language community and have never even been inside the home of one of them. English-speaking Canadian author Ron Graham, in his book *The French Quarter*, speaks of his childhood, in which the French Canadians were "as abstract as the Hindus I read about in Kipling or the Mau Maus."

Since the 1970s, an exodus of more than 300,000 English-speaking Canadians from Quebec has taken place. An official language act passed in 1969 was designed to reactivate the language equality between English and French that had been promised in the nineteenth-century constitution, but it has allowed the Quebec authorities practically the same unlimited power to promote French at the expense of English as was the other way round in the nineteenth century. Scores of laws have required the children of new immigrants and even those of indigenous Indians in the far north of the province to attend French language schools, demand a French-speaking staff, carry out business in French within large private business firms, and demanded French-only signs in stores and on highways and even in public places where various warnings are posted. Although some of this legislation was subsequently declared unconstitutional by Canada's supreme court, the effect has been to turn Quebec into an unfriendly place to live, work and raise children for English speakers unless they are also fluent in French.

For the almost 40 percent of Canada's population who are the descendents of Asian or European immigrants and not of French or British extraction, the clear preference for English has led to further segregation by language, strengthening the predominance of English in the prairie and west coast provinces. Enthusiastic attempts by the government to encourage a multiethnic, multilingual Canada among second- and third-generation Canadians as a means to defuse the Anglo-French rift have only backfired. The Canadian government has given considerable publicity to this formula as a distinctive feature of Canadian society, in contrast to the American melting pot. Most French Canadians are upset that Ukrainian or German speakers in the prairie province or Chinese and Japanese speakers in British Columbia should be rewarded or that resources are made available to them when historically Quebec was so badly treated by the Anglo elite.

The Uncertain Future

In reality, it is not Canada that has two official national languages. French is the national language of Quebec, and English is the universal medium of discourse in the rest of the country. Canada, even more than Belgium, may become the ultimate testing place for the disintegration of a state that was never a nation and will pose the question to English-speaking Canadians, "Are you Canadians?" (or simply English-speaking North Americans, like the 275 million U.S. citizens with whom you share much of a common way of life and culture).

Will English-speaking Canadians have enough sense of identity to preserve their claim to a distinctive nationality, or will the United States pick up the pieces and absorb a people with whom they share so much, including, first and foremost, language? Unlike in Belgium, where the Flemings are divided regarding the future of Flanders, with only a minority in favor of full independence and the unwillingness of the Netherlands to act as a Dutch-speaking fatherland, a majority of French Canadians see only one alternative to the status quo of remaining in Canada as a junior partner and that is full independence. How strong is the "maple leaf"? There is doubt it will last forever.

9

INDIA

The problems of multilingual India and South Africa appear to dwarf the problems encountered in Europe or Canada and can only be briefly touched upon. Both countries contain an enormous diversity of peoples who trace their ancestry back to different civilizations, languages, religions and tribal customs. India's size—a veritable subcontinent with a population in excess of one billion—has made a single, unified India as much of an impossible dream as were the attempts by the Roman Caesars, Napoleon, and Hitler to unify (conquer) all of Europe. Although the origin of one of the world's great civilizations is linked to Hinduism, India has a substantial Muslim minority (14 percent). It ranks as virtually the second largest Muslim state in the world, exceeded only by Indonesia.

English and Hindi as National Languages and the Other Sixteen Local Competitors

With its eighteen official languages (Assamese, Bengali, Gujarati, Hindi, Kannada, Kashmiri, Konkani, Malayalam, Manipuri, Marathi, Nepali, Oriya, Punjabi, Sanskrit [ancient liturgical language of Hinduism; not currently the spoken language of anyone], Sindhi, Tamil, Telugu, and Urdu), India probably deserves the title of the most linguistically diverse state in the world. Its major national language, Hindi, is the native language of less than one-third of the total population, and its associate official language, English, is effectively used by no more than 3 percent of the entire population, even though English accounts for more than half the books published there. It is no exaggeration to claim that, thanks only to English, India has managed to effectively stay united and progress due to the attraction of this foreign and European or even imperialist language that has earned an absolutely essential importance for a tiny, bilingual, English- and Hindi-speaking elite that dominates the country's cultural, scientific, commercial and literary life.

Before the British *raj* (rule), the civilization that had unified most of the region in what is today north India was the Islamic Mogul empire. The Moguls were Muslim invaders who arrived in India from present-day Afghanistan and used Persian in their court. "India" is derived from the Mogul word "Hind" for the entire subcontinent beyond the Indus River. The cry "Jai Hind" (India lives!) was sounded many times during the British "raj." In ancient times, the Sanskrit term *aryavarta* referred to the Aryan origins of the early Indo-European settlers. The official name of the country in the most widely spread indigenous language, Hindi, is *Bharat* ("supported" or "maintained" by the pantheon of Hindi gods). It is Bharat in Hindi characters along with the English "India" that appear on the country's postage stamps (Figure 16).

Figure 16. Indian stamp featuring portrait of Nehru with his name and the name of the country in both English and Hindi (Bharat).

The North-South Divide

Hindi is a modern language that traces its ancestry back to the sacred Sanskrit—a form of Indian Latin, the language in which the holy books of the Hindu religion were written in the flowing Devanagari script. The lighter-skinned Aryan peoples of northern India were themselves invaders who pushed the original darker and shorter peoples who spoke the Dravidian family of languages to the south of the subcontinent. This racial divide is still quite apparent in modern India. The terms "Indo-European" or "Indo-Aryan" apply to the languages spoken throughout most of Europe, Iran and northern India. The ancestors of the speakers of all these languages lived somewhere between the Alps and the Black Sea in eastern Europe and possibly Anatolia and moved in great migratory waves westward into Europe and eastward across Iran and the north

India plain sometime between 3000 BC and 1500 BC.[1] The similarities in many basic words for family members, numbers, the weather, animals and vegetation are readily apparent to even a casual observer today.

Before the arrival of the British, the ruling Mogul elite cultivated poetry and music in Hindi which borrowed extensively from Arabic and Persian, reflecting Muslim traditions and written in Perso-Arabic script. This language was called Urdu. Urdu also replaced Persian as the language of the Mogul court. And so there developed two languages with different scripts. These were actually one language when spoken, except for their higher vocabularies. This situation continues today and is further complicated by the recognition of more than a dozen local, official languages in various Indian states, the most important of which are Bengal, Maratha, Maharashtra and Bihar, each of which has in excess of fifty million speakers. In the south, the Dravidian family of languages dominates although there is some evidence that today's speakers of these languages are the descendents of people who lived farther north and were displaced by the Indo-Aryan invaders.

The four major Dravidian languages, Telugu, Tamil, Kannada and Malayalam, comprise 100 million speakers among them. Representatives from the southern region immediately challenged the supremacy of Hindi and staged demonstrations and hunger strikes, forcing the central government to back down from its original plan following independence to teach Hindi as the sole official language everywhere in the country. In October, 1953, four southern states received the right to reorganize governmental administration and education on the basis of their local languages.

Not unexpectedly, the southern region warmly supported the bill in 1963, giving English the special status of an associated national language. Opposition was strongest in the north, where Hindi activists viewed English as a threat to national unity. In the scattered mountainous regions of northern and central India, Mongoloid and other minority languages that do not belong to either the Indo-Aryan or Dravidian families account for millions of speakers, although these languages have a very limited range of written expression. Hindi's supremacy and its association with the dominant Hindu religion and civilization through the holy language of Sanskrit are sufficient indicators of Indian identity for only a plurality of the Indian population, scarcely a third of the total. Indian stamps always bear the name of the country in both Hindi and English—and only in these two languages. For the actual non–Hindi majority, the answer to the question "Who are we?" is more complex and for most of those who are educated at the university level today it includes a knowledge of English. Many have sufficient knowledge of Hindi or English to be able to progress in their career and business outside of the immediate environment, but the country's many problems—continuing high illiteracy (roughly 50 percent), issues of caste, religious tensions, separatist tendencies[2] and the conflict with Pakistan—threaten stability.

Religion, Alphabets and Languages

Following the end of Mogul rule in the eighteenth century, the British introduced English to India and continued using the language of the previous rulers—Urdu—for official purposes. But nationalist Hindus demanded that Hindi (essentially the same language as Urdu but in a unique Indian script) become the language of administration. Even Hindus whose native languages were not Hindi supported this argument. This debate between the Hindus and the Muslims continued right up to the independence of India in 1947. It was also aggravated by the language conflict arising from the two very different scripts.

Attempts at a compromise proposed by India's two great national leaders, Jawaharlal Nehru and Mahatma Ghandi supported the idea of one Hindustani language written in both scripts. The secularism of Gandhi and Nehru made every effort to avoid a particularism that favors one religious group over another, and it has succeeded in making India more stable and more tolerant than Pakistan. India has had Muslim presidents, Muslim supreme court justices, and Muslim captains of the national cricket team. Nevertheless, Sikh militants of Punjab felt strongly enough about their national struggle that they assassinated Prime Minister Indira Gandhi in 1984, and Tamil (from the south) extremists did the same to her son Rajiv in 1991. Muslim extremists, aided by outside forces and encouraged by Pakistan, seek to force India to withdraw from Kashmir.

India's problems are particularly severe because of numerous, mutually unintelligible dialects of Hindi and the very large non–Hindi-speaking populations. In order to secure Hindi's position as the sole official language of India, the nationalists claimed that all the Hindi dialects were one language. Of the different Hindi languages, only Punjabi got this recognition. Other Hindi languages are considered dialects and diverge considerably from the standard, Sanskrit-descended Hindi. The central government has accorded considerable autonomy to the local states to decide on their own official languages, although on the national level, Hindi and English are necessary for government service. Even today, schools in India that emphasize English are considered the best, and English is universally required for admission to Indian universities.

About one-third of secondary and higher Indian schools maintain English as their first language. For most of these students, English is their first language, and it is easier for them to communicate, read and write in English than in Indian languages, including their mother tongues. Nevertheless, in spite of grossly exaggerated statistics claiming that India is an English-speaking country, it is doubtful that more than 3 percent of the total population is capable of using English as the language of daily communication, as a research tool or as a language of literature.

English as the National and Neutral Meeting Ground

Nevertheless, in this multiethnic, multilingual and multireligious country where the Muslim minority constitutes 130 million people, English is a vital, neutral meeting ground. Some Indian states, such as Bihar in east India, have three official languages—Hindi, Urdu and Bengali—all recognized by the central government. The government also faces pressure from smaller groups speaking non-nationally recognized languages, and their speakers seek this recognition, often withholding support from the government on other vital issues.

National politicians risk being isolated in Delhi without fluency in Hindi, no matter how popular they are in their home states. The overwhelming majority of academics at Indian universities prefer to stay within their home state and language area. The dominant Congress Party has seen itself suffer humiliating defeats in various states in the south on the issue of making Hindi the sole official language and, ironically, within its own core region as a result of proposals to abolish English.[3] Has Hindi won a Pyrrhic victory in obtaining the title of India's national language?

Nevertheless, a look at the most popular entertainment form—the cinema—is clear proof that in spite of the 3 percent intellectual elite of the country, the Indian film industry (known as "Bollywood"), the most productive in the world, aims at the vast, Hindi-speaking majority and cooperates with the policy endorsed by the government to favor Hindi. All but a handful of close to a thousand firms produced annually in India are in Hindi or a simplified form of Hindi.

10

SOUTH AFRICA

The South African situation is in some ways similar to India. Following the end of white minority rule in 1994, the new authorities proclaimed that each of the major, native African languages would have national status and be taught in the areas where their speakers constituted the majority. Their use for judicial, legislative, and administrative purposes has also been increased in the local areas where there are large Black African majorities. This decision was made difficult by the reality that these languages have utility only in South Africa, in contrast to the former two official languages, English and Afrikaans. For decades the Union of South African, later renamed the Republic of South Africa, bore the inscriptions of the country's name in only these two official languages. Similarly, the country's flag contained the Union Jack and the Dutch tricolor, signifying that South African nationality comprised a white population descended from these two European origins in spite of the very large Black majority, with its diverse tribal languages and cultures.

The Origin of Afrikaans

In spite of the widespread assumption that South Africa is an English-speaking country, the role of national language for English is misleading. Of South Africa's eight million white citizens, Afrikaans speakers outnumber English speakers by a ratio of three to one (six million to only two million). The Afrikaaners are the descendants of Dutch settlers who began to arrive in the sixteenth century. Overwhelmingly rural, the Afrikaaners wrote their language more in accord with phonetic principles, and it thus began to deviate from standard Dutch. The absorption of many words from their Black African neighbors made it increasingly deviant. They wrote in Dutch and read in Dutch, but the spoken language gradually diverged from the standard Dutch of Europe. Historic documents suggest that as early as the late eighteenth century, settlers were speaking a language very similar to Afrikaans and very unlike proper Dutch. In 1875, a patriotic group of Afrikaans speakers from the

II. Multiethnic Countries

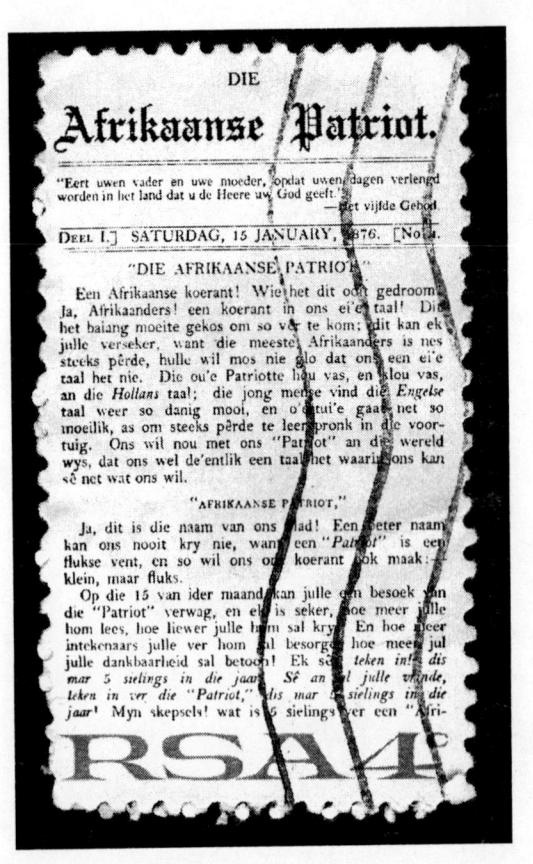

Figure 17. *The Patriot* in Afrikaans on a South African stamp.

Cape formed the *Genootskap vir Regte Afrikaanders* (Society for Real Afrikaners) and published several Afrikaans books, including grammars, dictionaries, religious material and histories. They also published a journal called the *Patriot* (Figure 17), which roused patriotism and pride in the Afrikaans language. Afrikaans absorbed diverse influences from the new African environment of the original Dutch settlers. It was influenced by African tribal languages, Malay, English, German and French Huguenot refugees. Afrikaans was first called "Cape Dutch," but the name soon became inappropriate as more and more settlers moved into the interior to find new farming land.

The perception of South Africa as an English-speaking country is due to the much greater utility English has for communication outside the country. Many Afrikaaners are literate and fluent in English as are many Black South Africans. During the last years of the apartheid regime, a large-scale switch in language loyalty occurred as many Blacks and "Coloreds" turned their backs on Afrikaans in much of the republic in the correct expectation that a multiracial society would give priority to the more useful international language.

The Decline of English Under the Nationalist Government

Native-born English speakers are much more concentrated geographically than the dispersed and rural-dwelling Afrikaaner population. Normally, this would mean less utility to serve as a national language, but in the South African situation, the worldwide prestige and utility of

English has made it a more desirable language. This was not the case during the administration of the country by the Nationalist Party, dominated by the Afrikaaners from 1948 until the end of the regime in 1994.

Moreover, English speakers in South Africa were always at a numerical disadvantage (outnumbered three to one by native, white Afrikaaners). Unlike the situation in Canada, it was the non–English speakers who eventually came to dominate the government. With a white voting majority backing the new apartheid policy of the South African Nationalist Party, South Africa was taken out of the Commonwealth, the official ties to the British monarchy were renounced, and the name of the country was changed to the Republic of South Africa. This led to a temporary ascendancy of Afrikaans, but the fall of apartheid resulted in a swing of the pendulum back to English as the most desirable official language.

It was not until 1925 that the government, dominated by the colonial establishment and put in place after the British victory against the Boer settlers between 1899 and 1902, recognized Afrikaans as an official national language alongside English. Many South Africans of Indian origin, the "coloureds" (mixed race), and some Black Africans in proximity to the whiter Afrikaaners adopted Afrikaans as a second language. English speakers were always much more ready to learn Afrikaans than English-speaking Canadians are to learn French. They had to be conversant in the language of the dominant group to participate in business, government, and the professions.

Although 95 percent of the language's words are related to Dutch, Afrikaans is a product of three centuries of linguistic mingling. Afrikaans became an important part of the identity of the Boers, the Dutch farmers who settled in South Africa. Stigmatized by the upper classes as ignorant and uneducated, the Boers fought back by refusing to speak English and by developing a nationalistic, Afrikaaner-focused identity. The language is common to ten million people in South Africa and Namibia, and many of its speakers are black in spite of the close association of the language with the apartheid regime. Many Black South Africans speak dialects rather than standard Afrikaans, spoken mainly by whites.

Afrikaaners believe that the language still has a part to play in the cultural diversity that is supposed to underpin the new South Africa. This view has even been expressed by several former Afrikaaner ministers, who were spokesmen for the apartheid regime for many years. The Afrikaaners are beginning to take more interest in the language's diverse multilingual roots and its variety of speakers and dialects, including those of Blacks and the "coloureds," Afrikaans remains the most widely distributed and the most widely spoken language in the country. Its significance in the creation of a new nation was symbolized by the construction of the largest monument to a language anywhere in the world, carved in granite on the slopes of Paarl mountain, overlooking Cape Town. A generation of Afrikaans-speaking, Black South Africans is also pushing for continued use of the language on the radio and in print, and they seek to redefine the role of Afrikaans. In the 1960s, South African English and Afrikaans popular folk songs achieved a measure of popularity through the talent of the husband and wife team "Marais and Miranda." They made many foreigners aware for the first time of the existence of a native, white culture in South Africa.

Afrikaans: Loss of Number One Status

If language were indeed the "soul of the nation," as von Herder and others maintain, it would stand to reason that Afrikaaners who are unhappy with the political changes that have occurred in South Africa would choose to return to the land of their forebears, the Netherlands. The reality is that most Afrikaaners in exile have chosen to emigrate to Australia, New Zealand, Canada, the United States, Germany and even Argentina rather than the Netherlands. Apparently many Afrikaaner farmers preferred the opportunity to find similar large farms or ranches where agricultural land and stock-raising opportunities are still available. This is not the case in the overcrowded Netherlands.

There are also small pockets of Afrikaans speakers in many large cities abroad. The South African case presents an interesting, unique example of the status of an official language severely downgraded with the loss of dominant political power by the white majority and apartheid regime. This has led to a renewed search for identity. An extremist fringe contends that the only alternative for the preservation of the nation is as an independent, white, Afrikaaner homeland, a grotesque reversal of the previous existence of the supposedly independent Black Bantu homelands in remote areas of the country. A majority appears to be rethinking the relationship of language and culture and for the first time acknowledges that the language is now the shared heritage of a multiracial community and that the "coloured" and Black speakers have a right and an obligation to contribute to it.

Xulu (Zulu) and Xhosa

Among the indigenous African languages, Zulu (eight million speakers) and Xhosa, the famous "click" languages, made known abroad largely by the talented singer Miriam Makeeba, are the principal ones. Another five languages, all regionally concentrated, are spoken by at least one million people. Zulu is spoken primarily in Natal Province State and in parts of the Transvaal and in one district of the Orange Free State.

Zulu is one of several, related Nguni languages that include Xhosa, its nearest relative. The two languages are mutually intelligible. However, a sharp distinction is made between the two for cultural, historical, and political reasons. There is a Zulu-based pidgin, known as Fanagalo. It is a mixture of English, Afrikaans, Zulu, and other African language vocabulary material, which is used as a lingua franca among mine and industrial workers. A Zulu language board determines a standard of written Zulu, but many Zulus consider it to be too conservative, favoring an archaic or highly stilted form of the language. Even during the period of white apartheid rule, instruction in primary education was in the native African languages. The Bantu Education Act of 1953 has been revised to take into account the new formal equality of all citizens.

Zulu is currently used in primary schools and then replaced by English, although it is studied as an individual subject in both primary and secondary schools in areas where Zulus are the majority. Most secondary schools serving Zulu-speaking students use English, and all education at the university level throughout South Africa is in English or Afrikaans. There are several Zulu language periodicals and newspapers. The South African Broadcasting Corporation has a domestic service in Zulu in both radio (up to about 120 hours per week) and television (15 hours a week by TV2). There is a considerable Zulu literature, and Zulu literacy is quite high—at 70 percent.[1]

The second most important language, Xhosa, is a national language in the Ciskei and Transkei regions. It is spoken by fewer people (6.5 million) but has a wider geographical dispersion, including most major urban areas. Both Zulu and Xhosa use the Roman alphabet. The role of Xhosa in education is quite similar to that of Zulu, but there has been more opposition expressed to de facto segregation and linguistic segregation and support for more progress and better integration into South African society by an earlier introduction to English. The elevation of the nine, native, Black African languages to the status of recognized national languages has not lessened the need for acquisition of English as the dominant language necessary for a career, government service, higher education, international trade and tourism.

PART III

The Celtic "Pygmy" Revivals of Welsh and Scots

What Is a Nation?

The term "pygmy" is not meant in any derogative sense but merely to give a graphic portrayal of the dimensions of a Celtic language revival that has been underway in Great Britain simultaneously with the mammoth strides made by the English language "giant" that has become almost universally recognized as the world's unofficial international language.

Any discussion or analysis of the debate raging in the UK over the further degree of local autonomy to be extended to Wales and Scotland, as well as rights concerning language use, must face an issue that has been avoided until now. Scotland and Wales have a considerable degree of individuality, which nobody can deny. The question remains, are they nations? What is a nation? Both Scotland and Wales participate in international football and rugby matches on the same level of representation as England. Does this make them nations? In Wales more than 20 percent of the population speaks Welsh fluently or with near fluency. Does this make Wales a nation?

In both Scotland and Wales, regional nationalist parties have won representation in the national parliament at Westminster. Both parties have a program that envisions eventual independence. The questions may be extended to a considerable number of peoples such as the Kurds, Armenians or Basques, who claim a separate history and unique language of their own but have no independent state, or the Palestinian Arabs, who have no special claim to statehood, separate language or other individuality distinct from the neighboring Arab peoples but claim they were dispossessed and were promised the right of self-determination in the past and therefore have the right to statehood. Poland disappeared from the map of Europe and was partitioned among the Russian, German and Austrian empires for more than a century and a half. Did this mean that there was no Polish nation for this period?

The number of such questions can be extended almost indefinitely.

Microstates such as Lichtenstein, San Marino, Monaco, and the Vatican are all independent with their own flag. Are they nations? There is hardly any unity on the answers to these questions. Any definition of "nation" must be subjective. Countless political scientists, anthropologists, sociologists, linguists and ideologists of every shade have disagreed on a definition. Let us look at just a few. As far back as 1882, the French philosopher and humanist Ernest Renan, in a lecture at the Sorbonne, expressed the view on nationalism that the existence of a nation is "a daily plebiscite demanding the renewed consent to continue life in common." He had in mind both the French citizens (who speaks a German dialect) of the Alsace region—and the Swiss.

As we have seen, Switzerland lacks the sufficient foundations of a common language, ethnic origin or religion, but it has become the common homeland of diverse peoples. Modern Switzerland is a functionally harmonious confederation in which none of the constituent cantons manifests any separatist ambitions. There is a common loyalty to the idea of a Swiss nation and state, embracing peoples who differ in various cultural attributes but who are united by common loyalty, democratic institutions and a shared history and sense of destiny. Many observers have addressed the distinction between nation and state but are far from unanimous.

States such as Switzerland or the United States, in spite of their success at mobilizing the loyalty of peoples of diverse origins into a single patriotic ideal, were held in contempt by both the kaiser and Hitler because, in spite of their successes, they lack what appeared to be the most important, old-world raison d'être—the attributes of an ethnic group or "folk" (a common biological descent) with the same language and predominant religion.

Most definitions that stem from an ideological commitment ignore any attempt at a rational or objective definition. It is most frequently kinship and the sense of family that figure in the praise of "nation" as a sacred and eternal concept: "A nation can exist only when there are people who are prepared to die for it…. Only when its sons believe that their nation is chosen by God and regard their people as His highest creation. I know that all people are equal. My reason tells me that. But at the same time I know that my nation is unique…. My heart tells me so. It is not wise to bring the voices of reason and of emotion to a common denomination."[1]

The term "nation" does, however, begin to grow pale and wax thin when stretched to cover the populations of microstates, the newly independent states created as part of the legacy of European colonial intervention without a continuous history dating back centuries. It seems most appropriate for peoples who have managed their own destiny for centuries (whether or not they were able to maintain political independence in the form of a sovereign state) and has been a factor in international relations as well as having created a significant, distinctive national literature or religious life over a long period of time, thereby immortalizing their way of life, history and social relations. A distinction may be made within this group between two categories—ethnic nations and political nations.[2] The latter would include Switzerland and the United States.

By this definition, many, but not all Scots and Welsh cling to a sense of identity that may or may not be simultaneously British but is definitely not English. The claim to nationhood by nationalists in both regions is a distinct political factor to be taken into account within the United Kingdom and, in the case of Wales, has resulted in considerable legislation ensuring language rights. These cover bilingual government forms, government-supported schools as well as radio and television programs in Welsh and bilingual road signs (Figure 18). In Scotland, the language issue is less apparent but Scottish nationalism, fed by a new oil wealth, is an even more significant political force. In the 1970s, the Scottish Nationalist Party ran a campaign featuring a poster with the trilingual slogan "It's Our Oil / It's Oor Yle / Is leinn an óla."

Although Scots is actually a remnant form of the language widely spoken in the lowlands that has been infiltrated by English, generations have suffered from the labeling of their native speech as "corrupt English." Though Gaelic speakers today are few, Kenneth MacKinnon, the author of an introductory text in Gaelic, argues that "The Gaelic speaking people came across the sea from eastern Ulster, and established their kingdom and their language throughout

Figure 18. Welsh bilingual road sign (photograph by Cherida Naughton).

what we now know as Scotland and even beyond. That is why, even today, there are few Scots who do not bear the surname or a forename of Gaelic origin, or do not live, work or travel past places every day whose names go back to that language."

With or without a deferential bow to Gaelic traditions, there are practically speaking no Scots who would deny today that Scotland is a nation, an ancient one, and by voluntary agreement (a formal treaty) merged with England to form Great Britain. Yet many Scots are still defensive about the conflicting desire to assert that they have the full right to be a nation once again with the realities of modern life. No Scottish national football team can hope to compete effectively in international matches, and most Scots realize that their separate national banknotes are often regarded with suspicion and cannot be used in most vending machines. The staff in English stores are reluctant to accept them in spite of the law guaranteeing that they are valid currency "within the United Kingdom." These problems affect many small nations that hold on to a distinctive national language as their only sure safeguard in the global village. In the words of Joshua Fishman,

> Home is where the tongue is. For all the pressures and rewards of regionalization, local identities remain the most ingrained. In most communities, local languages ... serve as a strong symbolic function as a clear mark of authenticity. The sum total of a community's shared historical experience, authenticity reflects a perceived line from a culturally idealized past to the present, carried by the language and traditions associated (sometimes dubiously) with the community's origins.... In each case, authenticity amounts to a central core of cultural beliefs and interpretations that are not only resistant to globalization but are actually reinforced by the threat that globalization seems to present to these historical values."[3]

11

WALES, WELSH AND PLAID CYMRU

In Scotland and Wales, the strongest symbolic function marking authenticity is support for the national football or rugby team. For a more committed minority it is political support for the local Nationalist Party, and for an even more dedicated minority it is language. Welsh and Scottish Gaelic are, like Irish, part of the Celtic family of languages. They were spoken not only in their present homelands but also in much of England at the time of the arrival of the Romans. The Celtic peoples fled before the Romans to the more peripheral, inaccessible mountainous regions of the British Isles. The same pressure was exerted on the original Celtic-speaking peoples by the newly arrived Anglo-Saxons who came from Germanic northwestern Europe in the barbarian invasions that toppled the Roman Empire in the 5th century AD.

One of the many ironies of history is that the ceremonial title "Prince of Wales," borne by the heir to the throne of England (and later Great Britain and the United Kingdom), was originally claimed by Llewelyn ap Gruffudd in 1267 and acknowledged by the English King Henry III. This native Welsh prince briefly established a single Welsh kingdom, something which had not been previously achieved despite attempts to resist the encroachments of first the Romans and then against Anglo-Saxon and Norman armies.

This brief period of independence was ended by the English king Edward I in a series of military campaigns between 1277 and 1295. The country however was divided into Crown lands in the north and west, ruled directly by the king, and numerous lordships under the control of powerful Anglo-Norman families in the border areas known as the Marches. However, rivalries and a struggle for power in Wales and the Marches sometimes involved alliances between local lords, whatever their first language. This was all the more so during the first two centuries of Norman rule, when the ruling elite spoke French and the peasantry, Anglo-Saxon.[1]

Nevertheless the Welsh people continued to speak their own language and felt themselves quite distinct from the English. They were also physically quite distinct—shorter in stature and darker in complexion than the Anglo-Saxons and Normans. Christianity had not entirely eradicated old pagan practices dating back to the priestly class of Druids, who had directed spiritual and tribal life in pre–Roman times. A major Welsh revolt (1400–1408) against King Henry IV further increased antagonism between the two peoples. Nevertheless, Wales did not enjoy the political identity and individuality of a state with a long history, such as Portugal. The ascension to the English throne in 1485 by a Welshman who became Henry VII (Henry Tudor) began a period of Anglicization, including the use of English in all administration and law.[2]

Thus, generations of Welsh choirs have sung with patriotic pride "God Bless the Prince of Wales" without feeling any division of loyalty between Wales and England. In 1536 Wales was formally integrated into England under the authority of the king by the Act of Union, and Welsh was explicitly forbidden as the language of administration and law. Welsh noblemen developed a fondness for all things English, but most common people continued their traditional way of subsistence farming and sheep raising in scattered hamlets and continued to speak their own language. Some scholars and gentry took an interest in literature, especially translation of the Bible and the Book of Prayer into Welsh. These achievements won the day for the Protestant reformation, but most Welsh rejected the radical, dour Puritans.

The popularity of non–Conformist (i.e., non–Anglican) Methodist, Baptist and revivalist independent evangelical chapels in Wales has had a profound influence on every aspect of Welsh life, including radical or liberal politics and a continued deep affection for the Welsh language. The Church of England and the pastors it sent to staff churches in Wales were often considered cold, uncaring and foreign by the majority of the people. The translation of the Bible into Welsh helped standardize a written form of the language that served as a model. Since the 1588 translation, more than 20,000 books have been published in Welsh, and undoubtedly the relative vitality of the language in comparison with other minor languages is due to the long tradition of literacy.

Nevertheless numerous commissions investigating the status of education in Wales in the nineteenth century, at a time of a major expansion of the state-supported schools, arrived at the conclusion that Welsh was a peculiar language isolating the mass from the upper portion of society, hardly a novel discovery when no university or institution of higher learning in the United Kingdom utilized Welsh as a language of instruction. The result was to discourage even primary education in Welsh, and many school teachers in Wales were authorized to hang a special school dunce sign labeled "NOT WELSH" around the neck of any child caught speaking Welsh during class instruction. Such measures stimulated the first mass reaction against further forced suppression of Welsh. The government became aware of and embarrassed by its policy, and in 1873, Prime Minister Gladstone attempted to court liberal public opinion by a public appearance at the Welsh cultural festival, the Eisteddfod, where he spoke respectfully of the language.

The Nationalist Reaction

Asked to name the three most internationally well known Welshmen of the twentieth century, the actor Richard Burton, the singer Tom Jones and the playwright Dylan Thomas, would probably qualify for this honor. Of the three, only Burton could speak some Welsh in his youth. Wales has been part of the United Kingdom and shared so much history with England that generations of the most talented, Welsh-born citizens of the United Kingdom have never hesitated to leave behind both language and homeland to make a mark for themselves on the much larger English stage.

In the words of language authority Ronald Wardhaugh, the situation in Wales can be summarized by "a fairly strong cultural but a very weak political nationalism."[3] In other words, this is precisely the opposite of the situation in Ireland. Public opinion among non–Welsh speakers has remained strongly in favor of non-coercive programs in support of the language. A 1995 opinion poll recorded a massive 88 percent of popular opinion claiming people's pride in the Welsh language, 83 percent in favor of bilingual public bodies and 68 percent of non–Welsh speakers agreeing that a goal of the government should be to "enable the language to become self-sustaining and secure as a medium of communication in Wales."[4] It can thus be argued that, in effect, Wales is a bilingual country but without the aggressive competition found in Norway or the sad, forlorn nostalgia and polite fiction of Irish's official status in the Republic of Ireland.

In the British census of 1901, the number of Welsh speakers was estimated at about 930,000 people, accounting for about half the population. Most of these were bilingual in English as well, although a significant minority of 16 percent were monoglot in Welsh. This did not set off alarm bells at the time, and even a form of home rule similar to the one being proposed for Ireland was considered of little appeal.

The continued emigration of the Welsh-born to industrial centers in Britain or abroad and the emigration of English and Irish workers to the coal fields in the South of Wales, however, was having a dramatic affect, along with the beginnings of English-language mass culture and communications such as film and the radio. The effects of the two world wars, television, increasing recreation and tourism and the choice of Wales as a retirement venue threatened to inundate Wales and devastate the Welsh language. In each succeeding census asking language questions, Welsh sank like a stone, falling to less than 20 percent today. English has penetrated to the degree that there is today a Welsh monoglot population of less than 1 percent.

The placid, rural lifestyle of most of the Welsh people was upset by the rapid development of coal mining in the great fields in the south of the country, which subsequently became closely tied to the national economy and witnessed a significant amount of investment, canal and railroad construction and migration to the coal field areas. With this movement came the rapid penetration of English.

By the 1930s, with the onset of the depression and the threat of another devastating world war, Welsh nationalism became active on behalf of the protection of the language, the rural countryside and the cause of pacifism. The Plaid Genedlaethol Cymru (Welsh National Party) had already been established in 1926 and resembled Sinn Fein and de Valera's idealization of a rural, pastoral, anti-industrial, anti-urban and anticapitalist nation which faces the threat of submergence under its continued status as part of the United Kingdom and is subject to continued domination of the English language over every important sphere of life. These views found little sympathy even among many Welsh speakers, the majority of whom lived in the more industrial, mining and urbanized areas of the southeast.[5] For fifty years, the dominant political force in Wales was the Labour Party, especially strong among the coal miners, and its program viewed the cultural and language issue as either of little importance or diversionary.

The Welsh language has been forced to make a continual retreat since the 1801 census, yet it remains today as the only language other than English which is commonly spoken among native-born citizens of the United Kingdom. It is also the most widely spoken or understood[6] of the modern, surviving Celtic languages. Official statistics from a handbook on the status of the language, "Cymdeithasol Cymru 1992: adroddiad ar y Gymraeg" published by the Welsh Office in March, 1995, show that 21.5 percent of the population of Wales (590,800 people) speak Welsh; 13.4 percent of the population of Wales claims to be fluent in Welsh, and 66.1 percent claim no knowledge of Welsh at all. It may also be said that Welsh ranks below Irish Gaelic in an official sense in that it is not a national language, but its practical utility is probably greater. In 1941, a petition signed by 400,000 Welsh people, calling for the Welsh language to be placed on an equal footing with English, was delivered to parliament. The petition was ignored. Without any separate, regional representation in parliament, however, Welsh nationalists argued that the central government could only throw the nationalist cause a few bones, such as recognition of Welsh in the courts (1944) or the creation of a special secretary of state for Wales (1960).

Until 1959, the nationalist Plaid Cymru was considered a joke but a remarkable turnaround in fortune occurred in the 1960s due less in part to a worldwide ethnicity revival and more in accordance with the related issues of environmental protection, conservation, feminism, the renewed pacifist cause against nuclear weapons, and devolution, all causes espoused by the nationalist movement. Ironically another factor aiding publicity to take special measures on behalf of Welsh was the investiture ceremony proclaiming the heir to the throne, Prince Charles, as Prince of Wales, in 1969, even though Welsh nationalists attempted to disrupt the ceremony. Charles had dutifully studied his oath and delivered it in near perfect Welsh, and both before and after the ceremony, he made public statements recognizing the "newfound vitality of the Welsh language," remarks that did not sit well with the government in London at the time.

The Bilingual Campaign

The core of Plaid Cymru support remains in the more rural north and west of Wales, but the issues raised in conjunction with renewed conflict in Northern Ireland and the growth of nationalism (unrelated to language) in Scotland focus on the issue once again of "Who are we"? The idea that Wales constitutes a separate nation that should recover its independence or that local authority should have the right to control migration from and into different parts of the UK are still unacceptable to an overwhelming majority of British voters.

A renewed activist campaign to promote a bilingual Wales began in 1952, when Trefor Beasley and his wife bought a cottage at Llangennech near Llanelli, an area where most of the population could speak Welsh. They received a letter in English with a demand for rates (a local tax). Mrs. Beasley wrote to the council requesting that the letter be sent in Welsh, and after the council refused, the Beasleys refused to pay their rates. This stalemate lasted eight years, during which time the couple were often summoned to appear before a magistrates' court and bailiffs were sent to their house to seize their furniture.

Finally, in 1960, they received a bilingual note. The case aroused national interest and was cited by Saunders Lewis, who demanded in a nationwide radio broadcast that all court summonses, election communications and other official documents be in Welsh. This speech was a historic watershed in the history of Welsh nationalism and proclaimed the need to rescue a culture in crisis. The campaign launched soon afterward to promote bilingualism focused on road signs, education (provision of Welsh-language schools), restrictions on the purchase of second holiday-homes by "outsiders," and a separate Welsh language television station. Part of the activities designed to promote these goals have been accompanied by violence—mostly against property but also bombing and arson, resulting in a few fatalities.

Embedded in Plaid Cymru and societies for the promotion of the language and its literature, is the slogan "A nation without a language is a nation without a heart." To those who subscribe to this view, neither Ireland nor Scotland has the essence of nationhood, a view which all Irish in the republic and most Scots would vigorously reject. No matter how multicultural, multiethnic or multireligious Britain has become due to post–World War II immigration, there is no foreseeable wish on the part of a great majority of people in England, Scotland, Wales and Northern Ireland to rid themselves of a thousand years of history, tradition and the identity forged between the monarchy, the Union Jack flag, the English language and the churches of England, and Scotland and the Anglican and Methodist prayers and hymns heard at all comprehensive state schools.

The Schools, Public Administration and Television

An increased use of Welsh in schools has been a major achievement and contributed to preventing the further loss of the language. Welsh is offered as a second language in many schools and is the language of instruction in more and more junior schools and in an increasing number of higher schools. A separate Welsh television channel began broadcasting on November 1, 1982, and many language courses have been made available by local councils for newcomers to learn Welsh. While road signs are purely window dressing (Figure 18), the progress made by the Welsh-language schools represents the hope of the future. The percentage of both the young (10–14 years old) and the very young (5–9 years of age) who are able to speak Welsh has increased from approximately 15 percent for both groups in 1971 to 25 percent in 1991, and in this same year 26.1 percent of all primary schools in Wales were defined as Welsh speaking.[7] Some high-level public jobs require bilingualism, meaning there are some positions for which knowledge of English is not a sufficient prerequisite in a part of the United Kingdom.

As of 1964, BBC Wales has been required to provide six hours per week of Welsh-medium television programming. Part of the campaign to pressure the BBC was a hunger strike by Gwynford Evans, a Welsh nationalist member of parliament. The separate S4C Welsh-language television station went on the air in 1982 and has been much more successful than similar attempts in Ireland or the Basque country due to the higher quality of independently produced programs. All local councils with a significant proportion of Welsh speakers now make all their literature available in both Welsh and English and often employ bilingual staff. A 1993 act required that English and Welsh be treated equally in the conduct of all public business.

A Welshman who chooses to vote for Plaid Cymru will argue with his fellow countrymen, only one-fifth of whom speak Welsh, that without national independence, Welsh culture is doomed in the face of the majority English domination of the United Kingdom. However, the popularity of the Eisteddfod festival, the continued success and appeal of massed Welsh choirs, the growth of a parallel, Welsh-language school system, an independent, Welsh-language television network all bode well for the survival of what makes Wales distinctive and makes even non–Welsh speakers aware that their cultural and historical heritage is alive, presenting the opportunity for an added dimension in their lives (without coercion), if they so wish. There is, of course, some grumbling, especially by non–Welsh speakers, and most of all among English vacation home owners who feel they are paying an exaggerated price for "luxurious" and "useless" public services.

12

SCOTLAND, SCOTS AND THE THREATENED DEMISE OF SCOTTISH GAELIC

How different the situation is on "yon bonny banks and braes" of Scotland. The "Scots tongue" or "Scots" or the "Scots language" is the term used by most Scots to describe the variety of English they speak. The languages originally spoken by the peoples of Scotland and Ireland were Scottish and Irish Gaelic. They were once one language. A common Gaelic heritage is shared by the two peoples in spite of many political ups and downs. Throughout much of the eighteenth century attempts were made by the authorities to suppress the native Gaelic language of the highlands, which was often referred to as the "Irish language." Strictly speaking, this was correct—Gaelic had been brought to the northern highland regions and outlying islands of Scotland by Irish settlers in the fifth century, whereas the South of Scotland received many migrants from among Germanic Anglo-Saxons, who invaded Britain after the fall of the Roman Empire.

What distinguishes the form of English spoken in most of Scotland is that it evolved in an independent state that existed alongside England for centuries. Had Scotland remained an independent state, it is likely that Scots would have evolved into as much a separate language from English as Portuguese is from Spanish. In the words of the author of the *Cambridge Encyclopedia of the English Language,* David Crystal, "Of all the varieties of English which have developed within the British Isles, there are none more distinctive or divergent than some of those associated with Scotland. The Scots language is unique because it was once the variety used in the late Middle Ages when Scotland was an independent nation; and it is unique because it has a clearly defined history of its own with a strong literary tradition."[1] In an innovative recent translation of the New Testament into Scots by William Laughton Lorrimer, only the Devil speaks in standard English.

The close association of lowland Scotland with England did not thoroughly erase its individuality, as reflected in a separate and militant Protestant Church, folklore, dress, music, the law and more convivial social relations, but it has probably been expressed most emphatically by the variety of spoken English so immediately recognizable. The English and lowland Scots have shared closely in an overarching British system of common values, historical experience and culture. On one level many Scots can take as much delight in a Scottish victory over the English football side as they can, and on another level celebrate the British victories at Waterloo, El Alemein, the Falklands and a thousand other battles.

Most young Scots today would assert that Scotland is a historic nation and deserves to be recognized as such within the European Union, rather than as a distinctive region such as Wales, Brittany, or Sicily or the Basque country, which have never fully enjoyed statehood in the past. In an uncanny resemblance to the Irish folk ballad "A Nation Once Again," many Scots echo the very same words in "The Flower of Scotland," which has become the unofficial national anthem.

The Jigsaw Puzzle of the British Isles

The traditional line of division between highlanders and lowlanders goes all the way back to Roman times and was drawn north of the River Tay, where Roman influence had not penetrated. The highland and lowland Scots, while still largely tribal and Celtic speaking, made common cause against the English, but by the Reformation, the highlanders remained Catholic and made common cause with their Irish "cousins," thus alienating the thoroughly anglicized lowlanders. As late as 1800, following the disastrous defeat of the Catholic Jacobite uprising, the proportion of highlanders north of the line still accounted for half of the Scottish population. By 1914, it had dropped to less than 10 percent.[2]

The still Celtic-speaking Catholic Scots felt dispossessed and culturally reduced to an inferior race. Many emigrated or fled to the more remote Gaeltacht of Ireland, while the triumphant Scottish Presbyterian church and the Crown sponsored a large-scale migration of loyal Protestant Scots-Irish to Ulster, in Ireland, to strengthen the Protestant cause there and loyalty to the United Kingdom. This centralized state was synonymous with the entire British Isles until part of Ireland was detached and became an independent state in 1920. In spite of the formal independence of a republic of Ireland, Irish citizens continued to be treated within the United Kingdom as if they were not foreigners and were still entitled to freely migrate, settle in, work and enjoy welfare benefits within a single society and economy as they had before 1920.

The English throne was bestowed by invitation on a Scot, James VI, who was invited to become king of England (under the new title of James I) in 1603, but the countries maintained a dual independence under a joint sovereign until formally united by the Act of Union (1707). The removal of the Scottish king to London made it imperative to standardize even more a common English to help unify the realm. Further decline of Gaelic was the result of the abandonment of much of the highlands for the grazing of sheep by large landowners. Many Scots saw little hope at home and were attracted to the great new areas of settlement under the British Crown in America, Canada, Australia and New Zealand. From a sociological viewpoint, The British Isles cannot be compartmentalized into the formally separate countries of England, Scotland, Ireland and Wales. The English language proved to be an important force for unity throughout the realm and was already dominant in both Wales, lowland Scotland and a large part of northern and southeastern Ireland by the time that all were united in the United Kingdom in 1707, and both native-born Scots and Welshmen have served as prime ministers of Great Britain.

English in various lowland dialects made a much more rapid penetration of Scotland than in Ireland or Wales. Scots nationalism is considerably stronger than the Welsh form, but there is no significant emotional tie to the Gaelic tongue with its numerically insignificant number of speakers in the highlands and in the Outer Hebrides, off the west coast. All Scots are justifiably proud that their variety of English has played an equal role with standard English in the formation of English literature. Gaelic devotees are even sarcastically called Albanians (derived from the Gaelic "Alba" for Scotland) which refers to the somewhat primitive nationalism associated with the tiny Balkan state. The Shetland and Orkney Islands were under Viking rule for a time and have retained some Norwegian elements. These areas were Norse speaking, and the late form of Norse which evolved there, called Norn (similar to Faroese), was replaced directly with Scots.

By the end of the thirteenth century, most lowland Scots were speaking some related dialect of the same Anglo-Saxon speech found in England. Scots with its different vowel modulations, a strong *ch* sound (as in loch), and a considerable vocabulary are familiar to any reader of the works of Robert Burns and Sir Walter Scott or to any fan of the films and books built around the character of James Bond, "Agent 007." Scotland continues to have its own laws and even its own distinctive currency (Figure 19), two obvious markers associated with nationhood.

The Scottish-Gaelic Literary Tradition and Lallans

Printed books in Scottish-Gaelic got a late start in Scotland. None existed before the absorption of Scotland into the United Kingdom

Figure 19. Scottish banknote, valid tender throughout the U.K.

(1707) or the Jacobite rebellion (1745). The first printed Gaelic Bible was published in the Irish form with the special Gothic letters that originated in the Middle Ages. Belles lettres in the format of an original Scottish Gaelic novel did not appear until the 1920s by which time the reading public had already been reduced to a small minority in the highlands.

In spite of continued out-migration to the more developed Lowland areas or England, the output of Scottish Gaelic literary effort has managed to keep pace due to renewed interest in learning the language by English-speaking Scots and Canadians of Scottish origin in Nova Scotia. As in Wales and Ireland, there is a renewed interest in the language as an essential element of a culture that is still vibrant in other areas of music, costume, dance and folklore as well as regionalist sentiment stimulated by the new Scottish parliament and activities of the nationalist party. Some Scots, aware of the daunting task of an attempt to revive Scottish Gaelic and unhappy with the vernacular Scottish way of speaking English with a limited vocabulary ("wee" for "small," "bonny" for "pretty," etc.) of distinctive words and intonation have attempted to create a more distinctive literary variety of the Scots language called Lallans (i.e., lowlands Scots English).

Most of the literary creativity in this form has been poetry. This clearly artificial attempt at a cultural renaissance has been labeled by critics as "plastic Scots," or "synthetic Scots." Several journals are published in Lallans, but there is no standard accepted form for spelling. The following example from the *Lallans Journal* (1977) still presents no difficulty for an English speaker: "The Scots Language Society offers prizes for scrievin in the Scots Tongue. Entries maun be original and ne'er afore prentit: They ma be (a) Poems up to 60 lines; (b) tales up to 3,000 words; (c) plays that tak nae mair nor 25 meenits to perform."[3]

But the following verse of poetry needs a special Lallans-English dictionary:

>The elbunk fankles in the course o'time
>The sheckle's no' sae souple, and the thrapple,
>Grows deef and dour; nae langer up and doun.

>The elbow gets clumsy in the course of time
>The wrist is not so supple
>And the throat grows deaf and dour, no longer up and down.

From "A Drunk Man Looks at the Thistle," by Hugh MacDiarmid (1892–1978), pen name of Christopher Murray Grieve, poet, critic and founding member of the Scottish Nationalist Party, 1926.

Another practical problem with Lallans is that, like Nynorsk, it was really not anyone's spoken home dialect but a literary construct. The argument in favor of a distinctive Scots as the national language of Scotland has relied on a nationalist interpretation of history. The influential pamphlet "Why Scots Matters" (1988) by Douglas McClure views the 1707 Act of Union with England as a deviation that prevented the development of a fully mature, codified written language. This view minimizes the major cultural and religious divides between highlanders (Catholic and Celtic) and lowlanders (Loyalist and Presbyterian, speaking a similar dialect to that of the people of Northumbria in the northeast of England). More Scots (lowlanders) fought with the English army at the battle of Culloden than among the highland rebels, who supported

Bonny Prince Charlie's attempt to restore Catholicism with French aid in 1745. The great religious divide extends in part throughout both Ireland and Scotland. The Presbyterian lowland and Catholic highland division, which stems from the last great rising of the clans in the 1745 rebellion, has been intensified by religious strife in neighboring Ireland. It is the background to the awesome football confrontation every year between Glasgow Rangers and Celtic. Many of Glasgow's substantial Jewish population always felt that they were the only Scots who could enjoy the match for the level of its play rather than the mayhem resulting from victory celebrations or a thirst for revenge by the losers.

Scots in Ulster

The Scots brought their languages, Scottish Gaelic and lowland "Scots," from their native Galloway and Ayrshire to Northern Ireland, where they still form the Protestant majority, and later to the backwoods and uplands of the American frontier of the Appalachians and Smokey mountains. These Scotch Irish have regarded Ireland as their home for the past three centuries, and their Presbyterian ministers were required by the church to learn Gaelic in many parishes, particularly in county Antrim, where Irish survived as a spoken language until the 1950s, refuting the assumption that it was only the language of Irish Catholics.

The Retreat of Scottish Gaelic and Scottish Nationalism Today

The percentage of Scotland's population who are monoglot speakers of Gaelic is now virtually zero. Unlike in Wales and Ireland there are practically no provisions for public services offered by local councils in Scotland to a separate linguistic community beyond language courses in a few primary and secondary schools. No more than a handful of primary schools in the highlands and islands offer Gaelic as the language of instruction. Gaelic usage is mostly confined to the home and church and geographically restricted within its own version of the Gaeltacht (known as the Gaidhealtachd in Scottish Gaelic). The average age of speakers is considerably above the average age in Scotland, and the home region continues to suffer out-migration in search of job opportunities and higher education. Many Scots regard Gaelic (like Yiddish today) rather like an elderly aunt whom you always promise to visit but somehow you never quite get around to it. Gaelic for Scots is a symbol of where the Scots came from and not a symbol of where they are going.

Beginning first with a sentimental reevaluation of highland culture and an appreciation of the distinctive Scottish contributions to English literature, a new ethnic nationalism that developed in the mid-nineteenth century has grown. Founded in 1926, the Scottish Nationalist Party now subscribes to full independence and won approximately one-third of the seats at the first election to the new Scottish parliament in Edinburgh. The apparent felt lack of a national language has led to pressure on the government to take a more positive role in the creation of new Gaelic-medium and bilingual primary schools, and increased subsidies for Gaelic-language programming on radio and television have multiplied significantly in the last decade, but the language is still effectively excluded from public administration. It is curious nevertheless that, Scots today, for all its essential role in the formation of a Scottish identity, has become restricted to folklore and the discussion of local issues. Standard English remains the acceptable written format for almost all areas of public life. For these reasons, the national language question is not an issue in Scotland today, and the Nationalist Party draws its strength from other grievances. Perhaps nowhere else among native-born English speakers is there so much use of a dual register, whereby speakers alternate between what is considered correct or proper speech for public events and is easily understandable by an audience of standard British or even American English speakers on the one hand and the local vernacular of Scots in a particular, regional variety that is considered authentic by one's colleagues, friends and neighbors on the other.

PART IV

Dialects or Languages ?

The Struggle for Unification and the Contrasting Experiences of Italian and the Scandinavian Languages

Whereas today no foreign observer doubts the claim to independence of three separate states in Scandinavia (Denmark, Norway and Sweden), yet accepts as perfectly reasonable that Italy is one nation, the cultural linguistic and economic differences existing one hundred and fifty years ago among different regions within Scandinavia were no greater than those within Italy. In fact, many Italian dialects[1] popularly spoken over wide regions of Italy in the mid-nineteenth century were mutually unintelligible, whereas speakers of the so-called national languages of Denmark, Sweden and Norway could with little effort understand each other.

Dialect clearly has a pejorative connotation. The *Concise Oxford Dictionary* defines it as a "Form of speech peculiar to a district, class, or person; subordinate variety of a language with distinguishable vocabulary, pronunciation or idioms." Obviously "subordinate" implies that it is of a lower order than a language. In dozens of political disputes involving speakers of a particular speech form, one side or another has claimed that the peculiarity of speech on the other side (in a territory considered part of the same homeland) is simply a minor variation of the same language. This is clearly not a logical and consistent yardstick to measure the distinction.

Dialects and Languages

Linguists have debated for generations what the critical distinction is between a language and a dialect and were long divided on the issue. More than forty years ago, Mario Pei summed it up best[2] by defining the three criteria most commonly used:

1. Political—The Official Language of Sovereign, Independent States
Language is that form of speech officially accepted by state authorities as the national patrimony and sanctioned for use in contracts, the

courts, the government, the army and all official institutions. Pundits had earlier retorted to critics of Yiddish as a jargon and dialect and said that it was disparaged simply because it lacked an army and a navy (i.e., an independent state) and thus could not qualify as a language but would do so immediately upon the proclamation of a Jewish state. Of course the great irony was that its historic rival and competitor, Hebrew, later deprived it of this opportunity. This would also mean for example that the languages spoken in the Baltic region and were originally considered only local, spoken dialects in Czarist Russia and were transformed into languages later when Latvia, Lithuania and Estonia became independent states.

2. Literature

The lack of a literature embodying the folklore, experiences and creativity of a group of speakers, no matter how large, is the second great criterion that results in a form of speech remaining a dialect. By this criterion, Pei was willing to define Brooklynese as a language but not Sardinian. This was of course facetious, but it does beg the question, how different does Brooklynese have to be from standard American English to qualify as a separate form of speech (i.e., how many words, local slang or deviations in pronunciation would be necessary to distinguish it). Pei argued that so many writers had written a body of fine autobiographical literature about their growing up in Brooklyn that it qualified as a language. What cannot be denied in Pei's definition is that for at least the last one hundred years, all the dialects without a body of written literature have been in decline, their number in constant attrition due to the achievement of national independence and the implementation of a national system of education requiring literacy.

3. Historical

Closely related to the first two factors is the historical one that originally there was no distinction made between naturally varying regional differences in local speech varieties before the growth of modern states that extended their control over large areas of territory. This occurred when one region became politically dominant, exerted its influence upon surrounding regions and became the seat of government, an educated elite, great universities, or church headquarters.

The Standard Language = Originally the Dialect of the Core Region

Through court patronage, successful writers, historians, poets and church figures set a national standard based on a local speech variety that became widely known. Often the location of major printing presses serving the court and other national institutions cemented this relationship. The historical criterion is the one that can most readily be docu-

IV. Dialects or Languages?

mented among the great national languages that can be traced back to the regional speech forms of the rulers who had the fortune to achieve political dominance over other regions. With a capital established as the seat of government, other institutions were drawn to this core region, and its speech forms were elevated into a national standard.

Part of the political power of this core region was the region's ability to extend its influence and prestige over more distant regions and diffuse its standard of speech into the national language to be taught in schools. With the advent of mass literacy, the national language did indeed become the standard over a much wider area than its initial scope. This process has been repeated many times with English, French and Italian, for example, in London, Paris and Florence (Tuscany). The national language is thus always a language that began as one of many regional dialects, grew, and became the accepted standard of all literary work, government documents and records, the courts and the army.

13

ITALIAN DIALECTS

The founder of modern Italian nationalism, Mazzini, commented on the inevitability of Scandinavian unification because he was aware of the similarity of their modes of Scandinavian speech. He faced a struggle in overcoming diverse, mutually unintelligible "Italians" spoken in Sicily, Rome, Naples, Venice and the northern alpine districts. The differences among these dialects were greater than those speech forms dividing Norwegians, Danes and Swedes.

As Mario Pei so astutely points out, without the historical accident of the mighty literary output of Dante, Petrarch and Boccaccio—three native Tuscans—occurring simultaneously in the first half of the fourteenth century and the subsequent powerful agency of the printing press, it is doubtful that this form of Italian would today be considered the model for the national standard, taught in schools all over Italy for more than a century and a half.[1] Additional prestige was assigned to this Tuscan variety as a result of the claim that it was the variety of modern, spoken Italian closest to Latin in its morphology and phonology (the appearance of the written word and its sound).

When Garibaldi proclaimed the independence of a United Italy in 1860, it was estimated that no more than 2.5 percent (600,000 out of a total population of 25 million) of Italians spoke the Tuscan dialect proclaimed as Italian and at least eleven other mutually unintelligible dialects were locally dominant. The shortage in teachers able to teach "correct" Italian was enormous, and it took decades before a national educational system with a unified curriculum in the official Italian could be implemented. Italian immigrants in the United States or Argentina often communicated with each other in English and Spanish respectively.

Ironically it was the Italian love of food—the oldest form of popular folk culture shared by all the diverse regions—that paved the way for a major breakthrough in unifying the written language and did more than a generation of schools, common administration, the armed forces and mass communications such as early radio. In 1891, a Florentine, Apelligrimo Artusi, wrote a best-selling cookbook, *La scienca in cucina* (Science in the kitchen), which excited palates all over the country. Local gourmet enthusiasts were anxious to learn the recipes of other regions, and the book went through continuous reprintings. It required the readers to be able to read the standard, national language, and for the first time many had an incentive to adjust their reading habits and improve their literacy in the standard language.

In the meantime, the history of an independent Italy has not been entirely successful in eliminating serious internal divisions that threaten the future unity of the country. In the past, Sicily and much of the south lagged behind whereas today agitation for an independent state of northern Italy presents a threat of secessionist sentiment or at least profound disappointment in the notion of an Italian Nation.

Italian authorities had also been very concerned about the German-speaking minority in the southern Tyrol, which had been annexed by Italy after World War I. The German language there was associated with an irredentist campaign to detach the region and return it to Austrian control. Rhaeto-Romansch[2] was not feared and in fact was totally disregarded as a harmless, local dialect by the Italian authorities, who were convinced it would wither away under the impact of education in the national language (i.e., Italian—the Tuscan-Florentine national standard). It is a Romance language and is spoken by almost 1,000,000 people on the Friuli plain northeast of Venice, to the east and west of the River Adige, near the borders with Slovenia and Austria, as well as by another 50,000 in the Engandine region of the Alps (the Swiss canton of Graubünden).

Lega Nord—Threat to Italian Unity

The contemporary regionalist party, Lega Nord, has won remarkable successes in the last several national elections, embracing between a fifth and a third of the popular vote in the industrial north Italian plain. The regions of Piedmont (Turin), Lombardy (Milan), Tuscany (Florence), Liguria (Genoa), the Valle D'Aosta on the alpine border with France, Emilia-Romagna (Bologna), Umbria (Perugia), Friuli-Venezia (Venice), Giulia (Trieste) and the Marche (Ancona) are closely associated with the greatest artistic treasures and the literary and scientific achievements of the Renaissance. Nevertheless, or precisely because of their glorious past, many residents are today profoundly unhappy after the experiences of more than one hundred and forty years of Italian unity, which they believe have been appropriated and misused by a corrupt and inefficient state apparatus.

For the Lega Nord, Italy cannot escape from recurring political and financial crises, and the domination of the state's interests by the "peninsula"—that is the centers of political power in Rome, the Vatican and the Mafia as well as the traditionalist south—of Naples and Sicily. Nationalism rests on the assumption of a metaphoric kinship, that people of the same nationality supposedly share—historic memories and aspirations, cultural similarities, language, loyalty and a belief in a common destiny, yet all of these have often been the outcome of determined and conscious efforts to create a sense of nationhood through a national system of education, modern mass means of communication and a framework of national laws rather than their prerequisites. Most of the independent states newly created since 1945 have been intensively concerned with the process of nation building to create the sense of solidarity, common culture and sense of history and destiny that had previously been achieved (and only partially) in such older European states.

Language as an Instrument of Political Geography

Nothing less than secession and establishment of an independent Padania will satisfy the Lega Nord. Pointing to the developments of the past decade, they confidently predict that Italy will follow the example of the dissolution of Yugoslavia, Czechoslovakia, and even the insistence by Ukraine and White Russia on political independence from the Russian federation after the break-up of the Soviet Union.

14

SCANDINAVIAN LANGUAGES: UNIFICATION TRIED AND REJECTED

Pan-Scandinavian sentiments envisioning a return to a single state have waxed and waned over the past century and a half. The current self-image of distinct and proud independent nations in Scandinavia blurs the historical record that for centuries the common regional cultures, languages and religion as well political union for varying periods of time could have led to a united state. It is only an accident of history that they did not remain united and become one country (and subsequently develop a sense of Scandinavia in the same sense as Italy, once also just a geographic expression). Whereas the Royal Danish national anthem still sings proudly of a naval victory over the Swedish fleet three hundred and fifty years ago, the Swedish anthem does not mention Sweden once by name but exclaims at the end "Jag vill leva, jag vill dö i Norden" (I will live and die in Norden), that is the north—a collective name, like Scandinavia, for the entire region. Anthropologist Thomas Hylland Eriksen[1] tells the following joke about the intensification of stereotyped national characteristics among the three Scandinavian countries to accentuate their sense of nationhood and how they are mutually dependent on each other to do so:

A Swede, a Dane and a Norwegian have been arguing all day over their respective national characters and repeating the typical stereotypes—the Swede is arrogant, aloof, industrious, neat, well groomed, rich and rational; the Dane is a decadent hedonist, quite lackadaisical, sloppy and a connoisseur of good food. The Norwegian is athletic, a nature lover, honest but a bit of a stupid country bumpkin. The three are then shipwrecked on a desert island.

A genie appears out of thin air, informing them that they can each have a wish granted. The Swede immediately says, "I want to go to my home, my large and comfortable bungalow with the Volvo, video and slick IKEA furniture." So he vanishes. The Dane then says, "I want to go back to my cozy little flat in Copenhagen, to sit on my soft sofa, feet on the table, next to my sexy girlfriend and with a six pack of lagers." Off he flies. The Norwegian, after giving the problem a bit of thought, tells the genie, "I suddenly feel so terribly lonely here, so I guess I wish for my two friends to come back!"

The Scandinavian states remain among the most politically stable in the world. They cooperate in many economic areas such as the joint SAS airline and are culturally, socially and linguistically quite similar but maintain a strong sense of political separateness. All three states jealously guard their independence even though their languages are mutually intelligible.

Part V

The Quarreling Cousins

In Moldavia, language is being shaped by a conscious policy to eliminate past differences in orthography (alphabets and spelling), pronunciation, vocabulary and effect a greater degree of unity covering vocabulary, pronunciation, spelling to emphasize "national unity" with Romania across current international borders. The reality is that considerable differences still exist in the spoken and written forms of Moldavian and Romanian. In Slovakia and the Czech Republic, Serbia and Croatia, Ukraine and Byelorussia, the reverse has occurred to accentuate differences following the division of a previously unified country.

15

SERBIAN AND CROATIAN (SERBO-CROATIAN) OR "A COMMON LANGUAGE DOES NOT A NATION MAKE"

This used to be the major language in use in the four former republics of Yugoslavia—Serbia, Croatia, Bosnia-Hercegrovina and Montenegro. It was also widely understood in the other two republics—Slovenia and Macedonia as well as in two other regions—Kosovo in the southwest bordering Albania, and Vojvodina in the northeast, on the Hungarian-Romanian border The language in spite of its hybrid name continues to be mutually intelligible in its spoken form throughout the region, although it has been written for centuries in separate alphabets, the Roman-Latin for Croatian and the Cyrillic for Serbian, hence the hybrid name.

The two scripts trace their use in this region back to the split in 1054 between the Catholic and Greek Orthodox churches. The slight differences in vocabulary are due to the greater influence of Latin on the western, or Serbian, form. Standard Serbo-Croatian as well as Czech, Slovak, Bulgarian and Russian derived much from a common "Church Slavonic," the language in which the holy books were translated from Greek and Latin by order of the Byzantine emperor in the ninth century. The written languages of the Serbs, Bulgarians and Russians all shared in the cultural milieu of orthodoxy, which was quite open to influence from Greek. In time, however, the written languages diverged to more loosely reflect the spoken vernaculars. Among many illiterate Serbian and Croat speakers, communication was often easier than among the more educated segments of the population.

In their respective home regions of Serbia and Croatia, the Serbs (10 million) and Croats (6 million) formed the two major ethnic groups in the former Yugoslavia, but a lasting antagonism based on religious differences, political rivalries and different cultural influences prevented Yugoslavia from maintaining a stable and lasting union. In the Bosnian republic, a third ethnic group based on religious differences, the local Muslim population, further aggravated the prevalent disunity in spite of speaking the same language. Serbs and Croats fought for possession of Bosnia in a shifting kaleidoscope of alliances. One mutually intelligible language among these groups with a divergent history, past hatreds, cultural and political orientations, antagonistic religions and traditions was not sufficient to create any sense of solidarity.

When Yugoslavia (meaning Union of Southern Slavs) became an independent state following World War I, Serbian in its Serbian-Cyrillic form was chosen as the most representative and used for training in the federal army. Serbia had won its independence from Turkey in 1878, but the other regions of the south Slavs (Slovenians, Croats, and Macedonians) as well as native Muslims, largely in Bosnia and speaking Serbo-Croatian, were divided between the Austrian and Turkish empires.

The history of Yugoslavia is a confusing one. The differences between the three minor regional dialects of Serbo-Croatian were not a barrier to communication. The dialect that was chosen by intellectuals to represent the standard written form of the language was the one employed by most Serbs, but none of the three variants overlapped exactly with the ethnic or religious divisions between Serbs, Croats and Bosnians. The Serb role as "big brother" leading the nation was resented. Religious, cultural and political differences eventually proved insurmountable. Yugoslavia could not become a united country as Italy, which overcame greater linguistic variation, nor could it evolve some sort of federal cooperative form of cantonal autonomy as in Switzerland. Tensions over language were only a result, not a cause, of disunity. An analysis of Yugoslavia and its chronic instability written in 1936 was both historically accurate and prescient:

> Almost from the beginning it was torn by domestic quarrels and split by fissures. The dominant political note ever since the War has been the angry quarrel between Serbs and Croats. The Serbs are a Balkan folk centering in Belgrade, Greek Orthodox in religion, semi-Turkish in culture and militant in spirit. The Croats centering in Zagreb, lived for centuries in the orbit of Vienna, and represented a more European culture and tradition. They are Roman Catholic.... The Serbs had a subconscious hatred of "European" Civilisation, which had been personified to them by German and Austrian invaders. The Croats, though Slav by race and language, were thoroughly Teutonised. The Croats called the Serbs Mexicans and bandits.... The Serbs replied that the Croats had done everything for independence for a thousand years—except fight for it."[1]

Under the old Hapsburg, dual Austro-Hungarian monarchy, the Croats were loyal citizens, and all three peoples were overwhelmingly Catholic. They shared much of the same tastes in art and architecture and many Croats believed that they would soon be invited to share in a triple monarchy as equals. Their hopes were pinned on the successor to the throne, the heir apparent, the Arch-Duke Ferdinand, who was however assassinated by a Serbian nationalist with dreams of uniting all the Slavs under Serbian leadership. This event, of course, was the spark that set off the First World War. When it became clear that the empire would fragment, it was natural for most Croats to assume that they, rather than the Serbs, would be entrusted to lead a newly united Slav state in the Balkans.

The Serbs had struggled to free themselves from centuries of oppressive rule by the hated Turks, and their status as a free nation encouraged them to believe in their role as the motivating force to unite the other Southern Slavs languishing under Turkish (the Macedonians and Bosnians) and Austrian rule (the Slovenians and Croats). The new Yugoslav state that emerged as the kingdom of the Serbs, Croats and Slovenians could not overcome the divisiveness of the past. Serbs looked toward the orthodox church and Russia and Greece as their spiritual mentors. The restive Albanian and Bosnian Muslim populations were included in the new state. They were the descendents of Slavic converts to Islam, and this only served to remind their Christian neighbors of the hated past when the Christian Slavs were ruled by Muslim Turkish overlords. The more austere Catholic Croats and Slovenians resented Serbia's central role in the new state and the royal Serbian house of Karageorgevich (Karadordjevic) on the throne. Nationalists on both sides became convinced that the other had frustrated their leading role and conspired with the great powers. First it was Serbia, when after achieving its full independence in 1878, Bosnia-Hercegrovina was severed from Turkish control and given to Austria-Hungary, with "Croat connivance." Following the Treaty of Versailles, ending World War I and creating the new Yugoslavia under Serbian control, it was the Croats who accused the Serbs of giving in to Italian demands for control of the Istrian peninsula and part of the Dalmatian coast, areas considered to belong to either Slovenia or Croatia.

World War II Rubs Salt into Old Wounds

The history of the turbulent kingdom gave further indications of failure to bring the diverse South Slav peoples together. Croat and Macedonian dissatisfaction with Serbian domination led to clashes, an assassination in parliament, withdrawal of Croat deputies and proclamation of self-rule in the Croat capital of Zagreb. The king, Alexander, was assassinated on a trip to Paris in 1934 by Croat gunmen. Attempts at reform and compromise included an official change of name to the Kingdom of the South Slavs (Yugoslavs), and finally, on the eve of World War II, a new federal constitution ostensibly granting a significant measure of autonomy. The move came too late however. Yugoslav resistance to the German and Italian invasion divided the country, and significant segments of the Croat and Albanian minorities collaborated with the invaders. A fascist, puppet Croat state was rewarded with control of Bosnia. Fierce Serbian resistance was met with a policy of reprisal and mass executions. Many Serbs still regard Croat complicity with the occupation and in the genocidal murder of several hundred thousand Serbs, Jews and gypsies in World War I as the ultimate betrayal.

The postwar Tito government policy instituted a revised model of the federal state and sought to achieve a convergence in languages between the Serbian and Croatian forms as well as teach it as a required second language for 25 percent of the country's population (Slovenian, Macedonian, Hungarian and Albanian). A writers' conference in Novi Sad was sponsored in 1954, in which participants from all ethnic groups issued a declaration, supported by the government, calling for resolving all differences in vocabulary, pronunciation, orthography, and the name of the language. The result of this declaration was the government sponsorship of new official dictionaries and orthographies for both forms of the language.[2]

The Collapse of Yugoslavia

Nevertheless, age-old rivalry between the diverse groups who considered themselves nationalities rather than ethnic groups tore the country apart. The Novi Sad declaration was repudiated later in 1970 by Croat writers and scholars presaging by more than twenty years the eventual turmoil and eventual breakup of the country. Attempts have been made since the 1980s to restore an old unique alphabet—the Glagolithic script, derived from "glagoliti"—"to speak"—dating from the 9th century. Linguists believe that this alphabet was derived from cursive Greek script and used in Old Church Slavonic in the areas of Bohemia (present-day Czech republic), Slovakia and Croatia.

A minority opinion holds that it may even have derived directly from Hebrew or the Samaritan Bible. Some early fathers in the Orthodox Byzantine church held it was too cursive and therefore undignified. It disappeared with the general acceptance of the Cyrillic alphabet but persisted in Croatia until the nineteenth century. Croat nationalists have suddenly revived its ceremonial usage following the disintegration of

15. Serbian and Croatian 169

ⴕ	ⴃ	ⴂ	ⴄ	ⴅ	ⴈ	ⴇ	ⴉ
a	b	v	g	d	ε	ž	dz
ⴊ	ⴋ	ⴌ	ⴍ	ⴎ	ⴏ	ⴐ	ⴑ
z	i	i	ģ	k	l	m	n
ⴒ	ⴓ	ⴔ	ⴕ	ⴖ	ⴗ	ⴘ	ⴙ
ɔ	p	r	s	t	u	f	x (kh)
ⴚ	ⴛ	ⴜ	ⴝ	ⴞ	ⴟ	ⴠ	ⴡ
ɔ	ts	č	š	št	w/ə	i	y
ⴢ	ⴣ	ⴤ	ⴥ	⴦	ⴧ	⴨	⴩
æ/e	yu	ɛ̃	yɛ̃	õ	yõ	f	i/v

Figure 20. Glalgolithic alphabet and an ancient monument on a Croatian banknote.

Yugoslavia (it even appears on currency Figure 20) as another step to further the distance between their language and Serbian. Committees with government support have begun to "purge" the Croatian language from Serb "corruptions." They have even borrowed coinages introduced by the profascist puppet state during World War II or searched obscure Glagolithic texts from the remote past to find them.

The bitterness and hatred engendered by the recent civil war in the Balkans that dismembered Yugoslavia has been matched in intensity by two other civil wars this century in Europe. Both Spain (1936–1939) and Greece (1947–1949) confirm the contention that a common national language is not an indication of national unity. Most Spaniards (with the exception of Basque separatists) and Greeks today believe that they have overcome the dissension and hatred of the past that threatened to disrupt a centuries-long coexistence within a single nation. Yugoslavia represents a case of a nation tacked together with artificial nails. The biggest one—a common language—was not enough to keep the pieces together.

Belgium, with its two distinct peoples speaking quite different languages, has remained bound together without enthusiasm but for lack of a viable alternative, a fear of "upsetting the cart," the reluctance of their neighbors to contemplate a new arrangement of the political map of Europe, and the power of inertia—sharing the same state for 170 years. The Swiss have achieved a sense of solidarity and stability after 700 years of common unity in spite of all the differences. Both the Southern Slavs and their northern neighbors (the Czechs and Slovaks) were not able to manage the same achievement with only a common or close language to share.

16

CZECH AND SLOVAK

By contrast, the union between the Czech Republic and Slovakia after several gradual separations ended in a "velvet divorce," without war, refugees, violence or economic upheaval, yet the history of once-proud Czechoslovakia bears an uncanny resemblance to Yugoslavia. The vision of the founders of the Czechoslovak state in 1920 was the basic nationhood of one people under some form of federalism and the function of the state as a democratic bulwark against German and Russian domination and totalitarianism. Both of these visions proved illusory.[1] The two languages are closely related, so much so that they are mutually intelligible, although with minor differences in the written alphabets of only three special letters. They are closer than the proximity of Spanish to Portuguese.

Like the Southern Slavs, the two Northern Slav peoples were separated for centuries under different regimes and cultural orientations. The Czech regions of Bohemia and Moravia were under German and Austrian rule and much more industrialized and literate. Religious reforms instituted the first nationally deviant form of Catholicism and later a partial acceptance of the Protestant Reformation. Slovakia remained under Hungarian rule and was entirely Catholic, more traditional and conservative, and much more rural. The history of the two languages is intertwined. Both descended from Old Czech, which dates back to the eleventh century and are considered different languages today only for political and historical reasons. Standard Slovak was codified relatively recently, in the early nineteenth century.

The founder of the Czech state, Thomas Masaryk, worked out the initial agreements with Slovak nationalists while both were in exile in America. Agreement was much easier between representatives of the two rival nationalist movements sitting in Pittsburgh in 1919 rather than in central Europe. Prior to the partition of Czechoslovakia in 1991, Slovak continued to be influenced by Czech in spite of efforts by purists to avoid a convergence of the two languages. Slovaks complained that the Czechs dominated the state in the interwar period (1920–1939). Literary activity, translations and the location of almost all publishing houses were centered in the Czech half. The Slovaks always felt they were treated as the "junior partner" or "little brother" and shared much of the same antagonism toward the dominant Czechs as did the minority groups of Germans and Hungarians. Slovak politicians at times cooperated with the German minority party in demanding greater autonomy.

Even during the great crisis of 1938, ending with the Munich agreement to satisfy Hitler's demand for annexation of the Sudetenland, with its large German population, many Slovaks did not feel solidarity with the state. On March 16, 1939, the German army occupied Prague, and the rump Czech state ceased to exist. In October, 1939, Hitler demanded autonomous zones for the Slovak and Ruthene minorities within Czechoslovakia. The shared interests of Slovak nationalists and the Nazis, who had destroyed Czechoslovakia and democracy, were not forgotten. Ironically, part of the "reward" that many Slovaks got was to return to their hated old masters – the Hungarians. In November, 1939, under German domination, Prague was forced to cede 4,600 square miles of Slovak territory to Hungary.

In the interwar years of independence (1920-1938), most Slovaks had refused to accept the self-designation of the country as the state of the Czechoslovak nation, contending that this formula masked Czech domination of the Slovaks. Several confusing federal formulas in new constitutions and new names, including a hyphen in "Czecho-Slovak," did not satisfy Slovak nationalists, who eventually forced a dissolution and separation of the state into two new independent countries without a referendum in either the Czech or Slovak areas. Like the Croats, the Slovaks have a long historical memory of domination, by Hungary. The presence in the new, independent Slovak state of a large Hungarian minority (over 10 percent and located in a narrow, contiguous belt along the country's southeastern border, where they are a majority in many localities) has led to a series of language laws to enforce the definition of "majority" and "minority."

The Slovak Language Laws

The preamble to the 1992 constitution states, "We the Slovak People together with members of national minorities and ethnic groups living in the Slovak Republic"[2] and thus distinguishes between different groups of citizens. It further states that the "exercise of rights by citizens of a national minority may not threaten the sovereignty and territorial integrity of the Slovak Republic or discriminate against other citizens." A series of language laws that banned bilingual road signs and non-Slovak first names has been challenged by the Council of Europe and rewritten. The Slovak National Council adopted law number 270/1995 on November 15, 1998: "On the State Language of the Slovak Republic," which declares Slovak to be more than just an "official language." It declares that The Slovak language is the most important distinctive feature of the uniqueness of the Slovak nation, the most valuable piece of the cultural heritage and expression of sovereignty of the Slovak Republic and the general means of communication for the citizens, which guarantees them freedom and equality in dignity and rights in the territory of the Slovak Republic.

Such restrictive legislation never existed in the old Czechoslovakia. The 1918 constitution had declared that the state language was Czechoslovak in two versions: Czech and Slovak. The Slovaks had always maintained this was a polite fiction. The Hungarian minority in particular objected to these laws, claiming they were being regarded as tenants in Slovakia rather than citizens. They demanded that they be allowed to use their own language in official documents in dealing with local authorities, road signs, and so on in areas where they constituted at least 20 percent of the population. Aware of the potential criticism from the European Union and the OSCE high commissioner on human rights, Slovakia amended some of the laws in 1999 after an emotional debate. Basically the 20 percent formula was adopted, but it is difficult to apply for the other two minorities – the more widely dispersed Ruthenians and the gypsy (Roma) population, whose language does not have a single codified standard, nor is there any specified demand for bilingual civil service officials in the minority areas. State schools provide a restricted syllabus in the minority language areas, where a non-Slovak language may be used as a language of instruction.[3]

17

Romanian and Moldavian

The third example of quarreling cousins at least demonstrates an attempt to patch up the quarrel. Moldova was the former Soviet Republic known as Moldavia and previously called Bessarabia when the area was a part of the Kingdom of Romania between 1920 and 1940. In 1991, Moldavia became independent. The new regime has cooperated with Romanian authorities to try and bring about a convergence of the two speech forms. During the period of Soviet rule in Moldavia, the Romanians criticized Soviet policies that sought to convey the distinction of a separate language of Moldavian as distinct from Romanian. This included the use of the Cyrillic alphabet and the introduction of many terms based on Russian or Ukrainian for Moldavian, a practice that made Romanians cringe in horror at what they regarded as a desecration of their sacred language, derived from Latin.

Romanians have always regarded with great pride their ostensible descent from the Roman province of Dacia and their long-term connections with French and Italian culture. At the time of Moldovan independence in 1991, about two-thirds of the population spoke the local form of Romanian. The remaining one-third was almost equally divided among speakers of Russian and Ukrainian.

Romania had long been under Turkish rule and achieved its independence quite late—in 1878. In spite of the pretensions looking to west Europe, it was Russia and Bulgaria that had the closest religious, linguistic and political links with the country and had actively sought to liberate the country from Turkish domination. The earliest Romanian documents and books were written in the Cyrillic script and date back to the fifteenth century.

Bessarabia had been ruled by Turkey for centuries until 1812, when it was forced to cede the rich agricultural land to Russia. The Czars thereby gained access to the rich lands of the Danube basin. Romanian linguists slowly began to reject Turkish and Russian influences and codify a standard literary language written in the Latin alphabet following the great liberal revolutions that swept through Europe in 1848.

Romania—World War I's Biggest "Winner"

The Treaty of Versailles awarded both Transylvania with its large Hungarian population and Bessarabia to Romania in 1920, based on the contention that a plurality of the population spoke Romanian dialects. In 1924 the Soviets formed the Moldavian Autonomous Region (MAR) out of a small part of the territory of the Ukraine on the left bank of the Dneister River, opposite Rumanian-occupied Bessarabia. The language spoken in much of this area was a heavily Ukrainanized and Russified form of Romanian. The intent was to provide a possible future excuse to claim back Bessarabia on behalf of their fellow Moldavians, implying that indeed the two peoples were two branches of the same tree. As the state with the largest territorial gains from the Treaty of Versailles, Romania forged close ties with France and French culture. Pronunciation of standard Romanian was based on the intonation used in Bucharest. This more closely resembles Italian than French, but the dialects of Moldavia in the northern regions more closely resembled Polish and Russian.

The Communist Party, Cyrillic Alphabet and New Dictionaries

The Soviet Union regained the province in 1940 as part of its strategy to protect its great port city of Odessa, located only a few miles from the 1920 border. The USSR merged Bessarabia with its own MAR creation to form the Bessarabian SSR. Following incorporation into the USSR, the use of the Latin alphabet was proscribed, and a consistent linguistic policy was instituted to emphasize the Russian and Ukrainian elements in Bessarabian speech and formalize them in the written language. A series of Moldavian dictionaries and grammar books published by the Moldavian Academy of Sciences in the USSR fixed a new literary standard in the russified, Cyrillic-script Moldavian. This policy of diverging from the standard Romanian based in Bucharest ignited a language conflict that sharpened in the period from 1950 to about 1980 and for a brief time reached a critical stage, when Romania was ruled by Nicolae Ceaușescu.

The nationalist communist dictator followed an extreme policy of Romanian nationalism and claimed that the former Bessarabia was a Romanian irredenta (territory waiting to be redeemed). The shoe was "now on the other foot," as Romanians claimed that their fellow Romanians were an occupied people within the USSR. Romanian maps and dictionaries all confirmed that the two peoples were indeed the same nation. These policies affected dissident groups in the Moldavian SSR, who petitioned their government in 1965 to convert all printing to the

Latin alphabet, a proposal that was immediately rejected. Under the glastnost and perestroika policies of Gorbachev, policies were relaxed and the Latin alphabet permitted.

Unity on the Basis of a Common Language?

The collapse of the USSR and the secession of Moldova in 1991 created the possibility of a merger between Romania and Moldova. Both governments and peoples appeared to be initially in favor, and intellectuals and writers proclaimed that their common language was the basis for reunification. However, by now Romania was in turmoil. Many Romanians also looked askance at the prospect of a very large, new Ukrainian and a Russian minority who would now be citizens of Romania, with their respective claims to "minority language rights."

There were other problems as well including the future status of the southern third of the former Bessarabia, which had been transferred to the Ukraine, the ethnic–Russian-inhabited border region along the Dniester region that had declared itself the independent Transdniestran Republic (TDR) and the presence of a Russian-speaking, Christian Turkic ethnic group, the Gagauz, numbering about 150,000. The TDR is usually referred to as a rogue state, a breakaway entity not recognized by anyone but able to enjoy some tacit protection from the Ukraine and Russia. It has been called a "black hole."[1] All of these potential headaches would create severe problems for Romania if it tried to absorb Moldova or the TDR. The minority groups are concerned that their status is jeopardized by the prospect of either eventual unification of Moldavia with Romania or linguistic pressure to assimilate. In 1989, a law on the official language of Moldova was passed, bestowing this title on Romanian and establishing language proficiency tests in five to seven years for all persons holding medium-high and high-ranking positions in the civil service. Russian remains the official language of the TDR.

"To Unite or Not to Unite—That Is the Question"

Like the other quarreling cousins, the Romanians were confident that language would help them reunite their nation, only to find out, like the Serbs and Croats and the Czechs and Slovaks, that, living in different states as well as under very different political and educational systems for a very long time, they had irrevocably drawn apart from each other. They were more like distant second cousins, and a common language could not make up for the time lost. Even if Romania had managed to convince the Moldavians to merge their country and reunite, it is likely that this "Romano-Moldova" would have been no more successful than the other hybrid states of Czecho-Slovakia and Yugoslavia had been. Distaste for Russian, the language of the former Soviet masters, remains strong, and a recent proposal by the government to make Russian a required second national language provoked demonstrations and riots.

PART VI

Ethnic or Regional Minorities: Bilingual or Using the "Wrong Language"?

A situation of noncoincidence of national identity and a popularly spoken tongue exists in several border regions in Europe. These include German speakers among the Danish minority in Germany, German-dialect speakers in France and Finnish speakers among the Swedish-minority community in Finland. In these three cases, a common discourse (speaking about the things we are all familiar with by virtue of living in the same country) is shared among citizens who do not share the same ethnicity. The language of common discourse is a "foreign" language for the minority or may even be the language of a traditionally hostile rival. This situation was once common before the rise of modern nationalism, when loyalty to a king or royal house, historic memories, educational and social opportunities, common interests, and so on were more important than language.

For most ethnic Swedes in Finland, or Alsatians in modern France, or among the Danish minority in south Schleswig in Germany today, language is not synonymous with nationality. In fact, in all three, it is citizenship and common loyalty to the state of which they are citizens which contributes to each generation of the minority becoming more and more fluent in the language of the majority. However, in two other cases, Romania and Israel, the minority has learned the language of a majority in state schools but to a large degree regards it antagonistically as the language of the enemy.

18

THE ROMANIAN-SPEAKING HUNGARIANS

The largest, linguistic-ethnic minority in Europe is the Hungarian in Romania, numbering at least 2.5 million people comprising almost 10 percent of the total population and almost 25 percent in the region of Transylvania. Their minority status and relationship to Hungary probably come closest to Von Herder's classical identification of nationality and native language. This area, to the south of the Carpathian mountains and east of the Transylvanian Alps, was originally part of the Roman province of Dacia, from which the Romanians trace their origin and language. It had, however, been part of the Hungarian kingdom since the tenth century, before falling first under Austrian rule, then Turkish and finally under the Hapsburg Austrian Empire for a second time.

The supposed Latin-Roman origin in Dacia of the Romanian people and their language is hotly disputed.[1] Many historians and linguists deny that there was any such ethnic-linguistic continuity and challenge proponents of the theory to present any document, artifact or even geographical place names that support this idea. The "true Romanians" are held to be interlopers who were nomadic shepherds that migrated into Transylvania from the western Balkans, in Illyria (present-day Adriatic coast of Croatia and Albania), as late as the fourteenth century. They were originally known as Vlachs, whose name was then transferred to "Wallachia," the traditional core area of the Romanian state located east and south of Transylvania.

The Debate Over Romanian Origins

As might be expected, language has played a key role in the various theories concerning Romanian origins. Critics of the Latin-Roman origin note that almost no Romanian words and expressions of supposed ancient Latin origin can be traced back to the second and third centuries A.D., when the last Romans withdrew from Dacia. Other vocabulary elements are of

Albanian origin. Several linguists, including a noted Rumanian, Ovid Densusianu (1873–1938), have placed the origin of the Romanian language in Illyria.[2] Such a view is anathema to most Romanians today, many of whom are unaware that a considerable number of Romanian words were coined by linguists from Latin over the last 150 years to consciously buttress the theory of Roman origins. The astute reader may have already guessed that the reason for the alternative spellings of Romania (present-official name) and the earlier "Rumania" is the insistence of the Romanian authorities on the vowel change as further "proof" of the identity of the modern nation with ancient Rome. Occasionally, one may see "Roumania," adopted by those observers who wished to take a politically neutral stance.

The Difficult Romanian-Hungarian Linguistic and Political Borders

In the seventeenth century, the Turkish occupiers followed a policy of favoring the Romanian population, a fact that many Hungarians never forgot. Under reinstated Hungarian rule, the Romanian-speaking population was made to pay the price for their perceived disloyalty and denied the right to schools in their own language. The difficulties of drawing a fair boundary are obvious from a look at the map that shows an isolated, noncontiguous, large Hungarian-speaking population (known as the Szeklers or frontier guardsmen) in the Szekely region of eastern Transylvania. This unusual distributional pattern was the result of the settlement of ethnic Hungarians, Germans and other groups of settlers in the territory on the eastern frontier of Austria bordering the Turkish Empire from the fourteenth to the eighteenth centuries. These diverse ethnic groups shared neither a common language, religion (most Hungarians are either Catholic or Protestant, and the Romanians are Eastern Orthodox) nor lifestyle (the Romanians were overwhelmingly rural, whereas the Hungarian and German speakers became increasingly urban).

In the Hungarian parliament before World War I, the Romanian population of Transylvania was almost totally unrepresented (1 deputy among 413, when in proportion to their share of Hungary's total population, they should have been entitled to 75)[3] although they experienced much less difficulty at the local level of administration from Romanian-speaking officials. As second-class citizens, almost all Romanians under Austro-Hungarian rule identified with the independent kingdom of Romania and sympathized with eventual secession and reunification with their fellow kinsmen, with whom they shared a common language. Largely for this reason, Romania opportunistically joined forces with the allies, reneging on its former agreements with the central powers, just as Italy did in World War I, and was rewarded with the transfer of huge territories including

Transylvania and its large Hungarian-speaking population following the breakup of the Austro-Hungarian Empire at the end of World War I. Many Romanians also felt a strong linguistic and cultural kinship with both France and Italy as fellow Latin states although differing in religion.

Romania has been fearful of a repetition of the events of August, 1940, which returned a large part of northern Transylvania to Hungary as a result of German-Italian intervention (Vienna Award) in order to secure Hungarian friendship with the Axis powers, In 1945, this award was revoked, and the entire region was ceded again to Romania. Romania's communist regime was forced to inherit the Marxist-Leninist program of a dual struggle to create a classless state ruled by the dictatorship of the proletariat and achieve full and equal rights for national minorities on the model of the Soviet constitution. In 1977, then leaders Nicolae Ceaușescu and Janos Kadar pledged "the full moral weight of the Romanian Communist Party and of the Hungarian Socialist Workers Party in applying socialist integration to the problems of nationalities. This will be based equality before the law, on Marxist-Leninist ideology, and on the Charter of the United Nations and facilitate the fraternal relations of the two socialist countries as a bridge between neighbors."

In spite of this grandiose rhetoric, practically nothing of any substance was done.

The Hungarian Minority Sparks the Anti-Ceaușescu Revolt

The catalyst that set off the uprising against the brutal communist dictatorship of Nicolae Ceaușescu in 1991 was the resistance of Hungarian Romanians in Timisoara (Hungarian "Temesvar") to the enforcement of more oppressive measures by further dispersal and assimilation of the population. The ethnic Hungarian Protestant pastor of the town openly criticized the move and was arrested, prompting demonstrations by groups of both ethnic communities that were fired on by the security police. This outrage unleashed the popular emotions of hatred against the communist regime and brought it crashing to the ground. This groundswell of common cause did not last long, however, and the new Romanian regime has permitted activities by extreme Romanian nationalist groups to harass the Hungarian minority.

Unable to deny mother-tongue education[4] to the large Hungarian minority, Romanian policy has nevertheless tried to divorce Hungarian native-tongue speakers from any contact with Hungary as if they spoke their own local dialect rather than a national language shared with another nation. Romanian authorities have taken extreme measures to bar access to all "foreign" Hungarian-language media as well as church activities and university programs emanating from Hungary. Visits by Hungarians to this sensitive area, annexed by Romania after World War I, are rigidly scrutinized and severely limited. In other areas of Romania outside of Transylvania and in the newly independent Moldova (part of Romania between the two world wars), there is no Hungarian-language education for mother-tongue Hungarian speakers.

Romania only briefly permitted a Hungarian-language university in Kolozsvar (Cluj), and Hungarian speakers are denied the opportunity to carry on a higher education at a Hungarian-language university in Hungary. Romanian resistance to permit any cross-border ties has even worked to the detriment of the small Romanian minority in Hungary. Under communism, Romania's policies towards the Hungarian minority have in fact been less liberal than in the interwar (1920–1940) monarchy, when a number of Hungarian journals championing minority rights were permitted. Romanian language and literature are compulsory in all grades of the Hungarian-minority schools, and the government has tried to legislate mandatory, Romanian-language history and geography courses. The Romanian language is a must in all government jobs, except in two Hungarian prefectures (Hargita, Covasna), where very low-grade municipal jobs have no language requirements. In private business, however, one must speak Romanian if the proprietor is Romanian.

Definitions of Language Loyalty and Nationality

The communist regime insisted on defining nationality by "mother tongue," except when inconvenient for them. To reduce the size of the Hungarian community, Jews were considered a separate minority and so registered in official census reports even if they reported Hungarian as their mother tongue. Jews who chose to identify Romanian as their first language were thus automatically listed as members of the Romanian nation. Few desired to take this step, however, as a result of Romanian compliance with demands that Jews wishing to emigrate to Israel be permitted to do so. The pattern of the Hungarian minority in Romania conforms to the classical model of a total correspondence between mother-tongue language and national identity. This entails repeated unsuccessful attempts by the majority in power to impose its language and culture on the minority, yet as we shall see from other historical examples, the situation is not marked by so much tension elsewhere.

Opposite: Figure 21. "Act on Hungarians Living in Neighboring Countries."

ACT LXII OF 2001 ON HUNGARIANS LIVING IN NEIGHBOURING COUNTRIES*

Adopted by Parliament on 19 June 2001.

Parliament

• In order to comply with its responsibilities for Hungarians living abroad and to promote the preservation and development of their manifold relations with Hungary prescribed in paragraph (3) of Article 6 of the Constitution of the Republic of Hungary,

• Considering the European integration endeavours of the Republic of Hungary and in-keeping with the basic principles espoused by international organisations, and in particular by the Council of Europe and by the European Union, regarding the respect of human rights and the protection of minority rights;

• Having regard to the generally recognised rules of international law, as well as to the obligations of the Republic of Hungary assumed under international law;

• Having regard to the development of bilateral and multilateral relations of good neighbourhood and regional co-operation in the Central European area and to the strengthening of the stabilising role of Hungary;

• **In order to ensure that Hungarians living in neighbouring countries form part of the Hungarian nation as a whole and to promote and preserve their well-being and awareness of national identity within their home country;**

• Based on the initiative and proposals of the Hungarian Standing Conference, a co-ordinating body functioning in order to preserve and reinforce the awareness of national self-identity of Hungarian communities living in neighbouring countries;

• Without prejudice to the benefits and assistance provided by law for persons of Hungarian nationality** living outside the Hungarian borders in other parts of the world;

Herewith adopts the following Act:

CHAPTER I
GENERAL PROVISIONS
Scope of the Act

Article 1

(1) This Act shall apply to persons declaring themselves to be of Hungarian nationality who are not **Hungarian citizens and who have their residence in the Republic of Croatia, the Federal Republic of Yugoslavia, Romania, the Republic of Slovenia, the Slovak Republic or the Ukraine, and who**

a) have lost their Hungarian citizenship for reasons other than voluntary renunciation, and

b) are not in possession of a permit for permanent stay in Hungary.

(2) This Act shall also apply to the spouse living together with the person identified in paragraph (1) and to the children of minor age being raised in their common household even if these persons are not of Hungarian nationality.

(3) This Act shall also apply to co-operation with, and assistance to organisations specified in Articles 13, 17, 18 and 25.

Article 2

(1) Persons falling within the scope of this Act shall be entitled, under the conditions laid down in this Act, to benefits and assistance on the territory of the Republic of Hungary, as well as in their place of residence in the neighbouring countries on the basis of the Certificate specified in Article 19.

A Hungarian Form of Zionism

The disastrous territorial losses suffered by Hungary produced the very large, Hungarian-speaking minorities in the Carpathian Basin, Central Europe and the Balkans. The communist regimes of Romania and Slovakia have followed a severe policy of repression and denial of cultural autonomy. As a result, the Hungarian government has enshrined in its constitution and the notable "*Act on Hungarians Living in Neighboring Countries*" laws (Figure 21), according special protection and most favored rights to citizens of the neighboring countries wishing to migrate, settle, reside, retire, work and study in Hungary in order to preserve their historical, cultural and national identity. This Hungarian version of the Israeli Zionist policy makes provisions to accord those "foreigners" of Hungarian origin access to institutions, services and benefits, make awards and provide assistance that enable them to preserve and promote the Hungarian language, literature, culture and folk art. Welfare assistance in the form of health insurance, scholarships, pensions and travel benefits are also generously made available to the less well-off citizens of Hungarian ethnic origin in the neighboring states.

The Csangos—Identity Subject to Language, Geography and Religion

Within the pre–World War I boundaries of "old Romania," in the historic district of Moldavia, on the eastern slopes of the Carpathian mountains live a still distinct group of about 250,000 Catholic (amidst their Orthodox and Romanian-speaking neighbors), largely rural and dispersed people, known as the Csangos (Ceangai in Romanian). The older generation speak an archaic and entirely oral Hungarian dialect. They have been separated for many centuries from Hungarian speakers in Transylvania across the Carpathians.

Many of their folk customs such as embroidery, costumes, weaving and pottery, mythology and traditions are Romanian, and the overwhelming majority consider themselves entirely Romanian in loyalty, quite distinct from other ethnic Hungarians in Romania, for whom language and ethic identity are one and the same. Their sense of nationality in the past was linked primarily with religion. Only about 50,000 have indicated "Csango" as their first or primary language at home. Romanian state officials and nationalists argue that this minority is proof of the tolerance of Romanian culture and the exaggerated claims of Hungarian nationalists and separatists. Only a small minority takes advantage of the option of sending their children to Hungarian language schools in Transylvania, across the Carpathians.

19

ALSACE-LORRAINE: GERMAN SPEAKERS WHO IDENTIFY WITH FRANCE

> Meine Leter ist deutsch,
> Sie klingt von deutschen Gesängen.
> Liebend den gallische Hane, treu ist
> Französisch mein Schwert.
> Mag es uder den Rhein und uber den Wasgau ertönen:
> Elsass heisset mein Land. Elsass dir pochet mein Herz.
>
> My lyre is German,
> It chimes with German songs.
> Loving the Gallic rooster,
> My sword is loyally French.
> Let it sound across the Rhine and the Vosges:
> Alsace is the name of my land;
> Alsace, my heart belongs to you.
>
> —Daniel Ehrenfried Stoeber (1779–1835)

This poem has a literal truth to it in the composition of the French national anthem, the Marseillaise, which was written by Lieutenant Claude Rouget de Lisle in Strasbourg, the capital of German-speaking Alsace in 1792. It was originally called "der Kriegsgesang der Rheinarmee" and sung by an Alsatian unit whose patriotic loyalty to France was unquestioned. Alsace and neighboring Lorraine present perhaps the most dramatic example that modern nationalism may find stronger support from common historic memories than from language.

The Alsatians, like the German Swiss, speak a dialect descended from the Alemanni tribes, who settled in both regions following the collapse of the Roman Empire. Standard German was elevated as the written High German language during a period when Germany did not exist as a united nation. Most of German-speaking Europe was a loose confederation of principalities, ecclesiastical states, minirepublics, and free cities, enjoying a large measure of self-rule within the Holy Roman Empire (800–1806). The area of Alsace, on the west bank of the Rhine, was an object of French expansionism seeking natural borders to provide strategic defense. France grew out of the West Franks, originally a German tribe who adopted the corrupted Latin speech of the conquered population of Celtic-Roman origin. The East Franks never lost their original Germanic speech but in between lay a contested area stretching from present day Belgium through the Ardennes and the Vosges hills overlooking the Rhine and Moselle valleys and then across Switzerland.

Early French Rule 1648–1870

Strasbourg played a brilliant part in German cultural life. The first Bible in German was published there in 1466, yet the great majority continued to speak their distinctive dialect. The Rhine region, like much of German-speaking Europe, was devastated by the Thirty Years War (1618–1648), and the Treaty of Westphalia placed Alsace under French protection, leading to eventual annexation. French rule did not interfere with local language usage, but the wealthy and literate classes found it advantageous to learn French. The glory and prestige of the French courts made French the most desirable language for international trade and diplomacy. The government insisted on all business contracts being written in French but did not demand instruction in French as part of public education in Alsace.

The French Revolution brought with it the promise of full equality for all citizens but insisted on a common language. Following the extension of public education, French was required as the medium of instruction, but German was also allowed to be taught. As early as 1848, the mayor of Strasbourg publicly asserted that even though Alsatians continued to use their home dialect as a medium of discourse socially and in the home, they were loyal to France.[1]

Alsace-Lorraine 1870–1918

Short-sighted, vindictive German policy following the Franco-Prussian war in 1870, in occupied France (1914–1918) and worst of all, during World War II, when Alsace-Lorraine was reannexed to Germany, permanently alienated many Alsatians, who were effectively bilingual but became more patriotically French. The Germans went beyond the purely German-speaking areas and annexed part of Lorraine around Metz to provide more strategic advantages and seize the rich iron deposits in the region. The newly united Germany (1871) insisted on instruction in standard German and took a harsh view of the lowly local dialect—almost as unintelligible as Schwyzerdütsch. Street, company and even family names had to be Germanized. Pierre became Peter, Henri became Hans, and Françoise, Fritz. In France, at the Place de Concorde in Paris, a mourning wreath was laid at the foot of the statue representing Strasbourg, one of the "nation's eight great cities."

France and Germany fought three terrible wars within the space of seventy years to redeem their lost territory Alsace, although many Alsatians regarded the two countries as their quarreling parents. During more than forty years under Prussian/German authoritarian rule, Alsace had always been a "Reichsland," directly under the control of Berlin, with an appointed rather than elected governor and local council. During this period, the trade connections between Alsace and the rest of France which had developed over the previous hundred years were disrupted. These policies increased the longing for a return to French rule. More than twenty-thousand Alsatians, instead of answering the mobilization call of the kaiser, left Alsace and volunteered for military service in France. Thirty-five thousand Alsatian men in the uniforms of both major adversaries were killed in action.

Under French Rule Again

Unfortunately, the French were also vindictive and pursued a similar, heavy-handed policy as soon as Alsace-Lorraine was regained. French became the sole medium of instruction from day one, and all documents in administration and the courts had to be in French, thus giving translators a substantial amount of business and encouraging everyone to rapidly learn French, but the results, under duress and coercion, were, of course, poor. Unavoidably, an Independent Party of Alsace was founded with a platform calling for independence and a "plague on both your houses."

The French Communist Party split into two factions, with the Alsatian wing favoring autonomy and even eventual secession. Nevertheless, the rise of the Nazi Party in Germany and its open call for a return of the lost territories alarmed most Alsatians. Most Alsatians were also horrified by Hitler's paganism, contempt of the Catholic church and vicious anti–Semitism. The small but highly respected Jewish community of Alsace traced its historic continuity back to the Middle Ages.

German victory in 1940 and the reannexation of the territories to Germany brought with it total reversal. Alsatians once again became German citizens and were immediately subject to military conscription. French was even scorned as a foreign-language subject in the schools. Speaking French in public could result in suspicion of treason, arrest and deportation. As in Flanders, some Alsatians supported collaboration with the Germans in the hope of winning regional autonomy, but the great majority quickly drew the conclusion that this was a hopeless illusion and that with an Allied victory, Alsace would once again be French. By the end of the war, the issue had been decided. The return of Alsace permanently to France was welcomed with relief. The conclusions of 1945 have not changed. "The German-speaking population of Alsace-Lorraine is an example, indeed, this seems to be the only instance in Europe of national feeling moving in opposition to language."[2]

In 1951, France adopted the Deixonne Law, allowing for several hours of instruction in local languages and dialects in the regions in which they were in use but expressly excluded German. Literacy and fluency in French is now almost universal in the large cities of Alsace-Lorraine and has also gained substantially in rural areas. It is now the first language of most Alsatians. Knowledge of standard German has declined significantly, although most Alsatians still speak dialect and can read German. Since the 1950s, German has been gradually reintroduced as an elective subject in the public schools.

Alsatian, French, German-Speaking and European (No Contradiction)

Interest in the dialect remains high. Its role as an important element in the local culture embracing folklore, costumes, music, dance, diet, architecture, and so on is acknowledged by all. Knowledge of standard German has also increased due to Strasbourg's role as one of the sites of the European Parliament and the council of Europe. Like Belgium, many Alsatians now view their bilingualism as a distinct advantage. Nowhere is the cause of a united Europe supported more wholeheartedly. As one observer remarked, the people seemed to have absorbed the best of both nations—a Teutonic spruceness and efficiency mixed with a Gallic stylishness and excitability.[3] No matter what the future of the union may have in store, almost all Alsatians are committed more than ever to the idea of being part of the French nation, even if they still speak a German dialect at home.

20

THE GERMAN-SPEAKING DANISH MINORITY IN SOUTH SCHLESWIG

Many German-speaking South Schleswigers feel a strong identity with Denmark, Danish history, culture and a lifestyle through the medium of German, which differentiates them from their neighbors who speak the same language (German) but identify with the history of Germany, its culture and way of life. We have seen that the definition of national self-identity as a concept has varied considerably over time. The original ethnic identity of individuals ceased to play a decisive role in determining loyalty, which changed from feudal lord and church to absolute monarch, to state and flag and self-serving economic or social interests. At different times these factors have swayed the population of Schleswig/Slesvig in one direction or another. There are some individuals who have identified with both national traditions and cultures and others who are so bilingual and bicultural that Schleswig as a whole is their first frame of reference. What is remarkable about the situation of the Danish minority in Germany (since the unification of Germany) in 1871 is that it has always been predominantly German-speaking.

Danish-Nordic Cultural Elements in South Slesvig (Schleswig)

Although predominantly German speaking for centuries, certain residual elements of folk culture in the popular subconscious revealing Danish-Nordic origins are still apparent. These include geographic place names (especially those ending in –by and –torp), family names (ending in –sen), colloquial expressions that indicate the indigenous population was not German (Han er så gal som en Tysker—literally, he is as crazy as a German), the layout of streets according to the compass directions, house and barn architecture, the use of wooden shoes with a full heel (compared to a wooden sandal with an open heel in neighboring Holstein), and many other customs and habits (see Eskildsen, 1946, op.

cit.). The area of Southern Schleswig initially settled by German speakers in the first great wave of German expansionism took place in the thirteenth century, whereas rural Schleswig remained primarily Danish in language, habits and customs. The wealthy, land-owning German nobility gradually acquired large estates throughout much of southern and central Jutland and brought with them German artisans, administrators, judges, lawyers, clerks and teachers who exercised a significant influence in the towns through their power in running municipal and guild affairs. Slowly the German language became the official administrative language in the schools and churches and then the vernacular throughout much of South Schleswig.

The Language Issue

Throughout the seventeenth and eighteenth centuries, the German nobility and wealthy merchants dominated the cultural life of Schleswig as well as Holstein and played an increasingly prominent role in the church and school system, both of which promulgated the use of German at the expense of Danish. Holstein was entirely German in language and culture. Local German noblemen, large landowners and powerful merchants played a major role in Danish affairs and politics and at first did not regard their German culture as an obstacle to their loyalty as subjects of the Danish king. In fact, many of them wrote poems in the German language, extolling the kingdom of Denmark and its royal house. As late as 1810, a patriotic subject of the Danish kingdom could express his loyalty to king and fatherland (Denmark) in the most ecstatic of terms (in German) as in the poems:

> "Wie gut ist ein Däne sein,und sich des Vaterlands zu freun!"
> O Dania, was glüht bei deinem Namen mir Wang' und Busen durch
> Ha! Das ist Dänenstolz, das ist die Liebe zu dir, mein Vaterland!"
>
> (How good it is to be a Dane and rejoice at the Fatherland)
> (Oh Dania, how my cheek and breast glow at mention of your name.
> It is Danish pride, my love to you, my fatherland!)[1]

Their attitude that German was the language of high culture and Danish only a rough peasant tongue permeated society at a time when their loyalty to the Danish ruling house was not in question. The diaries of several German pastors stationed in Schleswig in the eighteenth century reveal the contempt for those Danish-speaking peasants ignorant of German, as if their language explained a lack of morality. One of them, Christopf Heinrich Fischer from Saxony, was installed in 1730 as pastor of the local community in Hyrup (German, Hörup) in Angel, about fifteen kilometers southeast of Flensburg. By 1738, Pastor Fischer confided that his congregation had no morals and spoke no German. He wrote that his parishioners included many elderly people who were unable to understand German and so had no sense at all for true Christianity in theory or in practice. The same year Fischer was visited by his son, a student from Kiel. The two of them became involved in harsh words with several parishioners, who gave them a beating and officially protested to church authorities about the irresponsible and arrogant behavior of their pastor. Fischer actually left behind a record of his church sermon held on the first Trinity Sunday and diary, which was later cited in court proceedings held against him (he was finally dismissed in 1750) and is worth quoting at some length to indicate the social gap between the two classes and language users well into the late eighteenth century:

> When I came home and took my boots off in the study room, a great deal of blood ran out of them due to the many blows I had received which struck an artery. Ach! you thieves and robbers of the church, what pains I have had with this congregation. Oh God, you have sent me to hell where there lives a devil in almost every house of my congregation. It would have been better to serve the devil as a swineherd than to be the shepherd of souls for such Christians. You pack of devils and hell-raisers, have I not sought to teach you German? But to what avail when this devilish riffraff continues to speak its stupid Danish tongue throughout, even with children and servants.... What can please the Devil more than that you cannot say the Lord's prayer, cannot pray God's commandments or even sing a song when the service and all the actions designed to save the soul occur by means of the German language."[2]

The Appeal of German

Only during the nineteenth century, after German had largely displaced Danish from much of south and middle Schleswig, did the language divide come to play a major role in defining the newly established national movements. The oft-repeated and automatic assumption in many nationalist rivalries that language is the most distinguishing ethnic marker and the easiest recognizable component of national identity is not borne out by the case of Schleswig,[3] Alsace-Lorraine,[4] or Switzerland.[5] Even a recent and thorough guidebook[6] devoted to the peoples and cultures of Europe makes the mistake of identifying the national minorities on both sides of the present-day Danish-German border in terms of language as the "Danish-speaking minority of Northern Schleswig-Holstein and the German-speaking minority in South Jutland." An ironic expression of the gap between the deeply embedded

Danish folk character and the newly acquired German nationalist sentiment in Schleswig-Holstein was revealed by none other than the poet Hoffman von Fallersleben, the author of "Deutschland, Deutschland über alles"in 1845, who arrived in the city of Schleswig to meet with and congratulate the leadership of his "fellow German brother-tribesmen" for their resistance to the Danish crown and wound up noting in his diary that "It turned into a depressing meeting. These Schleswigers have almost nothing in common with us other than our language. The Danish soul is deeply embedded within them and emerges at every opportunity!"

The achievements of Germany's philosophers, musicians, writers, and scientists, the appeal of modern nationalism, the problems of an orderly succession to the Danish throne, and the attraction of a dominant Prussia all conspired to make Schleswig look southward. Danish continued to be spoken predominantly by those classes who had the least influence in the prevailing "high culture" of Schleswig—poor farmers and pockets of an urban proletariat in the few big cities—Flensburg (Flensborg) and Schleswig (Slesvig).

The Importance of Economic Interests and Social Climbing

In those more prosperous areas of Schleswig facing the Baltic—notably Angel, south of the line Sli estuary–Dannevirke–Trene River, the local dialect variety of Danish (Sønderjysk) was replaced by German as a result of socially ambitious farmers cultivating German. It was the language spoken in the home in order to give the children a social advantage in school, the church and "fine society." The wealthier farmers, who raised cattle driven for sale in northern Germany along the market trail known as the "hærvej" (ox road) more readily and willingly adopted German as the language of commerce and then at home. In contrast, the poorer farmers in middle Schleswig and near the North Sea coast retained their Danish longer, until the mid-nineteenth century. On the other hand, the population of the island Als and many of the smaller islands in the Little Belt were tied by church connections to the important cathedral and the bishop residing in Odense, on the island of Fyn. This helped preserve Danish language ties and associations.

The German definition of "minorities" as enshrined in the Weimar constitution of 1920 defined the term "*Volksteile*"employing foreign-language usage as the sole criterion and ensured that no barriers would be put in the way for the use of one's mother tongue in education, administration and the courts. This provision (article 113) adversely affected the Danish-minded minority more than others. Language had not been the major criterion for distinguishing national identity in south Schleswig, and Danish-minded parents were prevented from sending their children to Danish-language schools in south Schleswig unless able to pass stringent tests indicating proficiency in Danish.

The Nazis refrained from closing down the minority community's Danish-language newspaper, *Flensborg Avis*, but intervened several times to stop publication of its German-language supplement—*Der Schleswiger*. The Nazis claimed that a German-language newspaper was an aggressive attempt by the Danish minority to win souls among "true Germans." Nevertheless, the fact that 28 percent of Flensburg's population had voted for Denmark in the plebiscite when only 5 percent utilized Danish as their first language was always difficult to explain, given the general popular (but mistaken) view that language is always a reliable indication of national sentiment. Attacks against *Flensborg Avis* by ultranationalist Germans unable to understand Danish were particularly ironic in light of the fact that the social democratic press in Denmark openly criticized the paper for being too lenient, passive and uncritical in the face of the new Nazi regime's undemocratic steps.

The Minority Schools

The right to an education in a Danish minority school and the right to give a child a Danish name, to belong to associations holding public meetings in the Danish language were limited to German citizens who identified with the Danish minority and were able to prove their identity by such tests. The same rights were accorded the German minority in north Schleswig by Danish authorities solely on the basis of free will rather than any objective criteria. These two contrasting definitions of minority rights and the much greater size of the German-minded minority in Denmark resulted in a quite unequal contest.

Whereas after 1920, more than thirty German public schools and several private ones were established in Denmark, the German authorities in south Schleswig made it practically impossible for new Danish schools to get started. Approximately three-quarters of all applications from Danish-minded parents to send their children to the Danish minority school in Flensborg were rejected because the parents were unable to pass the language exam. In 1929, more liberal German authorities passed a new school bill, permitting enrolment in the Danish minority schools without any geographical requirement and permitted the establishment of such schools even in the southernmost region, where a Danish school was established in Tønning, near the Eider River.

VI. Ethnic or Regional Minorities

The Danish Minority Organization (SF), 1920–1939

The Danish minority organization Slesvigsk Forening (Schleswig Association), or SF, was repeatedly labeled by the German authorities as a front for social democratic and Marxist elements hiding their dissatisfaction with the new regime behind the guise of national minority rights. The large German majority in plebiscite zone 2 in 1920, especially in the city of Flensburg itself, was, in part, the result of the Marxist sympathies of Social Democrats, who regarded themselves as workers first and voted for their class interests rather than ethnicity or simply out of fear of becoming unemployed. Since the party's appearance, it had supported the internationalist Marxist dictum that "a worker's fatherland is the whole world" and supported the right of self-determination in north Schleswig. Many Danish-minded workers in south Schleswig became increasingly aware of their mistake in having voted to remain in Germany out of Marxist theoretical principles. They were however not alone.

The Schleswig case was not unique and resembled Burgenland,[7] where the Marxist Social Democratic party in what had been Hungarian territory agitated on the basis of class interests for the local proletarian population to seek the transfer of their territory to the new Austrian republic. The party argued that the workers' connections to Vienna, both in terms of jobs and commuting time, their literacy in German—a language of workers' solidarity in central Europe—and the need for the party to work within a wide organizational framework made Austria a better choice. Many Burgenlanders of Hungarian or Croat ethnic origin were convinced to vote in favor of transfer to Austria. In the view of Otto Bauer, leader of the party, the fragmentation of central Europe into competing national states was a backward step and a hindrance to proletarian solidarity. His view greatly influenced Social Democratic circles in both Denmark and Germany.

The Fate of the German-Language Supplement

Flensborg Avis was conspicuous among newspapers in Germany by its avoidance of editorial comment on Nazi anti–Semitism. It faithfully reported the anti–Jewish legislation without comment except for a few occasions when it dryly noted that these measures were designed by the government to uphold the "German sense of honor and racial purity." It must be also be borne in mind that the Danish government and its representative at the Danish consulate in Flensburg had warned the SF leadership and *Flensborg Avis* not to openly antagonize the Nazi regime or express sympathy on a community-wide level for Jews, Social Democrats and Communists who had been forced out of public positions or had fled to Denmark. This became even more acute after the Nazi prohibition against *Flensborg Avis*'s German-language daily supplement, *Der Schleswiger*, as a result of accusations that the paper had been openly circulated among groups of disgruntled communist workers in Hamburg's harbor, who then had distributed it to "unscrupulous elements" and bookshops throughout Germany, representing the anti–Nazi "confessional church" (led by the Reverend Martin Niemoeller until his arrest by the Gestapo together with more than 800 pastors in July, 1937). The Danish minority community in south Schleswig had thus been branded as an ally of the regime's opponents by some local Nazi politicians and revisionist circles anxious to recover north Schleswig. The Nazi government in Berlin however repeatedly assured the Danish government and the editors of *Flensborg Avis* that these measures were not intended to hinder the "authentic" Danish minority community but only to prevent it being exploited by opponents of the Nazi regime.

The Return of the Language Issue

Walter Bartram, the leader of the state coalition government between the Christian Democratic Union (CDU) and the party of German refugees in Schleswig-Holstein spoke out in 1949 against the growth of Danish schools in Schleswig and the specter of "children of parents living in a land of cultural homogeneity being ripped out of a linguistic and cultural community of 100 million people and led to another one of only 4 million whose language is nowhere understood outside that tiny country's narrow borders."

Clever German exploitation of the language issue was similar to the use the Nazis had made of the fact that the germanized Danes of Schleswig, who still felt an affinity to the Danish cause, culture, lifestyle and human values, spoke German as their first and habitual language.[8] Knowledge of Danish was often retarded by the opinion that German was the socially more refined, profitable, practical, and prestigious language (as it had similarly been among germanized Poles, Lithuanians, and Sorbs, or as French had been among the originally German-speaking Alsatians). Another factor often held accountable is the pronounced difference in the intonation of standard Rigsdansk (the national language, i.e., "Danish of the realm"), based on the eastern Danish dialects in Copenhagen and the local Sønderjysk, or South Jutlandic, based on west Danish dialects. The overwhelming dominance of Copenhagen made it difficult for peripheral regions to retain a sense of loyalty. The result was that neither Norway, Iceland, the Faeroes, Greenland, Bornholm nor south Schleswig were wholly integrated with the rest of the realm. Nevertheless, the same linguistic and socially perceived distance between peripheral Schleswig (with its variety of local Plattdeutsch) and the literary High German (Hochdeutsch) of the united country's cultural core also worked against integration.

The great wave of pro–Danish sympathies that swept south Schleswig after World War II led to the demand for new Danish-language schools but was nipped in the bud by strong counterarguments following Denmark's decision not to press for a new plebiscite. German authorities repeatedly focused on the language issue, claiming that loss of German—"a language of worldwide prestige"—in favor of Danish— a minority language of Europe's "Scandinavian periphery"—would be a tragic reduction of economic and social opportunities (repeating the same line of reasoning which originally had led many Danish speakers to switch to German in the eighteenth and nineteenth centuries). The Danish-minded minority in south Schleswig today is made up of primary German speakers, whose knowledge of Danish is as a second, spoken language or largely passive and confined to the written language. Since the war, knowledge of both the Danish language and literature has increased considerably. In 1947, a spelling reform of Danish did away with the previous practice of spelling nouns with capital letters. This move was due to a desire to distance Danish as much as possible from German as part of the general anti–German reaction during and immediately following the war.

The Danish Minority in Germany Today

In retrospect, the source of much intransigence over the question of Schleswig/Slesvig was the unwillingness to draw a border separating two peoples, cultures, lifestyles, languages, and traditions but built upon such grandiose ideas as "the integrity of the monarchy" or "forever undivided Schleswig-Holstein." Only when the border was considered as final have both sides accepted it and worked within its framework to ensure minority rights. The fine showing of the Südschleswigscher Wählverband (SSW), the party representing the Danish minority, in the last elections (February, 2000) is proof that the removal of any doubt regarding the finality of the boundary has been a precondition for achieving mutual recognition and tolerance and the stability of the Danish minority. The large German-speaking but Danish-minded minority community has made a long and painful journey from regarding south Schleswig as an irredenta to be redeemed by Denmark to a common "heimat" (homeland) for the territory's people, forming an economic, cultural and social bridge between Germany and Scandinavia.

21

THE SWEDISH-SPEAKING FINLANDERS

Alsace-Lorraine and south Schleswig were not the only regions in Europe where national self-identity and a preference or need for the "other nation's language" have been very powerful. The Swedish minority in Finland is unique. Finland is officially a bilingual country with guaranteed rights for the Swedish-speaking minority ("Finlanders" is a term sometimes used to distinguish them from the ethnic majority of "Finns"). These rights are, however, distinctly administered according to geographic location. In the autonomous Åland islands lying out in the Gulf of Finland, the Swedish-speaking population even enjoys an official monopoly that excludes the use of Finnish for all public purposes.

The Swedish-speaking minority in Finland constitutes about 6 percent of the total population. It is the only significant minority in Finland and is the result of Sweden's role as colonizer, conqueror and missionary power in much of Finland for more than 600 years. At one point in the seventeenth century, the Swedish minority constituted more than 16 percent of the population in Finland and in total numbers reached its maximum of about 350,000 people in 1940.

Today, the minority numbers less than 300,000 and there is a slow but constant migration back to Sweden.[1] It is geographically concentrated in three distinct areas, the west coast facing Sweden across the Gulf of Bothnia, the south coast adjacent to Helsinki and the Åland islands between the Baltic and the entrance to the Gulf of Bothnia, each with its own set of regulations regarding the use of Swedish for administrative purposes and the rights of Swedish speakers. The relationship between the two languages was dramatically altered when Sweden was forced to surrender Finland to Russia toward the end of the Napoleonic wars and with the independence of Finland after World War I.

Swedish and Russian Rule

The Swedes were encouraged by Pope Adrian IV (1155) to conquer Finland and convert the pagan tribal Finns to Christianity. Swedish sovereignty over Finland was recognized by the pope in 1216, and the king of Sweden was authorized to expand his control over the less-populated territories farther north and east. This brought Sweden into conflict with Russia and the Russian Orthodox church, which also wished to extend their influence over the Finnish tribes. For centuries, a small Swedish elite administered the country at a time when Finnish was only an oral language. Not until 1563 was the first Finnish book, an "ABC" primer, published, followed by the New Testament shortly thereafter. The great Finnish oral tradition of folktales was not gathered and recorded until 1835, when the first edition of the great epic poem, the *Kalevala*, was published.

Viking expeditions used the Åland Islands, a rocky, granite archipelago of 6,500 islands in the Gulf of Bothnia, only eighty of which are today inhabited, to expand its control over the Finnish mainland. Almost all Swedish migration and settlement was confined to the islands and narrow strips along the coast. By using these stepping stones, the early Viking explorations proceeded on to Russia and down the great river systems to the Black Sea. In 1362, the Christianized Finns were granted rights as Swedish citizens, and the country became a duchy within the Swedish kingdom in 1555. Swedish was used exclusively as the language of administration and the church.

Between 1720 and 1749, the Swedes lost control of much of Finland to an expansionist Russia, and by 1809, all of Finland, including the strategic Åland Islands, fell into Russian hands. The Russians at first made no attempt to force their language, culture or religion upon the Finns. Swedish remained the sole language of administration under Russian rule until 1863, when Finnish was accorded equal rights. In 1894, Russian was introduced as an official language in the administration, the courts and schools, and in 1912 Russian migrants resident in Finland were accorded equal rights, posing a threat to the national and cultural identity of the country. Whereas Finnish Swedes had the option of leaving Finland under Russian rule and returning to Sweden, the Finns had nowhere to go.

A Finnish nationalist movement struggled for recognition, and at the turn of the century, the great composer Jean Sibelius completed his famous composition "Finlandia" (1899–1900), symbolizing aspirations for Finnish independence. Many of the strongest supporters of Finnish nationalism and independence were Swedish speakers, who used their own language in patriotic pamphlets and journals of the time because few of them could write Finnish. By the end of the nineteenth century, the nationalist movement in Finland had been successful in encouraging a mass movement to use Finnish as a written language and in creating an educated, Finnish-speaking elite. At that time, Swedish speakers numbered about 350,000, forming about thirteen percent of the country's population and were still disproportionately influential and wealthy, but they no longer constituted a dominant aristocratic elite as they had done at the beginning of the nineteenth century. They are still, however, more urban and overrepresented in the professions and in higher education.

Independence and the Åland Islands Autonomy Act

The achievement of Finnish independence following the collapse of the czarist empire posed a difficult problem for the new Finnish republic. Control of the entrance to the Gulf of Bothnia and Finland's populated coastal area depended on control of the Åland Islands, which were wholly Swedish speaking and claimed by Sweden as vital to its defense. The conflict was successfully resolved by the League of Nations in 1920 and 1922, which awarded the islands to Finland, under the condition of full cultural autonomy, special rights for the Swedish-speaking inhabitants and a permanent status as a demilitarized and neutral zone. In recognition of this decision, the Finnish constitution enshrined the position of Swedish as one of the country's two official languages in 1922.

Since then, several revisions of the act of autonomy have expanded the competence of the local inhabitants. Only foreign affairs, the courts of justice, civil and penal law, customs and monetary services are controlled directly by the Finnish government in Helsinki. The islands are a kind of reservation for the protection of the Swedish language. Apart from marriage, settlement by Finnish citizens from outside the islands is strictly regulated to prevent any change in ethnic character and the sole use of Swedish as the official language. Residents of the Åland Islands carry Finnish passports marked with the designation "Åland Island resident," and the region has its own flag. This arrangement of regional citizenship and exclusion of what is the native official language of 94 percent of the country's population is quite unique. It discriminates against the main national language in favor of a minor national language.

A Common Patriotism

The Finlanders rallied to their country's defense in the 1940 winter war provoked by the USSR and then in the continuation war from 1941 to 1944. Thousands of volunteers from Sweden and among Finnish

Americans contributed an "international brigade" to the Finnish war effort. From the nation's undisputed leader and brilliant wartime hero, Marshall Carl Gustaf Emil Mannerheim, himself a Finlander of partly Swedish descent, to the non–Finnish-speaking Åland Islanders, the cause of Finland's independence was unquestioned. There was no sense of discrimination, special treatment or hesitation on the part of Finland's Swedish minority to defend the common homeland.

Bilingualism in Finland: Unequal Partners

In other areas of Finland, however, the rights of the Swedish-speaking minority are protected but not guaranteed. Finnish is an obligatory subject of study in the Swedish minority schools except those in the Åland Islands. On a national administrative level, the laws and ordinances are formulated in both languages, and the right to use one's mother tongue (Swedish or Finnish) before legal and administrative authorities in most relevant areas is guaranteed. Higher-ranking civil servants must pass competency tests in both languages. Once all this is said and done, it is still apparent that the Swedes in Finland, apart from the Åland Islanders, encounter problems as a minority in the rest of Finland. The authorities do not provide Swedish-language services in much of Finland where there are few or no Swedish speakers.

The country is divided into municipalities and these units of local administration are required to provide bilingual services for the Swedish minority; only where it constitutes at least 8 percent of the population. Once a municipality has been declared bilingual, it may revert to unilingual Finnish status if the number of Swedish speakers drops below 6 percent. This means, however, that a population register is maintained to ascertain who "belongs" to the Swedish minority. This used to be determined every ten years on the basis of a census and acceptance of a respondent's answer to the question "What do you consider your main language?"

As in every society, the influence of the majority is greater upon the minority than vice versa. Through intermarriage, national military service, employment and educational opportunities, more and more Finlanders acquire Finnish as their first language, and native-language fluency and literacy in Swedish continue to decrease. As a result of pressure from minority organizations, the question has been changed to "What is your mother tongue?"—a question which most Finlanders can answer honestly when reporting Swedish. This technique has enabled them to maintain their special rights, but it does imply a form of ghettoization. This is also the case with respect to military service. There is one brigade in the Finnish army set aside for Swedish speakers only.

21. The Swedish-Speaking Finlanders

As in Canada, where there is much less good will, bilingualism is frequently a failure in practice, no matter how fine the theory is. Although the laws protecting language rights for Swedish speakers in Finland are among the most generous in the world, apart from the Åland Islanders, Finlanders occasionally encounter situations where they live in dealing with authorities whose knowledge of Swedish is poor. As elsewhere, the good will of the majority can be strained to provide services that demand from them a level of language ability that is beyond the reach of many. There are also delays and extra expenses to provide costly interpretation and translation services if Swedish speakers insist on dealing with the courts in their own language. In reality, this means poorer services for citizens whose Finnish is not good enough for easy comprehension in a range of situations where language problems can easily arise, such as in legal cases in court and for medical care in hospitals. The press occasionally plays up embarrassing situations where young children, the retarded, or the elderly among the Swedish minority with very poor knowledge of Finnish have been treated abruptly or misunderstood by officials. Insistence on an education entirely in Swedish-language schools means careful selection of residence within Swedish-speaking municipalities to avoid very long journeys to schools.

Finnish is no longer obligatory for the Swedish speakers in the Åland Islands who, when required to sing the Finnish national anthem, do so in Swedish. The irony of this situation is double because the words were originally written in Swedish and subsequently translated to Finnish. Most Finnish students choose to learn Swedish as a useful foreign language, and many Finns delight in telling foreigners that their most famous personalities, the great composer Sibelius and the outstanding military hero Mannerheim, both spoke Finnish with an accent. The Finlanders regard Finland as their home, even those who do not speak its first national language. Several opinion surveys have shown that bilingual Swedish-Finnish

Figure 22. Bilingual Finnish stamp with the names of the country in both languages.

speakers in Helsinki and along the southwest coast of Finland feel more in common with their neighbors than with the Åland Islanders in their Swedish-speaking ghetto. University education is available in both languages but only in Finnish for a number of specialized fields.

The state radio and television produces a special Swedish-language service on a national level, but the number of broadcast hours is a fraction of the total. The Swedish-language press maintains more than thirty daily or weekly newspapers, and every year about 200 Swedish books are published in Finland. An additional problem for the minority is that their Swedish continues to be influenced by Finnish, often through bad translations, and this problem is magnified with each generation. Finland is a bilingual country with two official national languages, but there is a clear majority, and the identity of the nation is not in doubt. It is Finnish. Whatever the minor problems, there is probably more harmony and goodwill among the two language groups than in any other bilingual country. Finnish stamps bear the name of the country and many localities in both Swedish and Finnish versions (Figure 22).

22

ISRAEL'S HEBREW-SPEAKING ARAB CITIZENS

Israel, like Finland, is officially bilingual (Hebrew and Arabic), and, like Finland, the nation is not in doubt. Israel is defined as the "Jewish homeland." There is little doubt that sometime before the year 2030, a majority of the world's Jewish population will be Hebrew speakers. The relation between majority and minority is, of course, much more problematic, more so than in Finland, Canada or Belgium. The question of language remains a dilemma for the State of Israel whose attempts to forge strong ties with the Jewish Diaspora are still negotiated often clumsily through English, Spanish, French and Russian. No matter how Zionist or sympathetic many Jews in the Diaspora are toward the Israeli experiment, the great majority lack Hebrew, the fundamental common tool to experience the reality of Israel firsthand. As a compulsory second language in the Arab school systems of Israel, Hebrew is acquired as an essential tool of communication. There are twenty-five independent states and sheikhdoms in the Arab League, each of which has declared Arabic to be its official language (or one of its official languages). All of them, with the exceptions of Egypt, Jordan and Mauritania, are in an official state of war with Israel or are simply hostile with no diplomatic relations.

The Need for Hebrew in Israel

Many Jews in the Diaspora, even those who pray daily in Hebrew, are unable to read or speak modern Hebrew, whereas many of Israel's male Arab citizens are fluent and more literate in Hebrew than in Arabic. Walk into an Israeli Arab village café on a Saturday and see what newspapers they are reading. The great majority will be reading the leading Hebrew weekend papers (*Yediot Ahronot* and *Ma'ariv*). A successful Israeli Arab writer in Hebrew is Anton Shammas, author of the critically acclaimed novel *Arabesques*, but his work and name are totally unknown among Jewish communities abroad, and within Israel he is regarded with suspicion by both communities. The reasons for this are not difficult to understand. Like everywhere else, language choice in a free market is determined not by ideology but by practical utility—opportunity to work outside one's home in the national economy makes knowledge of the national language essential everywhere. Even during the time of the British mandate in Palestine (1920–1948), much Arab labor was employed in the Jewish sector of the economy, and some knowledge of Hebrew and even Yiddish or English by more skilled Arab workers was occasionally required.

Due to the political conflict and enmity between Israel and the Arab world and the low socioeconomic status of the Arab minority, Arabic ranks low on the scale of prestige even though it is of vital strategic importance for the Israeli intelligence services and the military. Arabic, along with Hebrew, is an official language in Israel. Most official documents in Hebrew are translated into Arabic. Arabic may be used in the courts and is the language of instruction in an autonomous Arab sector of public education. The name of the country appears in Arabic script on all banknotes and stamps, but the symbols of the state and the personalities honored on these are all Jewish (Figure 23). Hebrew is a compulsory subject in the minority schools, and all Israeli Arabs study it from the third grade to high school. Arabic is an elective within the Jewish schools in Israel and was the native language of many Jews who came from Middle-Eastern countries. About 40 percent of Israel's Jewish population stems from Arabic-speaking countries, and about one in eight Israeli Jews still uses Arabic as a first or second language daily.[1]

Hebrew's dominance is however even greater among Israeli Arabs than might be imagined due to the paucity and poor quality of Arabic textbooks, the Arab boycott against Israel and the fewer, less sophisticated resources at the disposal of the Arabic mass media via Israeli radio, television and the press. The Palestinian Arabic vernacular is the daily common speech of all Israeli Arabs. Modern standard Arabic is taught at school and, as in the rest of the Arab world, is used in all books and newspapers. Knowledge of Hebrew among Israeli Arabs, who comprise about 17 percent of Israel's total population (i.e., three times greater than the Swedish minority in Finland) is related directly to education, residence, sex and age. It is considerably more important for work outside the village, in higher education and for contact with the majority Jewish population. Knowledge is much greater among men and in the 30–55 age group.

The Arab minority is caught in the dilemma that an essential part of their identity as Arabs is related to language, but their own insistence on a separate Arabic-language education segregated from the Jewish

22. Israel's Hebrew-Speaking Arab Citizens

Figure 23. Israeli banknote with Arabic inscription on reverse.

majority accentuates their status as a discriminated minority. Certainly, fluency in Hebrew has been a tool of advancement for those Arabs who seek to go on for higher education in Israel, where there is no Arabic-language university, and due to the lack of the opportunity to study at Arab universities abroad. It also enables some Arabs to "pass" in Jewish society if they so desire, although this phenomenon has been halted or slowed down by the acquisition of some Hebrew by many Arabs in the areas under Israeli occupation since 1967.

Hebrew fluency is undoubtedly a marker of Israel Arab identity. A sample survey released in 2002 shows that only 30 percent or so of the respondents support annexing Arab settlements in the Triangle and Wadi 'Ara areas as part of an exchange of territory between Israel and the

Palestinian-state-to-be. The Arab-Israeli weekly, *Panorama*, reported only 9 percent of a cross-section of Umm al-Fahm (the largest Arab village in Wadi Ara) residents supported the idea. The head of the labor party's Israeli-Arab section, Ghaleb Majadla, said, "No one will prevent us from identifying with our people and their suffering and fighting on its behalf in legitimate ways. To the same extent, no one will take away our Israeli citizenship which is citizenship that we are entitled to and was not granted to us as a favor." Qassem Ziyad, a veteran teacher of Arabic who taught the language to thousands of Jewish students in the kibbutz educational movement, has decided to rally Arab regional leaders against any proposal for an exchange of territory with the Palestinian authority. According to Ziyad, "There have been several generations formed of Arabs with an Israeli social and civilian identity. We are part of the social fabric of the country and that's a fact. We serve it in the most positive sense of the word. So don't tell us to go to hell" (Middle East Media Research Institute; 5/2/02, No. 374; Israeli-Arabs Object to Ideas of Israeli-Palestinian Territorial Exchange).

The Irony of Correct Hebrew Pronunciation and Prejudice Toward Arabic

The relationship between the two peoples and language is an asymmetrical one. Arabs distinguish between the social necessity and desirability of communicating in Hebrew for many practical purposes, even though their relationship to Jews and the state of Israel may be hostile, whereas most Jews have a negative attitude toward Arabic as a result of the two peoples' mutual hostility. This is apparent even among the children of native Arabic speakers of Jews, who were expelled and whose property was confiscated in the 1948–1949 hostilities, when anti–Jewish disturbances occurred in Iraq, Syria, Egypt, Libya and Yemen following the defeat of the invading Arab armies.

Ironically, "correct" Hebrew pronunciation was modeled after Arabic by prominent linguists in the formative period of the Hebrew revival, including Ben-Yehuda. The distinct pronunciation of the guttural letters of the Hebrew alphabet, "ayin" and "ḥet" were originally used to function as a guide for correct spelling. These letters originally had the same pronunciation as the corresponding letters in Arabic. What was once considered correct Hebrew pronunciation is now largely regarded by the Jewish majority as a marker of lower-class origin and Arab or Eastern-Oriental Jewish identity. Another irony of this situation is that failure to pronounce these letters correctly leads to frequent spelling errors by the upper class and largely Ashkenazi (European origin) Jewish majority. In the view of Haim B. Rosen, one of the foremost Israeli authorities on linguistics and the Hebrew language, the European Jewish majority has considerably altered Hebrew in the direction of an Indo-European language in terms of grammar and syntax and noticeably in pronunciation: "By a singular historical accident, the group of speakers whose speech exhibits more puristically desirable features ("Semitic" tainted phonetics ... darker articulation..., etc.) are those which are considered non-prestige by others ... and by themselves. It is the speech habits of groups hailing from Eastern Europe that tend to be imitated by those coming from Oriental countries, while speech habits fostered by purist language policy-makers will not be observed normally other than by 'Orientals.'"[2]

One amusing anecdote of this situation is the solution found to the Hebrew translation of the great musical and film "My Fair Lady." How would the translators deal with Eliza Higgens's lower-class Cockney accent and dialect and her struggle to learn "proper" (upper-class) English? The first attempt was ridiculous because a proper pronunciation of Hebrew in the ears of the purists meant imitating the "lower-class" pronunciation of Hebrew employed by most Arabs and many Oriental Jews. Dan Almagor, the translator, wrote, "A Yemenite flower girl would speak Hebrew with an authentic accent closer to the way King Solomon and the prophets pronounced the words of the Bible than most university professors of Hebrew who migrated to Israel from Eastern or central Europe." The solution ultimately found was for Eliza to imitate the way Israeli children (i.e., of Ashkenazi origin) naturally speak Hebrew and copy their mistakes! Instead of a spoken "Oriental" Hebrew, Eliza was given an imaginary "ch" mispronunciation of the letter "resh" (the equivalent of "r"), which Prof. Higgins manages to correct after hours of training.

In spite of this prejudicial view, Arabic has made a significant contribution to Hebrew in both the classical golden age of medieval Spain and in modern Israel: "Arabic, indeed was a favorite source for new Hebrew words. As well as being an aid in explaining obscure Biblical terms for which reason, Ben-Yehuda and his colleagues made a close study of the language."[3]

The Druze and Circassian Minorities

Spoken Arabic in Israel has also made borrowings from modern Hebrew in slang, curse words, the Hebrew names of formal Israeli institutions and for patterns of social organization or technical terms that were largely absent from Arab village life and were introduced during the period of Israel's independence. Hebrew has also been more fervently embraced by the Druze community—70,000 Arabic speakers in Israel who were considered a heretical or deviant Muslim sect. The Druze sided with the Jews in the war for independence in 1948 and 1949 and have since voluntarily accepted the obligations of military service in the Israeli defense forces and the border police. The greater degree of social integration with the Jewish majority is also leading to greater use and fluency in Hebrew, so much so that many observers report spontaneous Hebrew conversations between Druze men or among youngsters at play or while watching football games without any Jews present.[4] Obviously, their shared loyalty, sense of common citizenship and language have also led to greater demands for real equality in every walk of life.

Yet, the Druze have their own flag, and their religious particularity remains unchanged. They are a minority within a minority, and their relationship with other Arabic-speaking Druze living in Arab states hostile to Israel is a cause of concern and suspicions among both Israelis and Arabs. There is a large Druze minority in Syria, a state which has been particularly hostile to Israel. The Druze claim of being a nation with a religious basis, somewhat analogous to Israel, presents a potential threat to both countries.

The 3,000 Circassians in Israel are non–Arab Muslims who settled in the Galilee region of Palestine at the end of the nineteenth century after fleeing from their homeland in the Russian-occupied Caucasus region to Turkey and Turkish-controlled areas in the Middle East. They were loyal subjects of the Ottoman Turkish regime and, like the Druze, have been on good terms with the Jews and loyally serve in the Israeli armed forces. All the men are fluent in Hebrew, and scores of Circassians have moved from their Galilean villages and settled in Israeli cities from Eilat to Haifa. They speak their Circassian language at home, but due to their physical isolation from other Circassian settlements in Jordan and Syria, they have readily given up Arabic and adopted Hebrew instead as the most practical means of common discourse.

Hebrew Literature in Arabic Translation

One hopeful sign among the general gloom regarding the prospects for a lasting, comprehensive peace between Israel and the Arab world was the translation in 1978 of an anthology of Hebrew literature into Arabic by the Egyptian author Salim Abd al-Mun'im, published in Cairo in 1978. Many translations of Arabic works had been made into Hebrew, but this was the first time any presentation of life and Hebrew literature in Israel was made available to Arabic speakers without editorial comment.

Unfortunately the translations were secondhand and made via an initial translation from Hebrew to English. Subsequent translations directly from Hebrew have been made and published in Egypt. These include the works of Israeli writers Michael Oz (*My Michael*), David Grossman (*The Yellow Wind*), Amos Kenan (*The Road to Ein Harod*) and Sammi Michael (*Victoria*). Michael was born in Iraq, made the transition from Arabic to Hebrew in the 1950s and has published a modern version of the Romeo and Juliet story involving a love affair between a new Russian Jewish immigrant who speaks a crude and limited Hebrew and a Christian Arab woman from Haifa whose Hebrew is flawless and is a devoted fan of Yehuda Amihai, one of Israel's greatest modern Hebrew poets. This book, *Hatzoztra beWadi* (Trumpet in the Wadi), in spite of, or possibly because of, its message of tolerance was not deemed appropriate for translation by Egyptian authorities into Arabic. It is a very poignant story of prejudice and role reversal and a comment on the nationalist aberrations that make language a political tool rather than a means of communication across barriers of nationality, sex, age and class.

The Hebrew works chosen for translation into Arabic by Egyptian publishers all typically reflect a critical view of Israeli society, particularly with regard to the status of the Arab minority, and were obviously approved for this reason. Nevertheless, the number of such works has been very limited. By contrast, many original Hebrew works have been translated into Arabic in Israel by both Jewish and Arab translators. However, they are not allowed to be imported or sold in the Arab countries. One fascinating aspect of the influence of their Hebrew-language education upon Palestinian Arab authors writing in Arabic and who grew up in Israel has been their use of Biblical motifs and their familiarity with some of the early Zionist-inspired Hebrew poets and authors. This is particularly evident in the work of the Palestinian poet Mahmud Darwish, who left Israel, and the Israeli Arab writer Emile Habibi, a former communist member of the Knesset (Israel's parliament): "In summary, it can be said that even though the echoes of Hebrew literature which reach us from the Arab world are few and usually negative, at least there is a de facto recognition of the existence of modern Hebrew literature ... they bear indisputable witness to the fact that Arab culture cannot ignore its existence and vitality, and that there are people in Egypt and other Arab countries willing to listen, and who, perhaps, in time will even be willing to enter into a literary dialogue."[5]

Hopefully, in the event of a more stable peace agreement, bilingual Hebrew and Arabic speakers among the Arab minority in Israel will form an important bridge in cultivating a new age of cooperation and mutual respect between these two ancient cultures and languages.

PART VII

Spanish versus Portuguese in Uruguay: The Case of Determined Government Planning to Avoid Bilingualism

23

URUGUAY: THE ORIGINS OF THE BUFFER STATE

In Uruguay, the national language was determined by government policy to favor one language—Spanish—over its competitor—Portuguese—and thereby prevent the development of a bilingual nation, a distinct possibility for this region on the left bank of the Rio de la Plata, which lay between the great centers of settlement and colonization in Argentina and those of Brazil. Like the great dispute between English and French speakers in Canada, the centuries-old rivalry between Spain and Portugal was transferred to the New World. The poorly defined and contested border between the Spanish and Portuguese empires had been in dispute since the "division of the world" agreed to between the two powers with the support of the pope by the Treaty of Tordesillas in 1494.

Like Belgium, Uruguay was established as a buffer state to avoid continual confrontations between the two major South American nations of Brazil and Argentina, near the strategic mouth of the La Plata River, where the Rio Parana and the Rio Uruguay join. At the beginning of Uruguayan independence in 1828, the country had a scarce population of only 75,000. Only one major city, the capital, Montevideo, existed. It dominated the country with 25 percent of the total. The rest of the population was widely scattered in a northwestern, Portuguese-speaking region and a Spanish-speaking south.

The government at Montevideo sought to encourage the spread of Spanish into the entire national territory by a planned program of establishing Spanish-language schools, extending the dominance of Montevideo and creating a sense of a shared culture with Argentina, based on common economic interests and a popular culture based on the tango. At times, however, Uruguayans have suspected that neighboring Argentina was acting like a domineering big brother or a huge magnet and that it would be an advantage to maintain good relations with Brazil to restrain big brother. Not until 1877, however, was Spanish made the official language of all public education throughout the entire national territory and a concerted effort undertaken to integrate the northern frontier region by enforcing elementary-school public education in Spanish.

It is Montevideo that had the original advantage of a better natural harbor suitable for large, ocean-going vessels. This geographic advantage over Buenos Aires should have made its side (the eastern) of the great estuary of the Rio de la Plata the major harbor and center of Spain's mid-latitude, South American, Atlantic-coast colony. The settlement of the eastern side of the great bay was delayed by the fierce resistance of the local Charrúa Indians, who killed all the first Spanish settlers. In 1680, the Portuguese, from their possession in southern Brazil, seeking to expand their empire, founded Colonia del Sacramento, near the mouth of the Uruguay River at the head of the Río de la Plata. It was not until forty years later, however, that the Spanish colonial regime based in Buenos Aires sent an expedition across the river to construct a military fort, Fuerte de San José, at the site of present-day Montevideo to exploit the natural bay and resist further Portuguese expansion. A Spanish expedition from Buenos Aires forced the abandonment of a small Portuguese settlement at the site in 1726.

In 1777, Spanish rule in the territory, then known as the viceroyalty of La Plata, around the great La Plata River bay, was established with its capital at Buenos Aires. Montevideo lagged behind and was used primarily as a port in Spain's African slave trade to supply labor for the Cuban sugar fields. This trade resulted in the presence of a small Black population settling permanently in the city and has contributed a distinctive sound to Uruguayan folk music (condombé) alongside the tango. Many Uruguayans feel Argentina has unfairly taken all the credit for both music forms.

Cattle introduced by both the Spaniards and Portuguese soon ran wild and created very large herds that provided a source of wealth in leather, hides, tallow, tinned beef and then fresh or frozen meat with the advent of the railroad and refrigerated ships. This enormous resource was exploited by the gauchos, nomadic herders who followed the herds and owed no allegiance to either authority. They resisted the control of both governments and even fought among themselves. Only gradually did the gauchos find it necessary to restrict the movement of the great cattle herds to afford easier and cheaper slaughter, processing and packing for markets in the cities and abroad.

As result of the Napoleonic wars, Britain became involved in the fighting in South America and captured both Buenos Aires and Montevideo temporarily after Napoleon had imprisoned Spanish king Ferdinand VII and invaded Spain in 1808. Local patriots in Argentina rejected the authority of the puppet viceroy and established a caretaker government to rule over the colony in the name of the authentic King Ferdinand but secretly aspired to independence from Spanish rule entirely. The Buenos Aires authorities could not establish control over the eastern bank and other outlying territories. The puppet Spanish viceroy moved his court to Montevideo and provoked dissension among local settlers. Uruguayan rebels joined in the revolt against Spain and believed that the "eastern bank" would have a large measure of autonomy in a federal type of government together with Argentina. They had always been dissatisfied by what they believed had been the policies of trade discrimination. At first, Argentina refused to acknowledge the right of the east bankers to secede.

The question remained unresolved when, in 1818, imperial Brazilian forces, still under Portuguese rule, invaded Uruguay. In 1821 Brazil, now independent, seized the country and annexed it as its southernmost Cisalpine province. This provoked Argentina to come to Uruguay's rescue and support a revolt against Brazilian rule. In spite of earlier having labeled the local Uruguayan leaders as separatists, gaucho rebels and anarchists, Argentina intervened to protect the territory from Brazilian subjugation.

Many Argentines feared that the Portuguese in Brazil would launch a new attempt to ensure control of the entire Rio de la Plata region. The conflict lasted from December, 1825, to August, 1828. In 1828, Lord John Ponsonby, envoy of the British foreign office, proposed making the Banda Oriental an independent state, as Britain was anxious to create a buffer zone between Argentina and Brazil to ensure its trade interests in the region. British mediation brought about a peace treaty that year, by which both Brazil and Argentina guaranteed Uruguay's independence as the República Oriental del Uruguay (Figure 24).

Its first constitution was adopted in 1830, and both its official name and its flag were designed to closely resemble that of Argentina in the ensign with a radiant sun on a field of blue-and-white stripes, a not-too-subtle hint that the two states had once been united and were close allies. Linguistically, the new state was divided. Montevideo and the coast were Spanish-speaking, while much of the interior was divided between speakers of Portuguese and a local mixture dialect named Portuñol (Portugues + Español). Argentina and Brazil retained the right to intervene in the event of a civil war and to approve the constitution of the new nation. For a time, two rival political factions, the Colorados (the "Reds") and the Blancos (the "Whites") attempted to steer Uruguay in a pro–Brazilian and pro–Argentine direction respectively until finally agreeing to maintain a strictly independent course.

The new nation originally was overwhelmingly rural with a dispersed population. Only with the advent of mass immigration from Europe,

218 VII. Spanish versus Portuguese in Uruguay

Figure 24. Uruguayan banknote.

primarily from Spain, the Canary Islands, Italy and central Europe, did Montevideo assume its totally dominant role. Today, the capital accounts for about 40 percent of the total population and dwarfs its nearest rivals. This made linguistic policy more difficult to institute. The planned schools to hispanicize the Portuguese-speaking north were few and far between and did not really get underway until several decades after Uruguay's independence.

Portuguese continued to be the more important language in much of the north, where smuggling of cattle and tropical and subtropical goods (sugar, coffee, tobacco, rice and citrus fruit) were a major source of income and supplied the new country with vital goods it lacked. The drift of the rural population to Montevideo and the proximity of Colonia del Sacramento to the border made speakers of Portuguese and Portuñol a factor in the population of Montevideo. Many *lusismos* (Portuguese words and popular expressions or their literal equivalents in Spanish but unknown elsewhere) crept into the popular speech of the capital. Later, in the 1850s, additional conflicts threatened to upset Uruguay's independence, and only Brazilian intervention saved Uruguay from conquest by the Argentine dictator Rosas. Brazil was rewarded with several treaties in which Uruguay confirmed "a perpetual alliance between the two countries" as well as Brazil's right to intervene in Uruguay's internal affairs; extradition of runaway slaves and criminals; joint navigation on the Río Uruguay and its tributaries and a tax exemption on Brazilian cattle and salted meat exports. These policies also increased the prestige of the Portuguese language, but the die had already been cast and there was no attempt to change the national language.

Portuñol

Nevertheless, the recently completed *Atlas Lingüístico del Uruguay*[1] confirms the existence of a twenty-five kilometer band across northern Uruguay, in which much of the population is either bilingual in Portuguese and Spanish or bilingual in Portuñol and Spanish. At first glance this seems strange given the more than 120 years of continued policy of "Spanish only" in the schools. The proximity of the border region to Brazilian television stations, coupled with the very small size of Uruguay, has contributed to a tendency to maintain the dialect and literacy, or even fluency in spoken Brazilian Portuguese. The continued existence of Portuñol may also be seen as an attempt by Uruguayans to reinforce a sense of national identity, particularly among young people, as a sense of rebellion against the views of the government's policy to learn to speak "correctly" and in order to feel separate and apart from their powerful Argentine neighbor.

The Military Dictatorship

Various Uruguayan ministers of education have declared Portuñol as a "vulgar" or "lower-class dialect" and that the policy of the ministry of education must be to ensure that both standard Spanish and Portuguese are taught and spoken well, whereas Uruguayan linguist Graciela Barrios, who defends the use of the Portuñol dialect and the language spoken by young people in Montevideo, has commented that "Behind the policies of managing the language there are discriminatory attitudes. When the government accuses young people of deforming the language, it is a sly way of saying—We don't like young people." For young people "the language of the frontier region is our cultural patrimony and must not disappear."[2] As late as the military dictatorship of the 1970s, Uruguayan linguistic and educational policy had reached such a negative attitudes toward Portuñol that huge signs were placed in the border area calling upon parents to "Speak Spanish—if you love your children. Remember—they imitate you!"

The Spanish spoken in both Argentina and Uruguay is quite similar, recognizable to all other Spanish speakers due to its distinctive Italian-sounding intonation, the use of "vos" instead of "tu" for the familiar form for the second-person pronoun "you," use of the Guaraní-derived word "che" ("man," frequently used as a familiar form of address like "hey, man!" in colloquial American slang) in familiar conversation and the pronunciation of the consonant "ll" as "sh." Diverse critics both in the government and among independent Uruguayan intellectuals have also attacked what they call "a slavish imitation" of "our powerful neighbor" (Argentine slang). This is the other side of the Uruguayan inferiority complex.

In the Shade of Buenos Aires

Resentment against Argentine assumptions that it speaks for all of the Rioplatense region, as if Uruguay were still a sort of half-forgotten "eastern bank" province, is strong. Many Uruguayans are angered that Carlos Gardel, without a doubt the greatest figure in the entertainment world of the popular tango song, was elevated into an Argentine national hero and that his probable birth in Uruguay was deliberately hidden by means of a falsified birth certificate. Gardel was the most famous but not the only artist, poet, writer or musician who crossed over to the "west bank" in Buenos Aires to find fame and fortune and was declared a true Porteño (native of Buenos Aires) but whose Uruguayan birth and roots were subsequently hidden.[3]

Today recognized as a monolingual, Spanish-speaking country, Uruguay reveals its dual heritage and the development of its national identity almost by accident as a result of its history as a lost province of both of its neighbors and then as a neutral buffer state. This is considerably more complex than the Belgian case. Belgian cuisine, art, national languages, even history belong to two coexisting but distinct older nations. In Uruguay, a new distinctive nation has been created which has a mixed heritage. It cannot be fully erased in spite of government policy to eliminate the Portuguese/Brazilian element. Although historically it was largely a matter of chance that the "eastern bank" became Uruguay, a proud nation has emerged and struggled to create an identity that is particularly its own between two neighboring giants.

Uruguayan historians today have even cast the original Charrúa Indian population that killed the first Spanish settlers as the heroic founders of the Uruguayan nation. The Charrúas thereby delayed the settlement of the "east bank" for another hundred and fifty years, allowing Buenos Aires to become the major port and settlement center of the Rioplatense region and leaving Montevideo to later developments. Much of this individuality was further defined in the twentieth century through political reforms. Uruguay established a functioning democratic system, full literacy, and universal free education; promoted social welfare benefits, protected essential liberties and provided a haven for refugees fleeing dictatorships in the rest of Latin America. Uruguay takes pride in calling itself the "Switzerland of South America." Winning the world cup in soccer several times, victories that included triumphs over their traditional rivals of Argentina and Brazil, also helped to cement the intense loyalty of its citizens to the smallest South American nation and developed the distinctive individuality of what originally had been just the Banda Oriental.

PART VIII

The Struggle with the Chains of the Past (Greek, Arabic and Turkish)

At first glance it may seem that both the division between classical and modern Greek and Arabic is similar to the situation that prevailed between biblical and modern Hebrew. This is not the case at all. When modern Hebrew was developed, starting 120 years ago, by Ben-Yehuda and a handful of visionary pioneers and mystics, there was no vernacular form of the language. The classical Hebrew of the Bible, Talmud or Golden Age of Medieval Spain had been preserved in a frozen, literary, written format of poetry and verse. Each period of literary Hebrew had distinguishing features. The modern Hebrew developed by Ben-Yehuda was nobody's spoken language learned at home from the immediate family or in a secular school. By contrast, Greek and Arabic have been continuously spoken languages that were widely diffused over an enormous area, each at least a hundred times larger than the modern state of Israel.

Each local variant of Arabic was spread by conquest, in comparison to Greek, the language of an international merchant class spread largely by migration and trade. Arabic, the language of the conquerors, was superimposed upon previously spoken languages—a process of slow language change that took centuries.

In the Arab world, almost all Arabic speakers were illiterate. Passages of the classical language from the Koran were learned by heart by most believers. These factors led to the dichotomy between language forms that continues to divide the Arabic-speaking world today and until quite recently constituted a major problem in the cultural and political identity of modern Greece. In Greece, among Greek speakers abroad as well as among Arabic speakers, there has been a diglossia, a dual use of two languages, each appropriate for a specific occasion and purpose.

24

THE GREEK DILEMMA: ANCIENT (ATTIC) VERSUS DEMOTIKE VERSUS KATHAREVOUSA

Greek, although the spoken language of only about 11 million people in Greece and Cyprus and perhaps an additional 1.5 million emigrants in a worldwide diaspora, has played an extraordinary part in the culture, philosophy, sciences and mathematics, religion, mythology, languages and literature of the western world. The earliest surviving texts in ancient Greek from the fifteenth century B.C. are inscribed on mud tablets. They represent the most ancient record of any European language. The modern Greek state has had problems reconciling the enormous ancient heritage with the present, small Balkan state: "The Greeks are particularly weighed down by the impediments of a cultural heritage that has for centuries been regarded as the pinnacle of human achievement. *Progonoplexia* (ancestor obsession) and *arkhaiolatreia* (excessive reverence for antiquity) are key elements in the modern Greek identity. Greek identity and the relationship of the present and the past is a common theme in literature. After all, Greece is the only country, Greek the only language and Greeks the only people that must be qualified by the adjective 'modern' in order to avoid confusion with the past."[1]

Attic Greek

It is precisely the prestigious role of their language that led to a modern dilemma regarding the most "authentic" version in an independent state. Ancient Greece had a cultural and political background very different from that of the modern nation-state. For much of the classical period (tenth to fifth centuries B.C.), Greece was fragmented into small city-states with their satellite colonies. Although there was a recognized unity of blood (common origin), a pagan pantheon of gods, legends, material culture, and to a large degree, language, each state had its own political system and cultural values. The various, rival city-states both traded and fought with each other through shifting military alliances.

The Greek-speaking peoples had evolved a number of regional dialects through successive southern movements through the Balkan peninsula, islands of the Ionian Sea and Asia Minor. The great classics of Homer (The *Iliad* and the *Odyssey*) were completed some time in the eighth century B.C. Towards the end of the classical period in the fourth century B.C., the dialect of Athens acquired wider acceptance in the Greek-speaking world due to its political leadership and cultural creativity.

The Koine

The city-state world of the Greeks was swept away in the great dynasty and empire established by Philip II of Macedon (382–336 B.C.) and his more famous son, Alexander the Great (356–323 B.C.), who came close to conquering the known ancient world. His empire stretched from Egypt across the Near and Middle East to India and Afghanistan. Greek became the most important language for commerce and administration even after the fragmentation of the great empire. The established elites of Athens, Sparta and the other city-states considered the new Macedonian rulers as half-barbarian and opportunists who sought to lend greater legitimacy to their new empire by employing the Attic dialect as the standard form of speech and written documents.

This variant became the common spoken Greek of the huge Diaspora throughout the eastern Mediterranean and Black Sea regions from Egypt to the Crimea. After Alexander the Great, the *koine*, or "common language," developed into an international language that remained current in the central and east Mediterranean regions and in parts of Asia Minor and Africa for many centuries.

This *koine* form of Greek spoken by a vastly larger population included many new subjects whose native language was not Greek. The result was an erosion, simplification of the grammar and corruption of the pronunciation. It became the language in which the Christian Gospels were written and then of the Greek Orthodox liturgy and church. Greek retained its prestige not only in the eastern half of the Mediterranean but also as the language of education, science, mathematics and philosophy studied by the Romans. The empire itself was divided in A.D. 395. The eastern half, known as Byzantium, established its capital at Constantinople (modern-day Istanbul), the cosmopolitan city founded by the Emperor Constantine the Great in A.D. 330. The Byzantines included many peoples of diverse origins for whom the *koine* became the common medium of discourse. Although the Byzantine Empire lasted until its destruction by the Turks with their capture of Constantinople in 1453, the Greek peninsula, islands and coastal areas of Asia Minor (Anatolia) were devastated by the Catholic crusaders and came under first Venetian and later Turkish rule. The Fourth Crusades ended in the Catholic Crusaders seizing control of the Byzantine Empire and sacking Constantinople in 1204, an event that made the Greeks and the orthodox church forever resentful and suspicious of the West. At the time of the Renaissance, the homeland of the Greek people lay subjugated, and its cultural creativity, literacy and progress disrupted. Not until 1821 was the beginning of a modern Greek state reestablished. Generations of Greek intellectuals had dreamed for centuries of a reemergent, glorious Greece, its language and orthodox church.

The Dark Ages

The expression of Greek culture, especially literature, had survived the dark ages of the Crusades, and Venetian and Turkish rule in isolated centers for brief periods (e.g., Crete during the sixteenth and early seventeenth centuries and later in the Ionian Islands after the fall of Crete in 1669), but much of the Greek mainland had to rely on a largely oral culture expressed in diverse dialects. A modern sense of nationalism arrived in Greece largely from visiting Europeans, who idealized the ancient past of the great philosophers, and the works of Homer and by the example set by successful Serbs, who had rebelled against Ottoman rule. Greek merchants from the port cities and the Aegean Islands along with the Phanariots, the class of professional administrators and translators who had served the Turkish court and claimed descent from the noble families of the Byzantine court, realized that Ottoman weakness would eventually be exploited by Russia, Italy, England and France and saw the opportunity for themselves in a future Greek state. Their idealized vision or great idea (*megali idea*) meant a greater Greece embracing the ancient Byzantine and Alexandrian empires.

The vision of a reunified and expansionist Greece raised the issue of "Who should we be?" Most of the leaders in the fight for independence and a new glorious Greek state imagined that the constitution, laws, educational system, serious literature and philosophic enquiry should be written in Attic Greek, the language of classical Greece, the language of Plato and Aristotle. This view was attractive abroad due to prestige of the ancient Greek civilization widespread then in Western Europe, immortalized by such famous personalities as the philo-hellenic English poet, Byron. The difficulties of reinstituting the cumbersome, classic Attic Greek were acknowledged, however, and the orthodox church was alarmed at what appeared to be a glorification and idolization of the pre–Christian pagan past. The Church had even objected to the practice of Greek nationalists naming their sons and daughters after the heroes of the *Iliad* and the *Odyssey* instead of the early Christian martyrs and saints.

Katharevousa and Demotike

One of the most influential of the Greek intellectuals and nationalists living abroad—the Paris-based Adamandios Korais (1748–1833)—was the first to pose a question that would divide his countrymen in an acrimonious debate for the next century and a half. Korais's solution was to adopt a compromise middle way, reforming the spoken language of his time on ancient principles and using it as a standard for formal, written Greek. The hybrid variety, known as *katharevousa*, literally "purifying language," thus came into existence and eliminated most words of foreign origin. Many Greek intellectuals were offended that during the long period of Turkish occupation, so many Turkish words had entered the speech of the common people that it had been reduced to a dialect.

Many Turcophone Greeks, known as Karamanli Christians, even wrote Turkish with Greek letters, further "defiling" their ancestral heritage." Some Greeks objected that the devised, "purified" language had not gone far enough, while others objected that *katharevousa* was too remote from the speech of the common people. The latter group of popularists proposed adapting and systematizing the common spoken language of the people, known as *demotike* ("democratic"). This would make spelling and grammar much easier for the common people. This speech form had been written down as early as the fourteenth century and even used in both Crete and Cyprus for more serious literary works but still lacked the backing of any official recognition. The issue of which Greek is the "purest" seemed unquestionable to supporters of *katharevousa*, but for proponents of the modern, national state idea requiring an enlightened population, the question was not one of purity to connect with a mythical past (the glory of ancient Greece) but rather of ease and the participation of all the people.

The Greek Language Rivalry

Ioannis Psicharis, a Greek scholar, was the first prominent figure to argue on behalf of the written, democratic Greek, closer to the medium of discourse used by most Greeks, and in 1881 succeeded in getting the first book published in this form in Greece. Disagreement between proponents of these two versions resulted in a continuous debate just as a similar controversy raged in Norway about the same time between supporters of Nynorsk and Dano-Norwegian. The weight of the Greek monarchy, government and most nationalists intent on achieving an even greater Greece objected to *demotike*. The nationalists were offended by the inclusion of words based on Turkish, Italian, French or Latin that had been integrated into the modern vocabulary.

Schools, scholars and newspapers were encouraged to use *katharevousa*. Some even imagined that the successful revival of Hebrew by the Zionist movement in Palestine was a model for *katharevousa* to follow, not grasping the essential difference between the two. Ben-Yehuda had evolved the basis for a modern spoken language based on the skeleton of the unchanged literary language, whereas Korais demanded acknowledgment of a "purified literary language." It was actually Psicharis's idea of a *demotike*, a democratic Greek, that sought a harmonization between the vernacular and literary languages that was nearer the concept of modern Hebrew.

The language question even led to rioting in the streets. In 1911, University of Athens students, encouraged by nationalist and government agitators, demonstrated in public against the proposal to translate the Bible into *demotike*. Treatises were written to convince the public that only *katharevousa* could preserve the cherished link to the glorious past of ancient Greece and the grandeur, purity, flexibility, subtlety and power of expression that had made the ancient language the most important in the world in its day. In 1913, Greece emerged as the "big winner" of the Balkan wars, with dreams of further expansion across the Aegean Sea. At the coronation of King Constantine I, nationalists called on the king to assume the title of Constantine XI Palaiologos, the last emperor of Byzantium.[2]

Katharevousa was imposed on the newly won territories of Thrace and Macedonia (1912–1913) even though it was remote from the vernacular spoken there. Greek nationalists were convinced that this was necessary to absorb a diverse population. In 1919 and 1921, a million ethnic Greeks fled from the coastal areas of the Aegean coast of Turkey and farther east in the Crimea, Armenia and the Caucasus following the Russian civil war and communist victory, and many Greeks saw an even greater role for *katharevousa* in integrating this new population.

Many of these refugees spoke little or no Greek or had lived for generations separated from the motherland. Their spoken language had become "polluted" with a mixture of Turkish, Albanian, Romanian, Macedonian-Bulgarian, Russian, and Armenian words. What greater mission could the nationalist cause have then to eliminate these "corrupting influences" and reinforce the sense of history and destiny implicit in the purer *katharevousa* form? This is alluded to in the great historical novel *Zorba the Greek* by Nikos Kazantzakis:

> Half a million Greeks are in danger in the south of Russia and the Caucasus. Many of them speak only Turkish or Russian but their hearts speak Greek fanatically.... They gather in the ports, scan the horizon anxiously for Greek ships to take them back to their Mother—Greece.... If we are going to save them and get them back to the part of our own free land where they will be the most use—that is, on the frontiers of Macedonia and further afield on the frontiers of Thrace, that is the only way we shall save hundreds of thousands of Greeks and save ourselves with them.... These inhabitants of the Pontus and the Caucasus, peasants of Kars, big and small merchants of Tiflis, Batum, Novo Rossisk, Rostov, Odessa and the Crimea are ours, they are our blood; for them as for us, the capital of Greece is Constantinople [pp. 160–161, Ballantine Books, 1965].

This Greek diglossia, or two-tier usage of a high literary and a popular spoken form, continued after World War II, although more and more critics attacked this division of the people into hostile camps. The final blow against *katharevousa* as the protégé of the establishment was the downfall of the conservative military junta in 1976. It is still used in legal texts and is crucial to an understanding of old books, church documents and older official records, but its association with the despised dictatorship has resulted in its fall from favor. Even classical Greek is no longer widely taught in Greek schools or as a required subject in what is still termed a "classical education" in the oldest West European universities. "Good" modern Greek is based largely on *demotike* but includes occasional *katharevousa* phrases in recognition of the importance of tradition.[3]

Cyprus and Macedonia

There are still a variety of dialects in Greece and Cyprus, but the resolution of the language debate, the transition to *demotike* for all newspapers, the increased influence of a standardized use of *demotike* in Greek films and television have all led to a greater sense of national solidarity. Ironically, *katharevousa* appears to be dying out more slowly in Cyprus than in Greece. The reason may be that Greek Cypriots, in their conflict with the Turkish minority on the island, identified with the most patriotic or nationalist *katharevousa* form to accentuate their sense of being the majority and that Cyprus had always been an integral part of Greek culture and history. The debate between the two forms had never been so intense on Cyprus, long a British possession, as on mainland Greece.

A further indication of the Greek sensibility to its ancient heritage has been the recent dispute over the former Yugoslav republic of Macedonia, a name the Greek government insists cannot be used by a foreign power. Further objections have been raised even to the right of the citizens of Macedonia to call their language Macedonian. For the Greeks, the name is part of the ancient heritage of the great hellenistic empire of Alexander the Great. Greek hostility to the Skopje (Macedonia's capital) government since the end of Yugoslavia is due to a fear of a threat to Greek territory and the implication that the ancestors of the Greeks were in part Slavic rather than "pure" Hellenes. In the end, the great majority of Greeks decided that *demotike* properly answered the practical question "Who are we?" rather than the abstract questions "Who were we?" and "Who should we be?"

25

ARABIC: THE KORAN VERSUS MODERN STANDARD VERSUS THE LOCAL VERNACULARS

Unlike the resolution of the conflicts in Israel, Greece, Malta, Norway and Ireland, the debate in the Arab world continues between those who cling to the notion that the Arabs are one nation, speaking a single national language and the reality of many local vernaculars and states. This hypothetical "one nation" must rely on the official language of an educated elite that is far removed from the spoken and mutually incomprehensible dialects spoken by large majorities in individual Arab countries spanning an immense area of the globe from Morocco to Iraq. The same type of conflict that existed in Greece for almost two centuries continues to plague not one country but the entire Arab world. A diglossia exists within diverse Arab societies.

On the higher level is the written standard based on the model of the Koran and supplemented with a modern vocabulary. It is the language of higher education, books, and the press and has a spoken form as well used primarily at international conferences and in serious speeches and formal talks. All Arabs consider it to be the fundamental pillar of an Arab nationalism that defines them as one nation. At the lower level, there are many local forms of spoken Arabic particular to specific counties or broad regions—Syrian-Palestinian, Egyptian, Moroccan, Iraqi, Arabian (i.e., in Saudi Arabia), Yemeni, and so on. These forms are only rarely encountered in written format, yet they are the real basis for each particular medium of discourse within the individual Arab countries. It is as if France, Italy, Spain, Portugal and Romania were to use Latin for higher education at the university level and all serious books and newspapers but speak their national languages in everyday life.

This dichotomy or schizophrenia is reflected in the political sphere. Numerous unions between diverse Arab countries heralding the unification of the Arab world have all failed. Nevertheless, as Raphael

Patai observed more than twenty years ago, "There can be no doubt that the Arabic language is the most potent factor in both the creation and the maintenance of this overriding myth of an Arab Nation, Arab unity, Arab brotherhood."[1]

The overwhelming majority of Arabs in more than two dozen independent states, sheikdoms and entities subscribes to the notion that whoever speaks Arabic is an Arab," implying that regardless of the present political fragmentation, the destiny of all Arabs is to be united in a single Arab nation-state. As part of this notion, there is a manipulated version of history concerning the entire region known as the Near East and Middle East, stretching from the northwest coast of Africa to the Tigris-Euphrates river valleys and including the historical civilizations of ancient Mesopotamia, Assyria-Akkadia, Babylon, the Fertile Crescent, Nile Valley and the North African states (the Maghreb). This immense and diverse area is viewed historically as the cradle of the Arab nation. In order to understand this distortion of history it is necessary first to acknowledge that a large part of the region was either only partially or briefly Arab or never Arab, either ethnically, linguistically or historically.

The great Persian and Ottoman Turkish empires that held political sway over most of the region from the time of the Crusades until World War I ruled over the Arabs and, even after accepting Islam, regarded the Arabs and their original homeland, the Arabian peninsula, as a backward, remote and primitive desert, far removed from the centers of urban civilization and creative achievements in the arts and sciences. The total number of Iranians (Persians) and Kurds who speak an Indo-European language, the Turks, Israelis and Berber-speaking peoples in North Africa almost equals the combined Arabic-speaking populations of all the Arab League states.

The Hamo-Semitic Family

The two indigenous civilizations of ancient Egypt and Mesopotamia-Babylonia each had their own distinctive languages (Coptic and Akkadian), writing systems and religions. Each had a continuous history thousands of years before their conquest by Arab tribesmen, and each retains significant non–Muslim (Coptic Christian, Assyrian) minorities, a deviant form of Islam (Shi'ite sect in southern Iraq) and non–Arabs (Kurds). In the Fertile Crescent (present-day Lebanon, Israel and Syria), the various forms of the western Semitic languages—Phoenician, Hebrew-Aramaic, Syriac—persisted from ancient times until well into the Middle Ages, and each of the present-day countries retains significant numbers of non–Muslims (Jews and Christians), deviant religious sects (Druze and Alawaites) and spoken (Hebrew) or liturgical (Aramaic) languages.

The Arabs, originally confined to the Arabian peninsula and largely excluded from the scene of ancient world history, emerged on the world scene in the seventh century A.D., following the death of Mohammed. Their expansion as a conquering military elite throughout the region occurred in much the same way as the Mongol nomads conquered China and established a new ruling dynasty. Even as late as the Christian Crusades to recover the Holy Land in the eleventh through thirteenth centuries, the Muslim forces were led by Kurds and Turks and not Arabs.

In the far west of the Muslim world, Berber tribesmen in Libya, Algeria, Tunisia and Morocco, speaking a mixture of their own indigenous languages or a newly imposed Arabic, swept into Spain, where they established Muslim rule for close to seven centuries. The entire region that we know today as the Near and Middle East was partially arabized as a consequence of the military success of a small, Arab ethnic minority. The imposed language was changed by the vast majority of subjects whom the Arabs conquered. They adopted the new language but subjected it to the stresses, strains and distortions imposed by their former native languages, Berber, Coptic, Greek, Aramaic and Syriac.

The political consequences of this arabization were brought to widespread fruition by British military aid to Arab Bedouin tribesmen in Arabia only in World War I. By raising an Arab revolt against the Ottoman Turkish Empire, the European allies sought to dominate the Near and Middle East through Arab proxies placed in power or on the thrones of Iraq, Jordan, Syria and Egypt.

Subsequent attempts by local elites to rid themselves of European domination indicated to them that it was to their advantage to emphasize their common Arab identity to magnify their negotiating leverage with the European powers and imposed a more intense cultural and political domination over the large Berber-speaking populations in North Africa. Arabic was most successful in supplanting and partially eradicating the closely allied languages belonging to the Hamito-Semitic family—Coptic in Egypt, Aramaic in the Levant, Fertile Crescent and Mesopotamia, and Syriac in Lebanon. In areas partially or never conquered by the Arabs and converted to Islam but speaking quite distinct languages belonging to other major linguistic families such as Turkish, Farsi (Persian), Pashtu, Uzbek, and Armenian, Arabic was studied only as liturgical language but did not supplant the indigenous languages. At various times, even in the heartland of the Arabic-speaking world, the ruling elites have wavered in their identification with the notion of an Arab identity. For many Egyptians, the term "Arab" was often used to indicate a Bedouin, or nomad, speaker of Arabic, to whom a different ethnic identity was implied. A significant number of Egyptian rulers were of Kurdish and Albanian origin who seized the throne and ruled the country. In the 1920s and 1930s many Egyptian nationalists were closely identified with the pre–Islamic heritage of Egypt that lay in its ancient pharaohnic civilization, and greater Syrian nationalists identified with the Phoenicians.

Even today in its commercial advertising on television, the Egyptian ministry of tourism bombards prospective European visitors with symbols of its non–Arab and pre–Islamic past—the pyramids, the Sphinx, tombs of the pharaohs, and so on. The very name of the country has been altered twice since 1958, from Egypt to the United Arab republic (following the merger with Syria in 1958), to the Arab Republic of Egypt under President Sadat). The last change prompted an open critical letter from Rif'at al-Asad, the brother of the late Syrian president, condemning the name change as symptomatic of Egypt's "abandonment of its Arab identity" and its "new course of particularism and Egyptianization."[2]

The Brief Fling with Wataniyah Nationalism

Great archaeological discoveries in Egypt, Mesopotamia and the Fertile Crescent briefly inspired a westernized minority among intellectuals in Egypt, Syria and Iraq, who toyed with the idea of a nationalism divorced from the Arab-Islamic connection. This was a movement that never enlisted the support of broad masses who were too tied to the concept of their primary identity as Muslims and their acceptance of the language of the Koran as fundamental to their religious heritage. A national identity based on a common territory and history as in the West never got off the ground. It made some initial progress in Egypt, the country with 3,000 years of pre–Islamic history and a recognized place in the history of the ancient world as the most formidable power in the Near and Middle East. Rafa al-Tahtawi, 1801-1873, was the first to espouse an Egyptian nationalism based on the heritage of the pharaohs.

A number of Egyptian intellectuals took up this idea in the twentieth century and argued that Egypt's particular identity and links with Europe were at least as important as the Arabic language and Islam. They included Salama Mousa, Taha Hasein, Muhammad Hussein Haykal, Abbas Mahmoud al-Aqqad, and Muhammad Sharaf, names that are forgotten today in Egypt. The missing ingredient in this Pharaohnism *(fir'awniyya)* was the lack of the language connection. Coptic, the language of ancient Egypt, had been preserved, ironically as the liturgical language of the Christian minority in Egypt, and as such was an anathema to Moslem opinion as the "language of the Christians."[3] The word "Coptic" itself is derived from the Greek word for Egyptian. It remained the language of the Egyptian masses until the Arab conquest of Egypt

Figure 25. This stamp honors the interpreter of the Rosetta Stone, Jean François Champollion.

in 642, although the ruling elite spoke Greek. It did not cease as a spoken language until a thousand years after the Arab conquest. Twenty-five of the alphabet's thirty-two letters stem from Greek (Figure 25). Thanks to the trilingual Rosetta stone (ancient hieroglyphics, Greek and Coptic), the key was found to the decipherment of the ancient Egyptian hieroglyphics and a much better understanding of ancient Egypt.

In Syria, Butrous al-Bustani spoke of the Syrian *watan* (heimat or homeland), the ancient home of the Phoenicians and Canaanites. This Greater Syria[4] extended across the entire western half of the Fertile Crescent and never recognized the subsequent division of the area after the collapse of the Ottoman Empire into Lebanon, Syria, Palestine and Jordan and across the sea to Cyprus. This homeland had also lost its original Phoenician-Aramaic-Syriac (and ancient Hebrew) languages.

Aramaic was the international language of the Middle East for a thousand years (fourth century B.C. to sixth century A.D.). Aramaic was originally written in the same alphabet as Hebrew (small parts of the Old Testament in the Books of Daniel and Ezra are written in Aramaic), and the later form of Aramaic known as Syriac, used for the translation of the Bible, has been preserved in the liturgy of the Maronite Catholic church, the Syrian Catholic, Syrian Jacobite churches and the Nestorian (or Assyrian) church. It is spoken in several dialects in a few remote Syrian and Iraqi villages, and three scripts are in use today.

A number of prominent Syrians, Antoine Sa'ada, a Greek Orthodox follower of al-Bustani, and Nnshu al-Uman both subscribed to the notions made popular in the two-volume history "La Syrie" of the noted Belgian Jesuit scholar and orientalist Henri Lammens[5] that neither race, blood, religion or even language but rather territory is the basis for the formation of a modern nation. Such a view was very attractive to Christian Arab intellectuals, who felt marginalized due to the close association of Arab nationalism with Islam. These ideas were adopted by the Syrian Social Nationalist Party[6] (SSNP), a serious political force in Syria until the mid-1950s. Several Lebanese Christian intellectuals such as

Charles Corm, Said Aql and others edited the journal *Le Revue Penicien* and argued for a Lebanese identity based not on religion but on the heritage of ancient Phoenicia. They wished to preserve their Christian identity and ties to western culture and the French language.

All these forms of patriotism based on a territorial identification of the nation as the mother of all her children are now of historical interest only. They could never compete with the much larger sense of Muslim identity. The Arab nationalist leaders who helped the Allies defeat the Turks in World War I did not recognize any divisions into such small entities as Lebanon, modern Syria, Palestine or Jordan. The French scholar of Middle Eastern life, Jacques Weuleresse, concluded in 1946 that

> For the peasant, the state is arbitrary, something that engages neither his life nor his heart; it is an inevitable curse that afflicts him. His absolute lack of patriotism is so striking because the reflexes of our French peasants are essentially patriotic. One searches vainly among Oriental [i.e., Syrian] peasants for the sacredness of the border of the holy defense of the ancestral land. His concept of the world does not extend beyond his tribe.... He knows no other community but that of religion. Interrogate a peasant in the Jazira, the Anti-Lebanon or in Ajlun, ask who he is and he will reply that he is of this or that tribe, of this or that village, a Muslim, Christian Orthodox or Druze; never will he tell you spontaneously that he is an Iraqi, Syrian, Lebanese or Jordanian.[7]

Ironically, these ideas did not made the slightest impact on the Palestinian Arabs, who claim an unbroken history in their homeland. Their rejection of the smaller Wataniyah nationalism was a strategy designed to win for them the total support of the Arab world. In fact, the idea that modern nationalism should be based on the roots of the ancient nation prior to the great religions of Islam, Christianity and Judaism, had its greatest success in Palestine, where the rebirth of the Hebrew language stimulated a growing interest in the ancient Hebrew-speaking world. The deviant Canaanite movement of Hebrew nationalists, who rejected the Zionist leadership and identification with world Jewry, carried on an underground struggle against the British. It found partial expression in the Irgun Tzvai Leumi (IZL, national military organization) and the Lohamei leHerut Yisrael (Lehi) also known as the "Stern Gang," after its martyred leader.[8] Extremists in the latter group ultimately rejected the Jewish religious basis for a reborn Israel but managed to win only a single seat in the first Israeli Knesset (parliamentary) elections in 1949. It too has since almost faded entirely from the political scene in Israel.[9]

The triumph of a pan–Arab identity promised greater leverage in the struggle against European colonialism and in attempts to gain popularity in Palestine and later to win political influence in OPEC and in support of the PLO against Israel. Two Arabic words are employed to translate "nation." The first, *Qawmiyya*, refers to the much larger notion of a mythical Arab unity, and the second, *Wataniyya*, to the much narrower idea of love of the homeland, or birthplace—what the Germans call the heimat.

The many failures of attempted mergers by Arab countries and the instability of others (Kuwait, Lebanon, Palestine, Algeria, Iraq) all clearly indicate that when push comes to shove, "Arab unity" and the "Arab world" are really empty rhetoric. Nevertheless, in terms of language, the political leadership of the Arab world has been grabbed by those who have claimed the right to lead or unite the entire nation. This was the charisma that first propelled Gamel Abdul Nasser, Egypt's mercurial leader, to become the acknowledged head of the Arab world, a mantle that has been subsequently claimed by Libya's Muammar Khaddafi and by Iraq's Saddam Hussein. When Egypt, the long-acknowledged leader of the Arab world signed a peace treaty with Israel, it was ejected as a member by a unanimous vote of the Arab League.

For the majority of ordinary citizens of the Arab countries with a grade school education or less, illiterate or semiliterate, the educational consequences of this policy has been an enormous gap between them and the dominant political and intellectual elites. Even the highly educated political elite find it a strain to use literary Arabic for any length of time, especially in stressful situations. Usually local dialectal features and words are interjected. Some speakers at public events wander back and forth between the literary and the colloquial forms. President Nasser was renowned for this.

He might begin in the classical form adapted to the modern world (i.e., the language of the Koran with the addition of a modern vocabulary known as "modern standard") and then abruptly switch to the colloquial Egyptian dialect. If Italian, French, Spanish and Portuguese national leaders or young people today facing career, educational and livelihood prospects had to maintain a double-language base, conditional in part upon their ability to command classical Latin, the results would be dire.

In Arab society, the value attributed to the language of the Koran is immense. The ability to use the modern standard form of the language based on the Koran and excel at rhetoric and evoke deeply intense emotions and its frequent use of exaggeration, overassertion and repetitiveness are highly valued literary forms, but they have retarded popular education and a more precise use of the spoken vernacular languages.[10] The consequences for adult illiteracy are obvious. It ranges from a low of about 10–20 percent in Lebanon and Kuwait to 35 percent in Iraq,

55 percent in Egypt to highs exceeding 75 percent (in some cases 90 percent for women) in such countries as Libya.[11] These are official statistics reported by the governments and no doubt underestimate illiteracy just as they overestimate population.

Even more ironic or strange from a Western point of view is the fact that many adults capable of reading the Koran (in the language of the seventh century A.D.) as a result of their religious education are unable to read any other material of practical or technical use or even a newspaper. It is no wonder that the distinguished historian Albert H. Hourani termed the Arabic language "the flawed mirror in which the Arabs see the world." This is the result of a situation in which creativity is more likely to be expressed in French or Berber in large parts of the Maghreb. They are the languages in which many people in the region think, write (French), speak (Berber), and dream.[12]

Arguments that the common vernacular and local dialect should be employed as the official national language have met with general hostility and the correct but circular argument that there is no value to learning to read a language in which practically nothing has been written.

More Arabs in the Maghreb countries are literate in French than in modern standard Arabic, and this has created great difficulties in following a coherent policy of education. In Morocco, for example, of four million speakers of French, almost a million are able to read the language whereas no more than one in thirteen adults can read classical (Koranic) or the modern standard version, in which textbooks are written; the situation in Algeria is similar.[13] Perhaps worst of all is the large Berber-speaking minority, whose second language may be French or Arabic but who receive practically no education in their own language. Recently, Berbers in Algeria have gathered the courage to openly protest this discrimination. Similar attempts were brutally suppressed in 1980. They too are met with the same argument—why teach in a language in which next to nothing has been written?

Early attempts by Morocco, Algeria and Tunisia after independence to scrap French as a language of higher education and administration in some ministries were quickly withdrawn. Obviously the argument works both ways. In spite of that fervent nationalism, French was necessary to maintain existing data bases, technical expertise, textbooks, teachers and communications with nearby Europe. This is the final irony. The nation cannot function with the national language alone, and insistence on identifying this speech form with the heritage of the 1,200-year-old Koran rather than the way most of the nation's own citizens speak has created a political impasse and social dilemma: how to bridge the gap between the diglossia of the political elite and the great majority of the people?

The state with the largest population and political clout in the Arab

League has always been Egypt and yet the appeal of Egypt's own historic civilization extending far back beyond ancient Greece and Rome has exercised a strong appeal for intellectuals who have become disenchanted and finally fed up with pan–Arab nationalism that has propelled Egypt into four disastrous wars with Israel (1948, 1956, 1967, 1973) over the issue of "Palestine." A new political group has founded a political party called "Egypt the Motherland" (Misr al-Um) that will represent those Egyptians who see their culture as distinct from the Arab peoples. According to spokesman Moshen Lutfi, "We are Egyptians and not Arabs.... The Arabs are our friends and neighbors and we have a common destiny, but we are not Arabs." The party openly calls for the abrogation of Egypt's Arab identity, forged by Muslim conquest and follows closely on the heels of similar statements by Libya's leader Khaddafi that Libya is an African state, not an Arab one.[14]

26

TURKISH IDENTITY FREES ITSELF FROM THE ISLAMIC/ARABIC YOKE

Until 1914, the Turkish sultan also claimed the title of caliph, or the religious spiritual head of the world's Muslims. Turkey ruled over a vast empire in the Balkans, the Middle East and part of the Caucasus region. It was not a state in the modern sense of the world but a religious community, the Islamic concept of a community of believers based on the teachings of the prophet (Ümmet-i Muhammed) embracing diverse peoples, traditions and languages. The loss of these territories and the dynamic leadership of Kemal Atatürk transformed Turkey into a modern secular state based on the ideal of the Turkish nation and defined by language and territory. The attraction of Persian and Arabic was due to the immense political-cultural achievements of the former and the religious heritage of the Koran of the latter for the Turks who were nomadic latecomers to the long-settled regions of the Near and Middle East.

Under the rule of both Seljuk and later the Ottoman sultans, a courtly etiquette and entrenched bureaucracy, an imperial diplomatic and literary language was fostered that became known as *Osmanlica*, or "Ottoman," remote from the daily speech of the people. Turkish is a Ural-Altaic language and was originally utterly distinct from the Semitic Arabic and Persian, an Indo-European language. Due to the pervasive influence of Arabic, which distinguishes nouns by masculine and feminine gender and insists on the agreement in gender of adjectives as well as Persian grammatical forms, Ottoman Turkish developed an unnecessary, borrowed complexity.

Atatürk realized that the close association of Islam and the Arabic language had retarded Turkey's development as a modern national state and successfully oversaw a radical reform replacing the Arabic alphabet with Latin letters (Figure 26), a step which greatly increased literacy in the country. The totally unsuitable Arabic alphabet was designed for a

VIII. The Chains of the Past

Figure 26. Turkish stamp honoring Atatürk teaching new Latin-based alphabet for the Turkish language.

language rich in consonants and poor in vowel sounds, precisely the opposite of Turkish.

It was not simply a different alphabet but involved the wholesale elimination of many Arabic and Persian loan words and phraseologies, which were replaced by new terms based on authentic Turkish roots in a way quite similar to what had been achieved in modern Hebrew.[1] Indeed the transformation of the Turkish language bears a remarkable similarity to the examples we have seen of Nynorsk, modern Hebrew and the *demotike* form of Greek. The reforms have been compared by the distinguished linguist Geoffrey Lewis[2] with a replacement of many "superfluous" English words of Latin-French origin with Germanic terms, such as "foreword" for "preface," "bravery" for "heroism," "chasing" for "pursuit," "leave" for "permission," "withdrawing" for "retreating," and so on.

The success of a modern, Turkish national identity with a dynamic leader, a great military hero who won the battle against Greek attempts to seize control of the Aegean coast and part of Anatolia, enabled Atatürk to personally convince the mass of the Turkish people to follow his formula toward a modern state, something which the Iranian Shah wanted to emulate. Farsi (the Persian language) is, like Turkish, a non–Semitic language but remains written in the Arabic alphabet, and the old heritage of an ancestral pre–Islamic religion (Zoroastrianism) and symbols (the rising sun and lion) have been swept away by the revolution and the Islamic clergy now in power.

Although attempts were made prior to Atatürk to reform, modernize and simplify Turkish and the constitution of 1876 officially promulgated Turkish rather than Ottoman as the national language, the effect was minimal. Namik Kemal, a noted Ottoman writer, observed shortly before his death in 1880 that barely one Turk in ten was capable of getting the gist of official proclamations and state laws because: "Our literature is swamped with locutions borrowed from several foreign tongues of east and west, which have damaged the flow of expression, while the style of composition has become totally detached from the particles and terms and forms of discourse and has fallen ... under the domination of another language.... While the three languages of which Turkish is compounded have attained a certain unity in speech, they still preserve their original forms in writing. Like the three persons of the Trinity, they are said to be united, but are in fact the reverse of integrated."[3]

Complicating the matter even further was the attraction of French for many would-be reformers in the Ottoman Empire, who saw it as a vital link to help Turkey modernize. Atatürk was by no means the first to realize the extent of the problem, but only he was capable by his immense dynamism and popularity to cut through the Gordian knot and with one stroke obliterate the foreign influences, change the unsuitable and difficult alphabet, stimulate mass literacy and turn Turkey toward the West. He personally toured the country with a blackboard and taught the new alphabet in dozens of villages (Figure 26). In November, 1932, the muezzins were ordered to chant the traditional call to prayer in Turkish instead of Arabic, a major break with Islam.

Turkish and the Turkic Languages

Although linked by language and a common historical origin on the steppes of central Asia the Turkish leaders realized that the modern state and sense of nationality created by Atatürk could not easily absorb the Turkic-speaking peoples in distant lands separated by centuries of a different political-economic development and cultural orientation[4] (Kazakhstan, Turkmenistan, Uzbekistan, Azerbaijan and Kyrgyzstan), in various central Asian areas of the Russian republic or among the mixed populations of Cyprus, Syria and northern Iraq. Even under the Ottomans, there was a movement of pan–Turkic nationalism mixed with Islamic fervor and Turkish racial distinctiveness that was encouraged by the sultans. In the declaration of war against the czarist empire in 1914, the sultan encouraged Turkic-speaking peoples to rise up and unite with "all branches of our race." In World War II anti–Russian sentiment and anticommunism were combined by pan–Turkic nationalists who had rejected Atatürk's limited "Anatolianism" as fundamentally flawed. This derogatory term referred to the heartland of the Turkish state in Asia Minor, a much smaller geographic area than the great regions of the Tigris-Euphrates valley, central Asia, the Caucasus and Ural mountains, around the Black, Caspian and Aral Seas and the approaches to China where Turkic-speaking people were distributed. They dared criticize him only in clandestine publications, however.

With his death and the great advances of German armies into central Asia, many pan–Turkish nationalists openly demonstrated for a pro–German foreign policy and Turkish entry into the war to "liberate

Turkdom." A major difficulty of pan–Turkish nationalism was, however, precisely the growing linguistic disparities among the Turkic peoples under Soviet rule, who were largely ignorant of the ongoing language reforms and new words introduced in Turkey and had their alphabets forcibly changed from either Arabic or Latin script to the Cyrillic alphabet.

The government reacted sternly, suppressing the pan–Turkish movement during World War II and imprisoning its leaders. After the war, these irredentist groups continued to agitate on behalf of a militant pan–Turkic nationalism. Criticism from the communist left labeled the manipulation with language as a bourgeois movement and far removed from the concerns and speech habits of ordinary Turks. Toward the end of his life, Atatürk became aware that some purists were going to extremes. He subsequently adapted his public speeches and writing to indicate that many traditional words and forms of address should be retained. This was made abundantly clear to him when visiting dignitaries found their Turkish interpreters and translators unable to deal with the torrent of new terms.

Turks have wisely avoided the temptation to create a "greater Turkey" in the same way as Yugoslavia or Czechoslovakia did with the southern and northern Slavs respectively. They have stuck to the course set by Atatürk and remolded their language accordingly. Turkish attempts to integrate with Europe and the secular character of the state have all helped turned the attention of most Turks toward the West.

Conclusion

Language Learning in the Free Market

People desire to learn another language (i.e., not the language they learned at home from their parents) because of the forces of the free market. There may be a host of reasons, all of which are deemed to be of utility and personal advantage. These are:

1. travel
2. education
3. career advancement
4. business and job opportunities
5. research and intelligence gathering
6. appreciation of another culture
7. social conviviality and convenience

The National Language—A Different Kettle of Fish

A different set of motivations is involved for an individual to learn a national language, the subject of this book. This language may or may not be the one our parents taught us as infants at home. We may have learned it as a matter of course, without any conscious decision, simply as a medium of discourse to communicate with others and participate as an equal member of a distinct society within the state where we make our home and living without necessarily making a political statement. Quite another decision is the conscious one on the part of an individual/state/government/movement to make a political statement and identify with a distinct historical entity known as a nation via the national language.

The creation of a national language is an integral part of attempts at nation building. It is more than just the language formally learned in school. It imparts conscious values to a host of words and concepts related to history and patriotism. It may vary significantly from the local vernacular spoken by family and neighbors as a medium of discourse. As we have seen, it differs in important ways among the different national varieties of the same language spoken in different countries (German in Germany, and Austria; or French as spoken in France, Haiti and Quebec; or English as spoken in England, Scotland, Ireland, Canada, and the United States), and so on.

An analysis of the national languages in the more than twenty countries examined here can serve to refute some of the most widely held assumptions about language and rectify some of the considerable popular confusion and misunderstanding of the role of language in national self-identity. The condition of multilingual states spans the entire gamut from threatening the continuation of a single state (Belgium and Canada) to the tranquil resolution and exemplary civic patriotism of Switzerland. Swiss speakers of French, German and Italian are not French, Germans and Italians who happen to live in Switzerland. Their loyalty to Switzerland, the outcome of 700 years of painful history entailing conflicts, wars and compromises is, nevertheless, very real and greater than a sense of community with speakers of the same languages in other states.

Nation Building

From Von Herder through Hitler to many present-day observers, language is held to be the determinant factor in national identity. The following quote from an American university's cultural geography textbook stresses that "nationality has become almost synonymous with language. The political map is nearly a duplicate of the language map."[1] A similar view on the relative rigidity of language loyalty holds that "Political, social, and economic structures are often closely related with linguistic usage, and distributional patterns of these phenomena tend to coincide strikingly with linguistic areal patterns."[2]

Nevertheless, language is only one and not necessarily the most important element in the historical evolution of nations. As Rustow[3] and Wardhaugh[4] point out, very few independent states are linguistically homogeneous. The most unambiguous examples of states with no sizeable linguistic minority can be numbered on the fingers of two hands (Hungary, Iceland, Portugal, Malta, Thailand, Japan and Korea). Only two generations ago many states such as the Netherlands, Austria, Germany, Sweden, Australia and New Zealand had very homogeneous populations. Today, large numbers of immigrants and refugees or "language revivals" to recover a lost indigenous culture have transformed these countries into multilingual states posing a challenge regarding the social and linguistic integration of minorities.

Conclusion

Nation building is a process which entails the winning of loyalties to a common ideal and a will to live together based first of all on a common identity and a single answer to the question "Who are we"? It often also involves a shared history (real or imagined), common values, ideals, and traditions. Speaking the same language has not prevented catastrophic civil wars among people who had previously been both equal citizens under the law and lived within the same political state for generations and who spoke the same language as did Americans, Spaniards, Russians, Chinese, Greeks, and Koreans.

Too often, the "cart is put before the horse" in the mistaken assumption that a distinct language is a factor calling for the establishment of a separate political identity. This was not only the basis of Von Herder's idea but has a long history going back to the Tower of Babel myth in the Bible subscribed to by the church. *Gentum lingua facit* ("language makes race") was already advanced by the medieval scholar Isidore of Seville,[5] yet it was always subject to the religious qualification of "belonging to Christendom," a condition which no multilingual Jewish or Muslim merchant, philosopher or scholar could meet in medieval Spain. Many of the cases examined in this book nevertheless show that a distinction of language was insisted on only when people first argued that it was incompatible or unnatural to speak the same language as "the foreigners." The desire for independence in Norway after 400 years of Danish rule was not due to a desire to preserve Norwegian. Neither was this the case in the struggle for Irish independence from Great Britain. Only after the clear manifestation to reassert Norwegian independence was apparent did Aasen feel the need to create a modified, constructed, neutral form of various geographically separated rural dialects and elevate it into a national language yet speakers of Nynorsk are no more Norwegian than speakers of Dano-Norwegian.

In spite of enormous efforts to establish Irish as a national language, the reality is that Irish nationality and identity do not depend on it. Irish citizens who speak English are no less Irish than their Gaelic-speaking countrymen and are no more Englishmen than are the Americans or Australians. Language was not the crucial element in the process of nation building or national unification but rather a sought-after goal of nationalists, whom we may call nation builders, who had a vision of a distinct identity to be enshrined on a political map that rarely coincided with the distributional maps of actual speakers. Speakers of Galician in Spain feel that they are Spaniards after centuries of coexistence and nation sharing in spite of the greater similarity of their language to Portuguese.

Many Jews were brought to Zionism as their national movement of liberation not by any affinity for Hebrew or Yiddish but from the realization that their self-designation as "equal citizens of the Mosaic faith" did not coincide with the social and political reality they encountered from many Germans, Poles, Hungarians, or Romanians, whose languages they shared.

In four dramatic cases, linguists and nationalists from among the same people were divided over the question of the most proper and fitting national language to answer the question "Who are we? In two cases (Ireland and Norway), the historical or "revived" national language has been divisive and is still a source of conflict. In the two successful cases where a historical language was revived or elevated in status (Hebrew and Maltese), it is quite unlikely that the two national movements might have otherwise mobilized the powerful force necessary to establish political independence and prevent foreign domination.

The same uncertainty over "Who are we?" continues to plague the Arab world, a region of great instability, shifting rivalries and perennial conflicts as well as high illiteracy, an unavoidable consequence of the gap between learning what amounts to a foreign language remote from the one spoken at home in order to be considered educated in one's own homeland.

A national language cannot be identified on linguistic grounds. It is ultimately defined by politics. Without political independence, the minor differences between the mutually intelligible Danish, Swedish and Norwegian national languages would qualify them in the eyes (and ears) of most observers to be nothing more than dialects. By contrast, the dozen or more regionally distinctive dialects and accents of "Italian" are more different from each other than Portuguese is from Spanish, neither of which is ever referred to as a dialect.

Language Manipulation, the Elites and the Masses

Political considerations fostering a sense of national solidarity across language divisions among citizens led to a decision to elevate a local dialect to the status of a national language for political reasons (Romansch in Switzerland). The use of language as a political football with various regimes alternately trying to differentiate and then amalgamate Czech and Slovak, Serbian and Croatian, Rumanian and Moldavian and Russian and Ukrainian demonstrate that the prevailing political framework and interstate relations are the deterministic forces in manipulating language to make people feel they either belong or do not belong to the same nation.

Language choice entails political consequences as well as the converse—that political choices lead to linguistic consequences even when not originally intended.[6] An example of the former was the adamant policy of the De Valera government in the Republic of Ireland to enforce its idealized vision of a reborn Irish language tied to a Celtic and Catholic identity that had no place for the Protestant majority in the north in spite of the fervent desire to reunite the entire country. An example of the latter has been insistence of the political leadership of the Arab countries to maintain a formal identification with an all-encompassing Arab identity (the "Arab World") that cannot accord the spoken vernaculars an equality of status and function in their societies.

Like the "chicken and the egg," it is often difficult to separate the two. The decisions of governing elites cannot remain divorced from the daily matters that are subject to the shared common medium of discourse prevailing among the masses. The vast majority of the Irish people have rejected the notion of a "reborn Irish" as have a large majority of the Norwegian people with regard to Nynorsk in spite of persistent, state-directed propaganda and lavish resources. Attempts by those who have shaped government policy to impose Hindi on a majority of the country's population or the continued naive belief in the utility of bilingualism in Canada at any cost have not as yet accomplished the fond hopes that national unity can be achieved together with tolerance.

A Third-World Example

Before reviewing our case studies, it is revealing to examine an example from one of many newly independent, third-world states that was until recently a European colony. The techniques of nation building and the often diametrically opposed views of elites and masses toward what constitutes both a nation and its language may be seen in the case of the U.N.'s newest member, East Timor. Ruled by Portugal as part of its heritage from the golden era of overseas exploration, the colony was among the most remote and backward. Education was almost entirely in the hands of the Catholic church and literacy barely exceeded 5 percent.[7] Some elementary instruction and church services were provided in the more than a dozen indigenous languages, the most widespread of which is Tetum. These purely local languages served no purpose in administrative functions, and the native elite that became active in the anticolonial struggle and led the campaign for independence was Portuguese speaking. Even in exile, these leaders sought to lead the struggle from a position of influence in the Portuguese-speaking world, namely Portugal itself and Brazil and with their colleagues in Portuguese Africa—Mozambique, Angola and the Cape Verde Islands.

Indonesian rule imposed in 1975 brought with it a much-expanded program of education in that country's national language, Bahassa-

Indonesian, to integrate the largely Christian population of the Timorese Island fragment. The result has been a major increase in literacy to nearly ten times the level under colonial rule, but the imposed new language is neither indigenous nor useful outside the political framework of Indonesia. The selection of Portuguese, a vestige of the colonial past and spoken by a tiny minority, is still viewed as a more successful choice for a national language because of its utility on a worldwide stage.

Von Herder's Thesis: The Scorecard

Let us return to Von Herder's view: "Has a nationality anything dearer than the speech of its fathers? In its speech resides its whole thought domain, its traditions, history, religion and basis of life, all its heart and soul." We can then apply it to our twenty-five case studies. Von Herder's thesis must be reformulated to answer three sets of questions.

(1) The first applies to present-day independent states. Do the peoples of these countries consider the "speech of their fathers" as the most important ingredient in the determination of their sense of nationhood? Question one applies to Part I.

Israel

The answer is a qualified no. Although Hebrew has played a major role in the creation of a new Israeli identity, it is not identical with the "speech of the fathers" (Yiddish) unless one goes back at least forty generations. It did, however, serve as an important element in the nation-building process in absorbing immigrants from many different geocultural and language backgrounds. A significant minority among the Jewish population is orthodox observant and does not subscribe to the view that Israel is simply a homeland with a national language shared by all citizens. For them, the essence of nationhood is divine election by God. The Torah is conceived of as a "movable territory" that evolved as a substitute for the loss of real territory and Jewish independence two thousand years ago. Jews thus effectively took their portable space with them into exile and replaced it with a real territorial definition of space only in modern times.[8]

Ireland

No, Not at all. For at least 99 percent of the Irish population, their sense of identity is not tied to the speech of their fathers. The future of Irish nationalism and the eventual reunification of the country will not depend on revival of the Irish-Gaelic language.

Norway

No, Not at all. For most Norwegians, the speech of their fathers was lost more than five centuries ago, and Nynorsk is not a substitute for 85 percent of the population. Their sense of nationality is not tied to which form of Norwegian they speak today, and resentment continues to grow against the Nynorsk version and its claim of being more authentic.

Malta

Qualified yes. It would be hard to imagine an independent Malta today, had most Maltese decided to adopt either Italian or English as their primary means of discourse. Maltese, like Hebrew, remains a unique expression of a distinct nation whose language is not shared with anyone else. Nevertheless, a referendum to join the United Kingdom won a plurality of votes at one point.

Greece

Qualified no. Exaggerated notions of identity between the ancient Greek world and modern state helped guide expansionist Greek nationalism only to become counterproductive later and create schisms. One could, however, look at the remote past and consider that the Attic, *koine* and *katharevousa* (i.e., "the speech of the grandfathers") was not sufficient as the basis for a modern state and that it was *demotike*, the most "impure" of the different forms of Greek, that finally became the medium of discourse for all Greeks.

The Arab Countries

Qualified yes. Even more than in Greece, exaggerated notions of a mythical identity helped create the ideal of the "Arab world" but are counterproductive today in developing a modern sense of nationality. Islam is still regarded by many Arabs as an essential part of their identity. If we look again at the remote past, it is obvious that the original "speech of the grandfathers" (Coptic and Aramaic-Syriac) was rejected along with the original pre–Islamic religious heritage. The modern states of Egypt, Syria and Iraq are thus in no way a continuation of their ancient forbears.

Turkey

Yes. The great majority of the Turkish people were never in doubt as to their national language. Atatürk's reforms were welcomed precisely because they were much closer to the common sense of ordinary speech even with a host of neologisms than the complicated, courtly, diplomatic-literary jargon in imitation of Arabic and Persian.

There is a different question to be asked of those people living in multiethnic states and those living as a national minority or regional minority in a state that was not originally the focus of their sense of nationhood.

(2) **Is my primary loyalty to the community with whom I share a common language? (Yes—i.e., the language of my fathers—or no, it is rather to those with whom I share the same citizenship.)**

Belgium

Yes for Flemings and no for Walloons. Most Flemings feel more of a sense of identity with their homeland in Flanders, secondarily with their fellow Dutch-language speakers in the Netherlands, and last of all with their Walloon French-speaking fellow Belgian citizens in Belgium. Most Walloons are ambivalent.

Switzerland

No, not at all. The sense of "Swissness" is not dependent on the identity of the speech of the fathers. It is the definitive case of a nation not dependent on a single language.

Canada

Yes for the Quebecois and no for Anglo-Canadians. The Quebecois feel a deep sense of identity as a nation based on the language of their fathers. Many English-speaking Canadians are ambivalent and uncertain as to their Canadian identity. There are two national languages in Canada, and in spite of gargantuan efforts to promote bilingualism, the two are the vehicles of two nations, not one.

Spain

Qualified yes. A minority of Basques and a majority of Cataláns and Galicians feel identity with the majority Castillians on the basis of a shared national language and history, yet there is a constant tension regarding how far to extend regional and linguistic identities.

India

No. Loyalty to India is not based on fluency in Hindi, although separatist groups demand more autonomy or independence. It is doubtful that English can ever be replaced by Hindi as the common medium of common discourse.

South Africa

No. Loyalty in South Africa is not based on fluency or literacy in either English or Afrikaans or any of the nine tribal languages. A fascinating question remains to be answered by future developments—Will Afrikaans evolve into a truly shared cultural possession of a multiracial society instead of an imposition by a ruling, white master race?

Italy

Qualified no. Many Italian dialects are spoken with major separatist sentiment in the north. Although standard Italian has gained considerable ground, it has not reduced the divisiveness of regional peculiarities and spoken local dialects. In Switzerland, the Italian-Swiss remain committed to the political idea of Switzerland and not to the nation of Italy.

Welsh in the UK

A qualified yes, but only for those Welsh who are nationalists and believe the fate of their nation is tied to the language. Can they convince the other 80 percent of residents in Wales that it is more than a provincial obsession? It is unlikely.

Scots in the UK

No, not at all! The Scottish Nationalist Party draws support for regional autonomy and eventual independence based on a range of economic and social issues but not language per se. In fact, the Scottish case is instructive in demonstrating the contradiction between the felt need for a national language and the need for a medium of social discourse. Fewer and fewer native Gaelic speakers are able to communicate in the language to the same degree as their parents. Nevertheless, a Gaelic renaissance, spurred by a nationalist mythology has led to more and more Scots learning the language formally in school and acquiring either a literary or rudimentary conversational knowledge of what is as much a foreign language as Latin is. In essence, they have learned Scottish-Gaelic in much the same way as early modern Hebrew speakers in Palestine or the first Esperanto speakers did.

Hungarians in Romania

Yes, but... This is the classic case that seems to unconditionally support the Von Herder thesis. The native language remains the preeminent means of determining nationality. The large Hungarian minorities in Romania, Moldavia, Slovakia and the border regions of Serbia and Croatia continue to look to Hungary for aid in preserving their national language and folk culture. Yet even here there is an ambivalent case—the Csangos. Many centuries of coexistence with the Romanian majority in Moldavia since the Middle Ages has created a gap with other Hungarian speakers, whose national culture and literacy were shaped in the kingdom of Hungary, the Austro-Hungarian Empire and the modern Hungarian state.

Alsatians in France

No, not at all. Many Alsatians for several generations spoke their German dialect but felt tied to the French nation. This is true today as more and more young Alsatians use French as their medium of discourse with fellow citizens.

Danish Minority in Germany

No, not at all. Even today, a majority of those who feel Danish continue to speak German as their everyday medium of discourse.

Finlanders (Swedes in Finland)

Qualified no. The Swedish minority has an option to return to Sweden. Nevertheless, those who live in the Åland Islands enjoy special protection of language rights and autonomy free from interference by the Finnish majority. Elsewhere the Swedish minority is almost entirely bilingual with a growing preference for Finnish as a first language. Both groups are loyal Finnish citizens.

The Israeli Arabs

Yes. Almost all Israeli Arabs and those Arabs in the Palestinian territories fluent in Hebrew still feel an Arab identity and loyalty to "the language of their fathers" and to the Arab forces/nations opposed to Israel. Their first language (Arabic) remains a focus of loyalty.

(3) **With regard to the three groups of "cousins," is or was a common (or very similar or nearly identical) language a sufficient basis to help create a sense of solidarity in a joint political framework?**

Serbs and Croats in Yugoslavia, Czechs and Slovaks in Czechoslovakia, Romanians and Moldavians in a Greater Romania

NO. The three sets of "quarreling cousins" are proof that national unity based primarily on language is very weak and cannot overcome diverse historical, economic and social differences.

Uruguay

State determined. Indecisive. Uruguay is in a class by itself. In the case of Uruguay, the only example of a new world nation built by immigration with very little input from the aboriginal population, the political leadership created the notion of a separate entity from Argentina and Brazil and chose the language of the center of settlement over the periphery. Opinion is divided among political and scholarly institutions as to whether Portuñol is a distinctive contributing feature of nationhood or a "vulgar" detriment. Its buffer-state origin enabled Uruguay to maintain its peculiar Banda Oriental separateness and develop a national profile of its own.

The Nation Building Device of a National Language

Von Herder had it backward. As with many other issues, there is a confusion between cause and effect. People are molded into a nation by a host of shared institutions and historical experiences. It has often been the conscious policy of those who construct a state by expansion and absorption of neighboring regions to embody the people's whole thought domain, traditions, and basis of life, its heart and soul in a particular speech form and through it interpret (or reinterpret) history.

This can be most clearly seen from recent history in the case of choosing Hebrew as the national language in Israel, but it is no less true in the nineteenth-century unifications of Italy and Germany. We have also observed those cases where the search for the national language in Ireland and Norway failed to convince a majority of the people that their identity was embodied in the much older, original language of the nation, but no one can deny that the "soul" of the Irish and Norwegian peoples is intact even when expressed in varieties of English or Danish.

The nation-building technique of ensuring the spread of the dialect chosen to be the most representative form of the national language often requires centuries. It is only in its early initial stage in countries like India and South Africa and has not been completed in older states such as Italy. It has met an impasse in Canada and Belgium, where there is no bridge between two distinct nations who inhabit the same state. It has worked out a compromise in such states as Spain and Sweden. It was insufficient to create (or recreate) nations embodied in states such as Czechoslovakia and Yugoslavia where history had intervened and separated the "brothers" for centuries into hostile cousins.

Finally, a people that initially was far along the road to integration in one nation and language switched course to another one, as occurred among the Alsatians. Exactly the same would have undoubtedly occurred among the Danish minority in Germany if the border had been changed after World War II. In Greece, Turkey and the Arab world, the meaning of "the speech of the fathers" has been interpreted in such a way that a remote, glorious past has impeded and retarded the development of national life. In our survey, only among the Quebecois and Arab nationalists does the language issue take unchallenged first place.

Recent research on the origins of nationalism in Western Europe emphasize the constructed or artificial nature of the modern nation as the embodiment of loyalty and identity of people initially sharing a common kinship[9] and subsequently reinforced by communication and then literacy. Benedict Anderson regards modern culture as the outcome of "print capitalism," before which religious affiliation was the paramount focus of community. It was literacy and the growth of a national literature that eventually constructed national cultures and shaped a common medium of discourse, a standardized literary form of what had been a local dialect in the capital region that was widely disseminated. This national language, along with common laws, was imposed by a centralized political authority and the printing press.

In addition to language (a subject of controversy for generations in Ireland, Israel, Norway and Malta), we have seen that other major factors such as love of the homeland—a common territory (as in Finland, Scotland or Uruguay), religion (Ireland, Israel and the Arab world have complicated their national identity by too close an identification with a specific faith), race (the Afrikaaner view under Apartheid and Basque extremists), a fascination with the glorious past (the glory that was Greece and the early Arab empires), inertia (Belgium), different cultural orientations and economic and political systems in force over a long period of time (Czech republic, Slovakia, Serbia, Croatia, and Moldova) or mutual self-interest and common values (Switzerland and the United States) have been equally important as language or more so.

A common language was not sufficient to hold together Spain's enormous empire in the Americas. As a result of the desire for independence, armed insurrection drove the Spaniards out from their six colonial dependencies in the Viceroyalty of New Spain (present day Mexico and Central America), the Viceroyalty of New Granada (present-day Venezuela, Colombia and Ecuador), the viceroyalty of Peru, the viceroyalty of La Plata (present-day Argentina, Paraguay and Bolivia) and the captaincy general of Cuba and Santo Domingo). The result was the emergence of seventeen independent countries. The political fragmentation occurred due to intense political rivalries and disparate geographical conditions which language could not bridge. In colonial Brazil, by contrast, Portuguese rule was replaced by an independent imperial Brazil ruled by an emperor who was able to command the loyalty of his subjects over an area as large and diverse as the Spaniards had ruled. The absence of any fragmentation was not due primarily to the existence of a common Portuguese language but rather the uncontested prestige of the emperor (Brazil became a republic only in 1888).

Language is a medium of communication, but only a constructed nonethnic language such as Esperanto (see Figure 11) has been totally free of the emotionally acquired connotations associated with the embodiment of a national culture and history linked with a specific state, flag and a patriotic call to arms in times of crises. During World War I, "sauerkraut" and "kindergarten" became unacceptable, and Americans were urged by various, self-proclaimed "patriots" to use such equivalents as "liberty cabbage" and "preschool education." The search for a national language is a critical part of a deeper issue of self-identity and must answer the question "Who are we?" The answers have been many, diverse, and sometimes shifting and contradictory.

CHAPTER NOTES

Introduction

1. Johann G. von Herder, *Über den Ursprung der Sprache* (On the origin of speech, 1772.)
2. Glynn Custred, "Alien Crossings" in *The American Spectator*, October, 2000, pp. 38–43.
3. Brian Weinstein, *The Civic Tongue: Political Consequences of Language Choice* (New York: Longman, 1983). This book deals with language as an instrument of access to or deprivation of political and economic power through education, employment, and administrative facility.
4. Richard Hartshorne, "The Concepts of 'Raison d'Être' and 'Maturity' of States; Illustrated from the Mid-Danube Area," *Annals of the Association of American Geographers*, vol. 30, pp. 59–60; 1940.
5. See Ronald Wardhaugh, *Languages in Competition* (Oxford and New York: Basil Blackwell, 1987), for an extensive bibliography.
6. *Language Policy and Political Development*, edited by Brian Weinstein (Norwood, N.J.: Ablex, 1990).

Chapter 1

1. See Reuven Sivan, "Ben-Yehuda and the Revival of Hebrew Speech," in *ARIEL, Quarterly Review of the Arts and Sciences in Israel*, no. 25, 1969, pp. 35–39; Jack Fellman, "Eliezer Ben-Yehuda," in *ARIEL*, no. 104, 1997, pp. 26–31, Jerusalem.
2. Ze'ev Jabotinsky, *Hebrew Pronunciation*, pp. 37–38. Tel-Aviv, 1940, HaSefer.
3. For a comparison of the similarities between the introduction of Esperanto and modern Hebrew, see Norman Berdichevsky, "Esperanto and Zamenhof," *ARIEL*, 1986, no. 64, pp. 58–71.
4. Ahad Ha-am, quoted in Benjamin Harshav, *Language in Time of Revolution* (Berkeley: University of California Press, 1993), p. 18.
5. For complete text see website: http//www.bibiblio.org/yiddish/Tshernovits/birnbaum-op.html.
6. The interwar capitals of Lithuania, Latvia and Estonia respectively.
7. For example, his translation of Edgar Allan Poe's poem "The Raven" is unparalleled and faithfully duplicates the meter, rhymes, and classical allusions. It is unmatched by translation into any other language.
8. Lucy Dawidowicz, *The War Against the Jews, 1933–1945* (New York: Penguin, 1975).
9. *Antologia shel HaSifrut HaLituait*, edited by Yitzhak Kissin (Kaunas, 1932).
10. Hebrew term, "the genius," used for Elijah Ben Solomon Zalwan, 1720–1797, of Vilna, a great Talmudic scholar and opponent of Hassidism.
11. See Joseph Heller, *The Stern Gang: Ideology, Politics and Terror, 1940–1949* (London: Frank Cass, 1995); and Nurit Gertz, "From Jew to Hebrew: The Zionist Narrative in the Israeli Cinema of the 1940s and 1950s," in *Israel Affairs*, vol. 4, nos. 3 and 4, Spring/Summer, 1998, pp, 175–199.
12. Benjamin Harshav, *Language in a Time of Revolution* (Berkeley: University of California Press, 1993).
13. Harshav, op. cit. p. 40
14. There is still a diversity of spelling forms; see pp. 36–38, "The Hebrew Spelling Dilemma"
15. Harshav, op. cit. p. 109.
16. B. Spolsky and R. L. Cooper, *The Languages of Jerusalem* (Oxford: Clarendon Press, 1991), p. 63.
17. Including the leading, most widely

circulated, newspapers today—*Ma'ariv* and *Yediot Ahronot*.

18. There are three sets of dual letters in Hebrew: P and F, B and V, and K and CH, which appear identical without nikud but have a different pronunciation, which depends on the preceding vowel or following consonant.

19. For a more thorough treatment of the changes in grammatical structure that characterize modern Hebrew as distinct from the ancient language, see "Israeli Hebrew" by David Tene in *ARIEL*, no. 25, 1969, op. cit.

20. See also the humorous article "Hebrew as She Is Spoke" by Hillel Halkin in *Commentary*, December, 1969, pp. 55–60.

21. Estimates from the 1897 census indicate that mother-tongue Yiddish speakers numbered well over 95 percent of all Jews in the rural area of White Russia and the Ukraine.

22. Reuben Alberg, "Kriyah yeilah bilvrit; HaKativ vehaKatav -haimhem dai tovim?" (Efficient reading in Hebrew, spelling and the alphabet: Are they good enough?) Pamphlet, Dfus Telegraf, Bnei-Brak, 1991, 69 pages.

23. Alberg, op. cit.

24. See "A Movable Feast" by Hillel Halkin in the weekly magazine *Jerusalem Report*, April 22, 1993.

25. Werner Weinberg, *Tikun HaKtiv HaIvri: Habaiya vehaNisyonot liftora* (The orthographic reform Hebrew: the problem and the attempts to solve it) (Jerusalem: The Hebrew University, 1971).

26. Eliezer Ben-Rafael, *Language, Identity and Social Division—The Case of Israel* (Oxford: Clarendon Press, 1994), p. 231.

27. John Geiple in *Mame Loshn: The Making of Yiddish*. (1982) takes the optimistic view that there are still upwards of four or five million speakers (or readers) of Yiddish worldwide. This seems exceedingly optimistic. The *1997 World Almanac and Book of Facts* lists the principal languages of the world (with over one million speakers) and includes Yiddish but without an exact figure—the only language in the table without one. Undoubtedly this is due to the difficulties of taking an accurate census when speakers are so geographically dispersed.

28. Table 2. Mother tongue of the population by nativity and parentage 1970. U.S. census.

29. Hillel Halkin, op. cit., p. 60.

30. See Part VI, Ethnic or Regional Minorities: Bilingual or Using the Wrong Language?

31. Chapter 5, "The Revitalization of Hebrew," pp. 57–73 in B. Spolsky and R. L. Cooper, *The Languages of Jerusalem* (Oxford: Clarendon Press, 1991).

Chapter 2

1. See *In Search of Ireland: A Cultural Geography* Brian Graham, ed. (London and New York: Routledge, 1997).

2. The language is also referred to as Irish-Gaelic to stress its common origin with Scots-Gaelic or "Erse" to specify the language rather than the use of Irish as an adjective.

3. *Ireland and the Irish: Portrait of a Changing Society* by John Ardagh, p. 296 (London: Penguin Books, 1995).

4. A reference to the heroic Greek resistance in ancient times to the Persian Hordes at the battle of Thermopylae.

5. "Political Structures, Social Interaction and Identity Change in Northern Ireland," p. 155, by Neville Douglas, Chapter 8, in *In Search of Ireland: A Cultural Geography* by Brian Graham, ed., op. cit.

6. See following sections on Malta and Norway.

7. Quoted in Ó h Ailín, "Irish Revival Movements" in S. Ó Túama, ed., *The Gaelic League Idea* (Dublin: Cork, Mercier, 1972).

8. *New York Herald Tribune*, March 17, 1960.

9. *Irish Advocate*, New York, February 19, 1955.

10. Interview with Nuala Ní Dhomhnaill in John Ardagh, *Ireland and the Irish: Portrait of a Changing Society* (London: Penguin Books, 1995), p. 300.

11. Quoted in John Ardagh, Ireland and the Irish, op. cit., p. 302.

Chapter 3

1. For an overview of the development of Nynorsk and the life of Aasen, see Lars S. Vikør, *The New Norse Language Movement* (Oslo: Folaget Novus, 1975).

2. See Niels Davidsen-Nielsen et. al., "Engelsk Eller Ikke Engelsk: That Is the Question," Dansk Sprognævns skrifter 28, Gyldendal (Copenhagen: Gyldendal, 1999).

3. Magne Oftedal "Is Nynorsk a Minority Language?" in *Minority Languages Today*, Einar Haugen, ed., pp. 120–130.

Chapter 4

1. It was Mizzi who, in a speech to the Maltese council of government in May, 1885, made the statement that "La lingua maltese é la maledizione del paese."
2. *Encylopedia Judaica*, vol. 5 (Jerusalem, 1971), p. 215.
3. See "The Punic Build-Up," in *Last Bastion: Sketches of the Maltese Islands*, by Eric Brockma (London: Darton, Longman and Todd, Ltd., 1961), pp. 206–217.
4. A. Cini, La libera scelta ossia la questione della lingua italiana in Malta secondo el Decreto-Legge del 26 settembre, 1901. Syracuse, p. 13.
5. Geofrey Hull, *The Malta Language Question*, op. cit., p. 115.
6. For research on this question, see Pietro Paolo Saydon, *The Development of Maltese as a Written Language and Its Affinities with Other Semitic Tongues*, 1928; Valetta, Malta, and P. Grech, "Are There Any Traces of Punic in Maltese?" in *Journal of Maltese Studies*, vol. 1 (Malta, 1961), pp. 130–138.
7. Rossini, *Malta on the Brink: From Western Democracy to Libyan Satellite*, London, op. cit., 1986, p. 2.
8. For the most complete work on the language controversy in Malta, see Geoffrey Hull, *The Malta Language Question* (Malta: Said International, 1993), p. 365.

Chapter 5

1. Henri Pirenne, *A History of Europe, from the End of the Roman World in the West to the Beginnings of the Western States*" (New York: Doubleday, 1956).
2. For a thorough analysis of Belgium's political crisis in the 1930s, see "Belgium," by G. Carpinelli, in *Fascism in Europe*, S. J. Woolf, ed., (London and New York: Methuen, 1981), Chapter 33, pp. 283–306.
3. *Vlaandern-Europa 2002. Een project van de Vlaamse regering*, Tielt, Lannoo, 1993.
4. John Fitzmaurice, "New Order? International Models of Peace and Reconciliation: Diversity and Civil Society";

report no. 9, pp. 1–13. Website for democratic dialogue, www.democratic dialogue.org/report9/report9d.htm
5. "New Order" in *International Models of Peace and Reconciliation* by John Fitzmaurice. Report no. 9. Internet www.democraticdialogue.org/report. For a thorough analysis of the language controversy dividing Belgium, see "Language and Nationalism: Comparing Flanders and Tanzania" by Jan Blommaert in *Nations and Nationalism* 2(2) (1996), pp. 235–256.

Chapter 6

1. Wardhaugh, op. cit., 1987, p. 3.
2. The referendum secured a clear majority in the French-speaking areas but was rejected in the heartland of the German-speaking cantons.
3. For an informative look at what makes Switzerland tick, see *Why Switzerland?* by Jonathan Steinberg (Cambridge University Press, 1996).
4. "Swiss" in *Guide to the Peoples of Europe*, revised edition, Felipe Fernandez-Armestro, ed. (London: Tomes Books, 1997), pp. 139–145.
5. "Herkunft der Kinder" by Elisabeth Liebl in *Atlas der Schweizerische Volkskunde*, Basel, Paul Geiger *et al.*, Schweizerische Gesellschaft für Volkskunde, vol. 2, part 4, plates 202–205.
6. See G. Thürer, *Free and Swiss* (London: 1970).
7. Daniel J. Elazar, *Two Peoples, One Land: Federal Solutions for Israel, the Palestinians and Jordan* (Jerusalem Center for Public Affairs, 1991), pp. 54–55.
8. See "Switzerland—A Model for Solving Nationality Conflicts?" by Bruno Schoch (Frankfurt: Peace Research Institute, PRIF Report 54/2000).
9. Also spelled Schwyzer-Tütsch.
10. Steinberg, op. cit., p. 3.
11. Also known as Ladin and Rhaeto-Romansch.

Chapter 7

1. John Hooper, *The New Spaniards* (London: Penguin Books, 1995) p. 409.
2. *The Basque History of the World* by Mark Kurlansk, (New York: Random House, 1999).
3. *The Jewish Chronicle* (London: May 31, 1957).

4. "Making Children Bilingual in a Land of Many Tongues," by I. Briscoe, in *El País*, English language supplement, Feb. 5, 2002, p. 3.

Chapter 8

1. Symbols of Scotland, Ireland and England respectively.
2. *The White Niggers of America* by Pierre Vallières (in English, translated by Joan Pinkham) (Toronto: McClelland and Stewart Ltd., 1971).
3. For the most thorough analyses of the Anglo-French rift in Canadian society today, see *Breakup—The Coming End of Canada and the Stakes for America* by Lansing Lamont (New York: W. W. Norton and Company, 1994); and *The Nine Nations of North America* by Joel Garreau (New York: Avon, 1981).
4. Official website of the Canadian government: "Our Official Languages: As a Century Ends and a Millennium Begins." Available as a publication marking the thirtieth anniversary of the Office of the Commissioner of Official Languages. © Minister of Public Works and Government Services, Canada, 2001. Cat. no. SF31-56/2001. ISBN: 0-662-65975-9.
5. This figure is based on an extrapolation. According to Jim Travers of "Southam News" and a Canadian press release in *The Province* (Vancouver), citing then Federal Language Commissioner Max Yalden, the total accumulated cost of the programs in 1982 was $4 billion since the inception of the act in 1969, thirteen years earlier, and that the annual cost estimated then was about $448 million. Projected to 2002, the total cost would reach $20 billion.
6. Ross McKay, "The Interactance Hypothesis and Boundaries in Canada: A Preliminary Study," in *Canadian Geographer*, XI, 1958, pp. 1–8.

Chapter 9

1. Terry Jordan, *The European Culture Area* (New York: Harper Row, 1973), Chapter 5, "The Geography of Languages" and Colin Renfrew, *Archaeology and Language: The Puzzle of Indo-European Origins* (London: Pimlico, 1987).
2. Especially among the Sikh religious and Punjabi-speaking minority.
3. Snehamoy Chakladar, "Language Policy and Reformation of India's Federal Structure: The Case of West Bengal," pp. 87–107, in Brian Weinstein, *Language Policy and Political Development*, op. cit.

Chapter 10

1. Grimes, B. F., ed., 1992, "Ethnologue: Languages of the World," Dallas, Texas, Summer Institute of Linguistics; M. McFerren, 1984, *Country Status Report: South Africa*. Washington, D.C.: Center for Applied Linguistics.

Part III

1. Written in solitary confinement by a Ukrainian nationalist, Valentine Moroz, "Report from the Beria Reserve" (Chicago: 1974), p.54, reprinted in *Ethnicity*, John Hutchinson and Anthony Smith, eds. (Oxford Readers, 1996).
2. For a thorough discussion and analysis of these forms of a nation, see "Ethnic and Political Nations in Europe" by Jaroslav Krejci and Vitezslav Velímsk, in *Ethnicity*, op. cit., pp. 209–221.
3. Joshua Fishman, "The New Linguistic Order," in *Foreign Policy*, Winter, 1998.

Chapter 11

1. A situation immortalized in the well-known novel *Ivanhoe* by Sir Walter Scott.
2. See Philip Jenkins, "A History of Modern Wales, 1536–1990" (London and New York: Longman, 1993), and especially Chapter 19, "A Nation Once Again?, pp. 385–406 for the role of the Welsh language in the preservation of Welsh identity and the national movement.
3. *Languages in Competition* by Ronald Wardhaugh, op. cit., p.86.
4. "The Cost-Effectiveness Evaluation of Minority Language Policies: Case Studies on Wales, Ireland and the Basque Country," by François Grin and François Vaillancourt. Monograph no. 2 (Flensburg, Germany: European Centre for Minority Issues, 1999), p. 17.
5. See "A History of Modern Wales, 1536–1990" op. cit. Today, most Welsh speakers are concentrated in the more rural North.
6. By more than half a million people. This figure refers to people in Wales. According to a letter to *The Times* by Harold Carter (Feb. 8, 1996) there may well be an additional 100,000 Welsh speak-

ers in the rest of the U.K. and additional speakers in countries where Welsh immigrants have settled, such as Argentina, Australia, Canada and the United States.
7. Grin and Villaincourt, op. cit., p. 17.

Chapter 12

1. *The Cambridge Encyclopedia of English*, David Crystal (Cambridge and New York: Cambridge University Press, 1995), p. 128.
2. "Highland and Lowland Scots," pp. 43–45 in *The Guide to the Peoples of Europe*, revised edition, Felipe Fernandez-Arnesto, ed. *The Times*, London, 1997.
3. Cited in *The Cambridge Encyclopedia of the English Language*, Crystal, David (Cambridge and New York: Cambridge University Press, 1994), p. 333.

Part IV

1. Most linguists would agree that "dialect" refers to the immediate geographical identification of a speaker by virtue of a distinct vocabulary and/or grammatical usage, whereas an "accent" refers primarily to a distinctive pronunciation identifying the speaker's geographical origin.
2. Mario Pei, *The Story of Language*, Mentor Book, New American Library, New York, 1965; Mario Pei, *Language for Everyone*, New York.

Chapter 13

1. Mario Pei, op. cit., 1965, p. 61.
2. See pages on the language situation in Switzerland.

Chapter 14

1. "Images of the Neighbour: Reciprocal Stereotypes in Scandinavia," Internet archive http://www.uio.no/-geirthe/Scandinavian_images.html.

Chapter 15

1. John Gunther, *Inside Europe* (London: Hamish Hamilton, 1936) pp. 382–383.
2. R. Bugarski and C. Hawkesworth, eds., *Language Planning in Yugoslavia* (Columbus, Ohio: Slavica Publishers, 1992).

Chapter 16

1. Stephen Borsody, *The New Central Europe: Triumphs and Tragedies* (New York: Columbia University Press, 1993).
2. Website of the Slovak Government at http://www.government.gov.sk/LISTA/sk_frame_vlada.shtml.
3. For a detailed account of the recent legislation in Slovakia, see "The New Slovak Language Laws: Internal or External Politics?" by Farimah Daftary and Kinga Gál, European Centre for Minority Issues (ECMI), Flensburg, Germany. Working paper no. 8, 2000.

Chapter 17

1. See "Breakaway—A Zone Uncontrolled by Any State: In Moldovan Province, Shades of Corruption," by Michael Wines, *International Herald Tribune*, March 13, 2002, p. 2.

Chapter 18

1. There is a massive and polemical literature on this subject. The novice reader is referred to the website: http://www.hungary.com/corvinus; see also B. Köpeczi, ed., *History of Transylvania*, Budapest, 1996. C. A. McCartney, *Hungary and Her Successors: The Treaty of Trianon and Its Consequences 1919–1937*, London, 1937. R. W. Cambridge, *A History of the Rumanians*, Cambridge, 1934.
2. Ovid Densusianu, *Histoire de la Langue Roumanie*, Paris, 1901.
3. *The World's Greatest War—From the Outbreak of the War to the Treaty of Versailles*, vol. XVI (*The Causes of the War*), Holland Thompson, ed. (New York and London: Grollier Society, 1920), p. 614.
4. The reader is referred to the comprehensive work by Karal Kocsis and Ezster Kocsis-Hodosi, *Hungarian Minorities in the Carpathian Basin: A Study in Ethnic Geography* (Toronto and Buffalo: Matthias Corvinus Publishing, 1995).

Chapter 19

1. Eugène Phillips, *Les luttes linguistiques en Alsace jusqe'en 1945* (Strasbourg: Culture Alsacienne, 1975), p. 107.
2. H. Munro Chadwick, *The Nationalities of Europe* (New York: Cambridge University Press, 1945), p. 8. The author is mistaken, however. See the following section on the Danish minority in Germany for a similar example of noncorrespondence between national feeling and first language commonly used as a medium of discourse.

3. "Guide to the Peoples of Europe," *The Times*, op. cit., p. 111.

Chapter 20

1. Cited in *Dansk Grænselære*, Claus Eskildesen, C. A. Reitzels (Denmark: Forlag, 1946), p. 140.
2. "Die Gemeinde hat keine Moral und spricht nicht Deutsch," by Claus Kühne; Slesvigland, no. 3, 1983, pp.87–88.
3. See Norman Berdichevsky, *The Danish-German Border Dispute: Aspects of Cultural and Demographic Politics, 1815–2001* (Bethesda, Md.: Academica Press, 2002).
4. Jean Gutmann, *The Significance of Territory* (Charlottesville: University of Virginia Press, 1973).
5. Terry Jordan, *The European Culture Area: A Systematic Geography* (New York: Harper and Row Pub.), pp. 189–193, "Switzerland and Belgium: Success and Failure Astride a Linguistic Border."
6. Fernandez-Armestro, Felipe, *Guide to the Peoples of Europe*, revised edition (London: Times Books, 1997), pp. 29–33. The author has thanked me for correction of the misperception of the Danish minority in South Schleswig being primarily speakers of Danish as their first or habitual language. There is also a confusing use of geographic terms. "Northern Schleswig-Holstein" refers to German South Schleswig, and "South Jutland" denotes Danish North Schleswig.
7. See Andrew F. Burghardt, *Borderland: A Historical and Geographical Study of Burgenland, Austria* (Madison: University of Wisconsin Press, 1962).
8. This is still the situation today in spite of the growth of the Danish Minority's Schools in South Schleswig since the end of the war; see Bent Søndergaard, "The Fight for Survival: Danish as a Living Minority Language South of the German Border," in *Minority Languages Today: A Selection from the Papers Read at the First International Conference on Minority Languages*, held at Glasgow University, 1980, pp. 38–143, Edinburgh Free Press.

Chapter 21

1. For a full discussion of the status of Swedish in Finland, see Mikael Reuter, "The Status of Swedish in Finland in Theory and Practice" in *Minority Languages Today: A Selection of Papers Read at the First International Conference on Minority Languages*, held at Glasgow University, 1980, Edinburgh Free Press, pp. 130–137, and Farimah Daftary, "Insular Autonomy: A Framework for Conflict Resolution? A Comparative Study of Corsica and the Åland Islands," in *The Global Review of Ethnopolitics*, vol. 1, no. 1, Sept. 2001, pp. 19–40.

Chapter 22

1. *Language, Identity and Social Division: The Case of Israel*, by Eliezer Ben-Rafael (New York: Clarendon Press, 1994), p. 209.
2. Haim B. Rosen, "Israel Language Policy, Teaching and Linguistics," in *ARIEL* no. 25. 1969, pp. 92–112, op. cit.
3. Reuven Sivan, "Ben-Yehuda and the Revival of Hebrew Speech," in *ARIEL*, no. 25, 1969, pp. 35–39, op. cit.
4. Chapter 13, "The Case of a National Minority" in *Language, Identity and Social Division: The Case of Israel* by Eliezer Ben-Rafael (New York: Clarendon Press, 1994), op. cit.
5. Sasson Somekh, "Echoes of New Hebrew Literature in Arab Culture," in *ARIEL*, no. 105 (Jerusalem: 1997), pp. 30–33.

Chapter 23

1. La Facultad de Humanidad y Ciencias de la Educacion de la Universidad de La Republica, Montevideo. Adolfo Elizaicin and Harold Tühn, eds.
2. Graciela Barrios, quoted in "Detras del manejo de la lengua, hay actitudes discriminatorias," Servicio Informativo Iberoamericano: Organizacion de los estados Iberoamericanos., October 1999, by Gustavo Laborde, pp. 1–4 (posted on the internet).
3. See Daniel Vidart, "La Trama de la Identidad Nacional," vol. 3, *El Espiritu Criollo*. Ediciones de la Banda Oriental, Montevideo, 2000.

Chapter 24

1. *Guide to the Peoples of Europe*. The *Times*, 1997, op. cit., Greeks, pp. 210–211.
2. Notwithstanding the fact that Constantinople, conquered in 1453, had been renamed Istanbul and continuously ruled by Turkey as their capital for more than 460 years.

3. For an informative account of the development of modern Greek, including changes in grammar and vocabulary, see *The Development of the Greek Language* by W. Moleas (London: Bristol Classical Press, 1989); the article on Katharevousa by P. Mackridge, "Background to Contemporary Greece," vol. I, M. Sarafis and M. Eve, eds. (London: Merlin Press, 1990); and Greek: A History of the Language and Its Speakers, Geoffrey Horrocks (London & New York: Longman, 1997).

Chapter 25

1. Raphael Patai, *The Arab Mind*, revised edition (New York: Charles Scribner's Sons, 1973); revised edition, 1983, p. 42.
2. Nissim Rejwan, "Egyptians and Arabs: The Continuing Controversy," *Midstream*, January, 2001, pp. 6–9.
3. E. A. Wessin, "A Lonely Minority: The Modern Story of Egypt's Copts" New York, 1965.
4. Daniel Pipes, "Greater Syria: The History of an Ambition" (Oxford and New York: Oxford University Press, 1990).
5. Henri Lammens, *La Syrie: Précis historique* (Beirut: Imprimerie Catholique, 1921).
6. I. Z. Yanak, *The Syrian Social Nationalist Party: An Ideological Analysis*, (Cambridge, Mass: 1966).
7. Jacques Weulresse, *Paysans de Syrie et du Proche-Orient* (Paris: Gallimard, 1946), pp. 84–85.
8. Joseph Heller, *The Stern Gang: Ideology, Politics and Terror 1940–1949* (London: Frank Cass, 1995).
9. Ya'acov Shavit, *From Hebrew to Canaanite; Aspects in the History, Ideology and utopia of the Hebrew Renaissance—From Radical Zionism to Anti-Zionism* (Jerusalem: Domino Press, 1995).
10. See "Under the Spell of Language," Chapter IV in Raphal Patai, *The Arab Mind*, op. cit., pp. 41–72.
11. According to the *Information Please Almanac*, 1997 edition.
12. See Gilbert Granguillaume, "Language and Legitimacy in the Maghreb," pp. 150–166 in Brian Weinstein, *Language Policy and Political Development*, op. cit.
13. R. Wardhaugh, *Languages in Competition*, op. cit., p. 183.
14. Israeli news service Arutz-7, "New Egyptian Party 'We Are Not Arabs,'" Arabicnews.com, Nov. 7, 2003.

Chapter 26

1. Jacob M. Landau, "Language Policy and Political Development in Israel and Turkey," pp. 133–149 in Brian Weinstein, *Policy and Political Development*," op. cit.
2. Geoffrey Lewis. *The Turkish Language Reform: A Catastrophic Success* (Oxford: Oxford University Press, 1999), pp. 2–3.
3. Cited in Lewis, op. cit., p. 13.
4. "Turkey's Ostpolitik: Relations with the Central Asian States," by Philip Robins, in David Menashri, ed., *Central Asis Meets the Middle East* (London: Frank Cass, 1998), pp. 128–149.

Conclusion

1. Terry G. Jordan, *The European Culture Area* (New York: Harper and Row, 1973), p. 129.
2. Philip Wagner, "Remarks on the Geography of Language," in *Geographical Review*, 48 (1958), pp. 86–97.
3. D. A. Rustow, "Languages, Nations and Democracy," in *Les états multilingues: problèmes et solutions*. Quebec, J.-G. Savard and R. Vigneault, eds., Les Presses de l'Université Laval, 1875.
4. Ronald Wardhaugh, *Languages in Competition*, op. cit.
5. See Robert Bartlett, "Language and Ethnicity in Medieval Europe" in *Ethnicity*, John Hutchinson and Anthony Smith, eds., op. cit., pp. 127–132
6. Jonathan Pool, "Language Regimes and Political Regimes," pp. 241–257, in Brian Weinstein, *Language Policy and Political Development*, op. cit.
7. See Michael Richardson, "A Language Challenge for Timorese Schools," in *International Herald Tribune*, May 24, 2002, p. 7.
8. Chris C. Park, *Sacred Worlds: An Introduction to Geography and Religion* (London and New York: Routledge, 1994); see also E. Maier, "Torah as Movable Territory," in *Annals of the Association of American Geographers* 65 (1975), pp. 18–23.
9. Benedict Anderson, *Imagined Communities: Reflections on the Origin and Spread of Nationalism*, revised edition (London and New York: Verso, 1991).

BIBLIOGRAPHY

Alberg, Ruben. *Kriyah yeilah bilvrit: HaKativ vehaKatav -haimhem dai tovim?* [Efficient reading in Hebrew, spelling and the alphabet: Are they good enough?], pamphlet (in Hebrew) *Dfus Telegraf*, Bnei-Brak, Israel, 1993.
Appel, Rene, and Peter Muysken. *Language Contact and Bilingualism*. London: Edward Arnold, 1987.
Aquilina, Joseph. "Languages in Contact in Malta." *Journal of Maltese Studies*, 12 (1978), pp. 45–62.
Ardagh, John. *Ireland and the Irish: Portrait of a Changing Society*. London: Penguin Books, 1995.
Arutz-7. "New Egyptian Party 'We Are Not Arabs.'" Nov. 7, 2003. Available on Arabicnews.com.
Askelund, Jan, ed. *Mål og Makt: Det Norske Samlaget*. Oslo, 1971.
Baker, Colin. *Attitudes and Languages*. Multilingual Matters Series, No. 83. Clevedon: Multilingual Matters, 1992.
Banhos Campo, A., et al. *Galiza-Portugal, uma só nação*. Lisbon: Nova Arrancada, 1997.
Baron, G. A., *Semitic and Hamitic Origins*. Philadelphia and London: Milford, 1934.
Barrios, Graciela. Quoted in "Detras del manejo de la lengua, hay actitudes discriminatorias." Servicio Informativo Iberoamericano, Organización de los Estados Iberoamericanos. October 1999. Internet posting.
Bartlett, Robert. "Language and Ethnicity in Medieval Europe," in *Ethnicity*, ed. John Hutchinson and Anthony Smith. Pp. 127–132.
Ben-Rafael, Eliezer. Chapter 13 "The Case of a National Minority" in *Language, Identity and Social Division: The Case of Israel*. Oxford and New York: Clarendon Press, 1994.
Berdichevsky, Norman. *The Danish-German Border Dispute: Aspects of Cultural and Demographic Politics 1815–2001*. Bethesda: Academica Press, 2002.
_____. "Esperanto and Zamenhof." *ARIEL*, 64 (1986), pp. 58–71.
_____. "Hebrew vs. Yiddish: The Worldwide Rivalry." *Midstream* (July–Aug. 2002), pp. 12–16.
_____. "Why Hebrew?" *Israel Affairs*, vol. 2, no. 2 (Winter 1995), pp. 95–114.
Blakart, Rolv Mikkel. *Språk er makt*. Oslo: Pax Forlag, 1973.
Blommaert, Jan. "Language and Nationalism: Comparing Flanders and Tanzania." *Nations and Nationalism* 2/2 (1996), pp. 235–256.
Bokmålsforbundet—Velkommen til Bokmålsforbundet. Website: www.allverden.no/polorg/bokmal/.
Borsody, Stepehn. *The New Central Europe; Triumphs and Tragedies*. New York: Columbia University Press, 1993.
Bowan, C. M. *The Greek Experience*. New York: Mentor, 1957.

Bibliography

Bra, Gerardo. "Donde Nació Carlos Gardel?" *Todo es Historia*, 329 (December, 1994), Buenos Aires, pp. 84–92.
Brass, Paul. *Ethnicity and Nationalism: Theory and Comparison*. Newbury Park, Calif.: Sage, 1992.
Briscoe, I. "Making Children in a Land of Many Tongues." *El País* English language supplement (Feb. 5, 2002).
Brockman, Eric. "The Punic Build-Up," in *Last Bastion: Sketches of the Maltese Island*. London: Darton, Longman and Todd, 1961, pp. 206–217.
Bugarski, R., and C. Hawkesworth, eds. *Language Planning in Yugoslavia*. Columbus, Ohio: Slavica Publishers, 1992.
Burghardt, Andrew F. *Borderland: A Historical and Geographical Study of Burgenland, Austria*. Madison: University of Wisconsin Press, 1962.
Bwrdd yr iath Gymraeg/Welsh Language Board. "A Bilingual Policy: Guidelines for the Public Sector." Cardiff/Caerdydd. 1995.
Calvet, Louis-Jean. *Les politiques linguistiques*. Paris: Presses Universitaires de France, 1996.
Cambridge, R. W. *A History of the Rumanians*. Cambridge and New York: Cambridge University Press, 1934.
Canada. Official website of Canadian Government: "Our Official Languages: As a Century Ends and a Millennium Begins." Office of the Commissioner of Official Languages. Minister of Public Works and Government Services, Canada 2001. Cat. no.: SF31-56/2001. ISBN: 0-662-65975-9.
Carlevaro, Tazio. *Cxu Esperanto Postvivos la Jaron 2045?* Hans Dubois. 2000. Bellinzona, Switzerland.
Carmichael, Joel. *The Nature of Arab Nationalism*. New York: Midstream, 1958.
Carpinelli, G. "Belgium," in *Fascism in Europe*, ed. S. J. Woolf. London and New York: Methuen, 1981. Chapter 33, pp. 283–306.
Chakladar, Snehamoy. "Language Policy and Reformation of India's Federal Structure: The Case of West Bengal," in *Language Policy and Political Development*, ed. Brian Weinstein. Pp. 87–107.
Crystal, David. *The Cambridge Encyclopedia of English*. Cambridge and New York: Cambridge University Press, 1995.
———. *The Cambridge Encyclopedia of Language*. Cambridge and New York: Cambridge University Press, 1987.
Chadwick, H. Munro. *The Nationalities of Europe*. Cambridge and New York: Cambridge University Press, 1945.
Cohen, Leonard. *Broken Bonds: Yugoslavia's Disintegration and Balkan Politics in Transition*. Boulder: Westview Press, 1995.
Cooper, Robert. *Language Planning and Social Change*. Cambridge and New York: Cambridge University Press, 1989.
Custred, Glynn. "Alien Crossings." *The American Spectator* (October, 2000), pp. 38–43.
Cymdeithasol Cymru 1992: adroddiad ar y Gymraeg, Wales. March, 1995.
Daftary, Farimah. "Insular Autonomy: A Framework for Conflict Settlement; A Comparative Study of Corsica and the Åland Islands." European Centre for Minority Issues (ECMI), Flensburg, Germany. Working Paper no. 9, 2000.
———, and Kinga Gál. "The New Slovak Language Laws: Internal or External Politics?" European Centre for Minority Issues (ECMI), Flensburg, Germany. Working Paper no. 8, 2000.
Daoust-Blais, D. "Corpus and Status Language Planning in Quebec: A Look at Linguistic Legislation in Progress," in *Language Planning: International Perspectives*, eds. J. Cobarrubias and J. A. Fishman. Berlin, New York, Amsterdam: Mouton Publishers, 1983, pp. 237–234.

Davidsen-Nielsen, Niels, *et al.* eds. "Dansk Eller Ikke Dansk? That Is the Question." Dansk Sprognævns Skrifter 28. Copenhaegn: Gyldendal, 1999.
Dawidovicz, Lucy. *The War against the Jews, 1933-1945*. New York: Penguin, 1975.
Douglas, Neville. "Political Structures, Social Interaction and Identity Change in Northern Ireland," in *In Search of Ireland: A Cultural Geography*. Brian Graham.
Dyer, Donald L. *The Romanian Dialect of Moldova*. Lewiston, N.Y.: Mellen Press, 1999.
Edwards, John. *Multilingualism*. London: Routledge, 1994.
Elazar, Daniel J. "Two Peoples, One Land: Federal Solutions for Israel, the Palestinians and Jordan." The Jerusalem Center for Public Affairs, 1991.
Elizaicin, Adolfo, and Harold Tuhn, eds. *Atlas Linguistico de Uruguay*. Montevideo: La Facultad de Humanidad y Ciencias de la Educación de la Universidad de la Republica.
Eskildsen, Clause. *Dansk Grænselære*. Denmark: C. A. Reitzels, 1946, p. 140.
European Centre for Minority Issues (ECMI). "From Ethnopolitical Conflict to Inter-Ethnic Accord in Moldova." Conference held in Flensburg, Germany, and Bjerremark, Denmark. September. 1997. ECMI Report no. 1.
Fellman, Jack. "Eliezer Ben-Yehuda." *ARIEL*, no. 104 (1997), pp. 26–31. Jerusalem.
Fernández, Tomás, and Juan José Laborda (coordinators). *España: Cabemos Todos?* Alianza—ensayo. Madrid, 2002.
Fernandez-Armestro, Felipe, ed. "Highland and Lowland Scots," pp. 43–45, and "Swiss," pp. 139–145, in *The Guide to the Peoples of Europe*, revised edition. London: The Times, 1997.
Fishman, Joshua, *et al.* (eds.) *Language Problems of Developing Nations*. New York: John Wiley and Sons, 1968.
_____. "The New Linguistic Order." *Foreign Policy* (Winter, 1998).
_____. *Reversing Language Shift*. Clevedon: Multilingual Matters, 1991.
_____. *The Rise and Fall of the Ethnic Revival: Perspectives on Language and Ethnicity*. Berlin: Mouton, 1985.
Fitzmaurice, John. "New Order? International Models of Peace and Reconciliation-Diversity and Civil Society." Report no. 9, pp. 1–13. Website for Democratic Dialogue, www.democratic dialogue.org/report9/report9d.htm.
Floor, Dennis J. "Switzerland in Arms," in *The Neutrals: World War II*. Alexandria: Time-Life Books, 1983, pp. 28–63.
Garreau, Joel. *The Nine Nations of North America*. New York: Avon, 1981.
Geiple, John. *Mame Loshn: The Making of Yiddish*. London: Journeyman Press, 1982.
Gertz, Nurit. "From Jew to Hebrew: The Zionist Narrative in the Israeli Cinema of the 1940s and 1950s." *Israel Affairs* 4 (3–4) (Spring/Summer, 1998), pp. 175–199.
Gordon, Cyrus H. *Before the Bible: The Common Background of Greek and Hebrew Civilizations*. London: Collins, 1962.
Gordon, D. C. The Arabic Language and National Identity: The Cases of Algeria and Lebanon," in *Language Policy and National Unity*, W. R. Beer and J.E. Jacob, eds. Totowa N.J.: Rowman and Allenheld, 1985, pp. 134–150.
Graham, Brian, ed. *In Search of Ireland: A Cultural Geography*. London and New York: Routledge, 1997.
Granguillaume, Gilbert. "Language and Legitimacy in the Maghreb," in *Language Policy and Political Development*, ed. Brian Weinstein. Pp. 150–166.
Grech, P. "Are There Any Traces of Punic in Maltese?" *Journal of Maltese Studies* 1 (1961), Malta, pp. 130–138.
Grimes, B. F., ed. "Ethnologue: Languages of the World." Dallas: Summer Institute of Linguistics, 1992.
Grin, François. "The Cost-Effectiveness Evaluation of Minority Language Policies:

Case Studies on Wales, Ireland and the Basque Country." ECMI Monograph no. 2. November, 1999. European Centre for Minority Issues, Flensburg, Germany.
_____. "Language Policy and Multilingual Switzerland: Overview and Recent Developments." ECMI Brief no. 2. European Centre for Minority Issues, Flensburg, Germany.
_____. "Towards a Threshold Theory of Minority Language Survival." *Kyklos*, 45 (1992), pp. 69–97.
_____, and François Vaillancourt. "Case Studies on Wales, Ireland and the Basque Country." Monograph no. 2, 1999. European Centre for Minority Issues, Flensburg, Germany.
Grintz, J. M. "On the Original Home of the Semites." *Journal of Near Eastern Studies* 21 (1962), pp. 186–205.
Gunther, John. *Inside Europe*. London: Hamish Hamilton, 1936.
Gutmannn, Jean. *The Significance of Territory*. Charlottesville: University of Virginia Press, 1973.
Halkin, Hillel. "Hebrew as She Is Spoke." *Commentary* (December, 1969), pp. 55–60.
_____. "A Movable Feast." *Jerusalem Report* (April 22, 1993).
Harshav, Benjamin. *Language in a Time of Revolution*. Berkeley: University of California Press, 1993.
Haugen, Einar. *Language Conflict and Language Planning: The Case of Modern Norwegian*. Cambridge: Harvard University Press. 1966.
_____. "Language Fragmentation in Scandinavia: Revolt of the Minorities." Chapter 9 in *Minority Languages Today: A Selection from the Papers read at the First International Conference on Minority Languages*. Glasgow University, 1980, pp. 38–143. Published by the Edinburgh Free Press.
Hartshorne, Richard. "The Concepts of 'Raison d'Être' and 'Maturity' of States: Illustrated from the Mid-Danube Area." *Annals of the Association of American Geographers* (1940) vol. 30, pp. 59–60.
Heller, Joseph. *The Stern Gang: Ideology, Politics and Terror, 1940–1949*. London: Frank Cass, 1995.
Herder, Johann G. von. *Über den Ursprung der Sprache* (On the origin of speech), 1772.
Heyd, Uriel. *Language Reform in Modern Turkey*. Jerusalem: Israel Oriental Society, 1964.
Hindley, Reg. "Defining the Gaeltacht: Dilemmas in Irish Language Planning," in *Linguistic Minorities, Society and Territory*, ed. C. H. Williams. Clevedon: Multilingual Matters, pp. 66–95.
Holmes, Janet. *An Introduction to Sociolinguistics*. London: Longman, 1992.
Hooper, John. *The New Spaniards*. London: Penguin Books, 1995.
Horon, A. G. "Canaan and the Aegean Sea: Greco-Phoenician Origins Reviewed." *Diogenes* 58 (1967).
_____. *Eretz HaKedem: Madrich Histori uMedini LaMizrach HaKarov* (The land of Kedem: A historical and political guide to the Near East). Tel Aviv: Hermon Publishers, 1970.
Horrocks, Geoffrey. *Greek: A History of the Language and Its Speakers*. London and New York: Longman, 1997.
Hull, Geoffrey. *The Malta Language Question: A Case Study in Cultural Imperialism*. Valetta, Malta: Said International, 1993.
Hutchinson, John, and Anthony Smith. *Ethnicity*. Oxford Readers. Oxford: Oxford University Press, 1996.
Hylland Eriksen, Thomas. "Images of the Neighbour: Reciprocal Stereotypes in Scandinavia." Internet archive http://www.uio.no/-geirthe/Scandinavian_images.html. 1998.
_____. "The Nation as a Human Being: a Metaphor in a Mid-Life Crisis? Notes on

the Imminent Collapse of Norwegian National Identity," in *Siting Culture*, eds. Kirsten Hadstrup and Karen Fog Olwig. London and New York: Routledge, 1997.
_____, "Reflections on European Identities and Scandinavian Minorities." Contribution to the IFLA Satellite meeting in Aarhus, Denmark. August 26-28, 1997.
Jabotinsky, Ze'ev. *Hebrew Pronunciation*. Tel-Aviv: HaSefer, 1940, pp. 37-38.
Jacob, J. E., and D.C. Gordon. "Language Policy in France," in *Language Policy and National Unity*. W. R. Beer and J. E. Jacob, eds. Totowa, N.J.: Rowman & Allenheld, 1985.
Jászi, Oscar. *The Dissolution of the Hapsburg Monarchy*. Chicago: University of Chicago Press, 1929.
Jenkins, Philip. *A History of Modern Wales, 1536-1990*. London and New York: Longman, 1993.
Jordan, Terry. *The European Culture Area*. New York: Harper and Row, 1973. Chapter 5, "The Geography of Languages."
Katzner, Kenneth. *The Languages of the World*. London and New York: Routledge, 1995.
Kazantzakis, Nikos. *Zorba the Greek*. New York: Ballantine Books, 1965.
Kenan, Amos. "Envy Tyre." *Yediot Ahronot* (June 18, 1982.) Israeli daily newspaper.
Kissin, Yitzhak, ed. *Antologia shel HaSifrut HaLitait*. Kaunas, Lithuania, 1932.
Köpeczi, B., ed. *A History of Transylvania*. Budapest: East European Monographs, 1996.
Krejci, Jaroslav, and Jaroslav Velimsk. "Ethnic and Political Nations in Europe," in *Ethnicity*, ed. Hutchinson and Smith. Pp. 209-221.
Kühne, Claus. "Die Gemeinde hat keine Moral und spricht nicht Deutsch." *Slesvigland* 3 (1983). Pp. 87-88.
Kurlansky, Mark. *The Basque History of the World*. New York: Random House, 1999.
Labrie, Normand, and C. Quell. "Your Language, My Language or English? The Potential Language Choice in Communication among Nationals of the European Union." *World Englishes*, vol. 16. 1997, pp. 3-26.
Lafont, R. *La Révolution Régionaliste*. Paris: Gallimard, 1967.
Lammens, Henri. *La Syrie: Précis Historique*. Beirut: Imprimérie Catholique, 1921.
Lamont, Lansing. *Breakup—The Coming End of Canada and the Stakes for America*. New York: W. W. Norton, 1994.
Landau, Jacob M. "Hebrew and Arabic in the State of Israel: Political Aspects of the Language Issue." *International Journal of the Sociology of Language* 67 (1987), pp. 117-133.
_____. "Language Policy and Political Development in Israel and Turkey," in *Policy and Political Development*, ed. Brian Weinstein. 1990, pp. 133-149.
_____. *Pan-Turkism in Turkey: A Study in Irredentism*. London: C. Hurst, 1981.
Lega Nord. Padania: The Foundations of a Nation. Website: www.leganord.org/eng/re,ake.htm.
Lewis, Bernard. *The Arabs in History*. New York: Harper and Row, 1966.
Lewis, Geoffrey. *The Turkish Language Reform: A Catastrophic Success*. Oxford: Oxford University Press, 1999.
Liebl, Elizabeth. "Herkunft der Kinder," in *Atlas der Schweizerische Volkskunde*, vol. 2, part 4, plates 202-205, ed. Paul Geiger *et al*. Basel: Schweizerische Gesellschaft für Volkskunde.
Lodares, Juan Ramón. *Gente de Cervantes: Historia human del idioma español*. Madrid: Taurus, 2001.
López Mira, Alvaro Xosé. *A Galicia Irredenta*. Ediciòns Xerais de Galicia. 1998.
Loughlin, John. "Regionalism and Ethnic Nationalism in France," Chapter 8 in *Centre-Periphery Relations in Western Europe*. Pp. 207-235.

Bibliography

MacAoidh, Garbhan. "La Gaela Lingvo en Skotlando." Pamphlet. Kardo and Glasgow: Polyglot Publications, 2001.
MacKinnon, Kenneth. *Gaelic—A Past and Future Prospect*. Edinburgh: The Saltire Society, 1991.
Mackridge, P. *Background to Contemporary Greece*, vol. I, ed. M. Saraphe and M. Eve. London: Merlin Press, 1990.
McCartney, C. A. *Hungary and Her Successors: The Treaty of Trianon and Its Consequences, 1919–1937*. London, 1937.
McClure, Douglas. "Why Scots Matters: The Scots Language Is a Priceless National Possession." Pamphlet. Edinburgh: Saltire Society, 1988.
McFerren, M. "Country Status Report: South Africa, 1984." Washington, D.C.: Center for Applied Linguistics.
McKay, Ross. "The Interactance Hypothesis and Boundaries in Canada: A Preliminary Study." *Canadian Geographer* XI (1958), pp. 1–8.
McLeod, Wilson. "Gaelic in the New Scotland: Politics, Rhetoric and Public Discourse." *Journal of Ethnopolitics and Minority Issues in Europe* (Summer, 2001).
McWhorter, John. H. *The Power of Babel: A Natural History of Language*. London: William Heinemann, 2001.
Maier, E. "Torah as Movable Territory." *Annals of the Association of American Geographers* 65 (1975). Pp. 18–23.
Maugué, P. *La Particularisme Alsacien, 1928–1967*. Paris: Presses d'Europe, 1970.
Menshri, David, ed. *Central Asia Meets the Middle East*. London: Frank Cass, 1998.
Milon Megiddo Hadish (Hebrew-English dictionary) Tel Aviv: Megiddo Pub. Co. Ltd. 1990.
Mizzi, Lewis. *What Is the Maltese Language?* Valetta, Malta: Progress Press, 1923.
Moleas, W. *The Development of the Greek Language*. London: Bristol Classical Press, 1989.
Moroz, Valentine. "Report from the Beria Reserve," Chicago, 1974; reprinted in *Ethnicity*, eds. John Hutchinson and Anthony Smith. Oxford Readers, 1996, p. 54.
New Statesmen, special issue, 5(207) June 19, 1992. Devoted to regionalism in Europe and geography of languages. Pp. 24–31.
Norges Mållag "Globaliseringa, språket og maten." Website www.nm.no//side.efm/1660/33423.
Oftedal, Magne. "Is Nynorsk a Minority Language?" in *Minority Languages Today*, ed. Einar Haugen.
O'Túama, S., ed. *The Gaelic League Idea: Dublin, 1972*. Cork, Ireland: Mercier.
Paredes, Xóan M. "The World Seen from the Corner: The Galician Globalisation." *Chimera*, 16 (2001). Department of Geography, UCC Cork, Ireland.
Park, Chris C. *Sacred Worlds: An Introduction to Geography and Religion*. London and New York: Routledge, 1994.
Patai, Raphael. *The Arab Mind*, revised edition. New York: Scribner's, 1983.
Pei, Mario. *The Story of Language*, revised edition. New York: Mentor Books, 1966.
Phillips, Eugène. *Les luttes linguistiques en Alsace jusqu'en 1945*. Strasbourg: Culture Alsacienne, 1975, p. 107.
Pipes, Daniel. *Greater Syria: The History of an Ambition*. Oxford and New York: Oxford University Press, 1990.
Pirenne, Henri. *A History of Europe, from the End of the Roman World in the West to the Beginnings of the Western States*. New York: Doubleday, 1956.
Poleshcunk, Vadim. "Multiculturalism, Minority Education and Language Policy." ECMI Workshops held in Estonia and Latvia. ECMI Report no. 10. August, 2001. European Centre for Minority Issues, Flensburg, Germany.
Pool, Jonathan. "Language Regimes and Political Regimes," in *Language Policy and Political Development*, ed. Brian Weinstein. Pp. 241–257.

———. "The Official Language Problem." *American Political Science Review* 85, pp. 495–514.
Preca, Annibale. *Saggio intorno alla lingua maltese come affine all'ebraico.* Malta: Micallef, 1880.
Purves, David. *A Scots Grammar: Scots Grammar and Usage.* Edinburgh: The Saltire Society, 1997. (See introduction.)
Rejwan, Nissim. "Egyptians and Arabs: The Continuing Controversy." *Midstream* 47 (January, 2001), pp. 6–9.
Renfrew, Colin. *Archaeology and Language: The Puzzle of Indo-European Origins.* London: Pimlico, 1998.
Reuter, Mikael. "The Status of Swedish in Finland in Theory and Practice," in *Minority Languages Today: A Selection of Papers Read at the First International Conference on Minority Languages.* Held at Glasgow University, 1980. Published by Edinburgh Free Press. Pp. 130–137.
Richardson, Michael. "A Language Challenge for Timorese Schools." *International Herald Tribune*, May 24, 2002, p. 7.
Rosén, Haiim B. "Israel Language Policy, Teaching and Linguistics." *ARIEL* 25 (1969), pp. 92–112.
Rossini, Enzo. *Malta on the Brink: From Western Democracy to Libyan Satellite.* London: Hyperion, 1986.
Rustow, D. A. "Languages, Nations and Democracy," in *Les états multilingues: problèmes et solutions*, J.-G. Savard and R. Vigneault, eds. Quebec: Les Presses de l'Université Laval, 1875.
Sasson, Somekh. "Echoes of New Hebrew Literature in Arab Culture," in *ARIEL* 105 (1997).
Saydon, Pietro Paolo. *The Development of Maltese as a Written Language and Its Affinities with Other Semitic Tongues.* Valetta, Malta, 1928.
Schoch, Bruno. "Switzerland—A Model for Solving Nationality Conflicts?" Frankfurt: Peace Research Institute, PRIF Report 54/2000.
Seton-Watson, H. *Language and National Consciousness.* London: British Academy, 1981.
Shaheedaeg, Haseeb. "The Hebrew of Arabs in Israel." Paper delivered at Third Nordic Conference on Middle Eastern Studies: Ethnic Encounter and Cultural Change. Joensuu, Finland, June 19–22, 1995.
Shavit, Ya'acov. *From Hebrew to Canaanite: Aspects in the History, Ideology and Utopia of the Hebrew Renaissance—from Radical Zionism to Anti-Zionism.* Jerusalem: Domino Press, 1995.
Sivan, Reuven. "Ben-Yehuda and the Revival of Hebrew Speech." *ARIEL* 25 (1969), pp. 35–39.
———. *Leksikon LiShipur HaLashon* (Better Hebrew usage). Tel Aviv: Karni, 1969.
Smith, Anthony D. *The Ethnic Origins of Nations.* Oxford: Blackwell, 1984.
———. *The Ethnic Revival.* Cambridge: Cambridge University Press, 1981.
Spolsky, B., and R. L. Cooper. *The Languages of Jerusalem.* Oxford: Clarendon Press, 1991.
Steinberg, Jonathan. *Why Switzerland?* Cambridge: Cambridge University Press, 1996.
Stephens, M., ed. *Linguistic Minorities in Western Europe.* Llandsul, Wales: Gomer Press, 1976.
Sukhwal, L. *Modern Political Geography of India.* New Delhi. 1985.
Søndergaard, Bent. "The Fight for Survival: Danish as a Living Minority Language South of the German Border," in *Minority Languages Today: A Selection from the Papers Read at the First International Conference on Minority Languages.* Held at Glasgow University, 1980. Published by Edinburgh Free Press. Pp. 38–143.

Sørenson, Knud. *Engelsk i dansk: Er det et must?* Copenhagen: Munksgaard, 1995.
Tagil, Sven, ed. *Ethnicity and Nation-Building in the Nordic World.* London: Hurst and Company, 1993.
Tene, David. "Israeli Hebrew." *ARIEL* 25 (1969).
Thompson, Holland, ed. "The World's Greatest War: From the Outbreak of the War to the Treaty of Versailles," vol. XVI in *The Book of History Series.* New York and London: Grolier Society, 1920.
Thürer, G. *Free and Swiss.* Coral Gables: University of Miami Press, 1971.
Trudgill, Peter. *Language in the British Isles.* Cambridge: Cambridge University Press, 1984.
Unwin, D. W. "The Price of a Kingdom, Territory Identity and the Centre-Periphery Dimension in Western Europe," in *Centre-Periphery Relations in Western Europe.* eds. Y. Meny and V. Wright. London: Unwin Hyman, 1995.
Vail, Leroy. "The Creation of Ethnicity in South Africa," in *Ethnicity* by Hutchinson and Smith. 1996.
Vallières, Pierre. *The White Niggers of America* (in French). Toronto: McClelland and Stewart, 1971.
Vidart, Daniel. "La Trama de la Identidad Nacional," vol. 3 of *El Espíritu Criollo.* Ediciones de la Montevideo: Banda Oriental, 2000.
Vikør, Lars S. *The New Norse Language Movement.* Oslo: Forlaget Novus, 1975.
_____. *Vegen frem til ett norsk.* Oslo: Landslaget for språklig samling, 1968.
"Vlaandern-Europa 2002: een project van de Vlaamse Regering." Lannoo: Tielt, 1993.
Wagner, Philip. "Remarks on the Geography of Language." *Geographical Review* 48 (1958), pp. 86–97.
Wakin, E. *A Lonely Minority: The Modern Story of Egypt's Copts.* New York: W. Morrow, 1963.
Wardhaugh, Ronald. *Language and Nationhood: The Canadian Experience.* Vancouver: New Star Books, 1983.
_____. *Languages in Competition.* Oxford and New York: Basil Blackwell, 1987.
Webster, D. E. *The Turkey of Atatürk.* Philadelphia: American Academy of Political and Social Science, 1939.
Weinberg, Werner. *Tikun HaKtiv HaIvri: Habaiya vehaNisyonot liftora* (The orthographic reform of Hebrew: The problem and the attempts to solve it). Hebrew University. Jerusalem. 1971.
Weinstein, Brian. *The Civic Tongue: Political Consequences of Language Choice.* New York: Longman, 1983.
_____. "Francophonie: Language Planning and National Interests," in *Language and Power*, ed. C. Kramarae *et al.* Beverly Hills and London: Sage, 1984, pp. 227–241.
_____, ed. *Language Policy and Political Development.* Norwood, N.J.: Ablex Publishing Corporation, 1990.
Weulresse, Jacques. *Paysans de Syrie et du Proche-Orient.* Paris: Gallimard, 1946, pp. 84–85.
Williams, Colin. *Linguistic Minorities. Society and Territory.* Clevedon: Multilingual Matters, 1991.
Williams, Mark. *The Story of Spain.* Malaga, Spain: Santana Books, 1992.
Zuwiyva-Yamak, Labib. *The Syrian Social Nationalist Party: An Ideological Analysis.* Cambridge and London: Harvard University Press, 1966.

INDEX

Aasen, Ivar 47, 57, 64
Adige River 158
Adrian IV, Pope 200
Afghanistan 139, 226
Afrikaans and Afrikaaners 89, 129–133
Akkadian 233
El Alamein 147
Åland islands 9, 199–204
Al-Aqqad, Abbas Mahmoud 235
Alba and "Albanians" (Scottish Gaelic-Nationalists) 148
Albania and Albanian 165, 167–168, 181–182, 229, 234
Alberg, Reuben 37
Albert King of Belgium 82, 83
Al-Bustani Butrus 236
Alemania (German-speaking Switzerland) 99–102
Alexander the Great 226
Algeria 234, 239
Alicante 109
Almagor, Dan 209
Al-Mun'im, Salim 210
Alsace, Alsace-Lorraine and Alsatians 99, 136, 187–190, 199
Al-Tahtawi, Rafa 236
Al-Uman, Nnshua 236
Americans and American English *see* USA
Amihai, Yehuda 211
Amur valley 34
Anatolia 125, 227, 242–243
Ancona 158
Andalucia 106, 211
Andorra 249
Angola 249
Antrim, County 151
Antwerp 21, 80, 82, 89
Apartheid 130–131, 256
'Aql, Said 246

Arabic, Arabs, Arab nationalism 5, 9, 14, 15, 29, 30, 35–37, 41–45, 67–72, 232–244, 205–211, 232–240, 251
Arafat, Yasser 42
Aragon 104–106
Aral Sea 243
Aramaic 232–236, 251
Aran 49
Arana, Sabino 113–114
Argentina 3, 9, 34, 215–221
Aristotle 227
Armenian and Armenians 135, 229, 234
Artusi, Apelligrimo 137
Assamese 124
Assyrians 233–236
Atatürk, Kemal (Mustafa Kemal) 241–244
Athens 9
Attic Greek 224–227, 251
Australia 3, 4, 51, 53, 148, 246
Austria and Austria-Hungary 10, 16, 18–20, 23, 93, 99–101, 158, 182, 196
Axis powers 98, 183
Azerbaijan 243

Balearic Islands 67, 106, 109–111
Balkanization 148, 166–167, 170, 181, 186, 225–226, 229, 241
Bantu Education Act 133
Barrios, Graciela 219
Bartram, Walter 197
Bashevis Singer, Isaac 19
Basques, Basque (Vasco), or Euskera 14, 20, 32, 42, 63, 103–105, 112–115, 252
Beasley, Trefor 143
Belfast 48
Belgium 7, 9, 20–21, 55, 75, 77–92, 100, 119, 123, 170, 188, 190, 205, 215, 246, 252, 255–256

Index

Ben-Avi, Itamar 26, 38
Bengali 124, 126, 128
Ben-Shazar, Zalman 16
Ben-Yehuda, Eliezer 14, 24, 26, 28–29, 38–39, 47, 49
Berbers 233–234, 239, 248
Bergen 57, 60
Bessariabia 174–176
Bethmann-Hollwegg Chancellor 83
Bharat 125
Bhassa-Indonesian 214
The Bible 16, 28, 29, 37, 39, 55, 68, 69, 79, 140, 149, 168, 188, 209, 223, 229, 236, 247
bilingualism: in Belgium 83–101; in Canada 130–136, 146; in Finland 209–215; in Israel 215–222; in South Schleswig (Slesvig), Germany 198–208; in Spain 115–127; in Uruguay 223–230
Birnbaum, Nathan 18
Birobizhan 36–38
Black Plague 56
Black Sea 25 125, 200, 226
Blancos 217
Bnei Brak 39
Boccaccio, Giovanni 157
Boers *see* Afrikaaners
Bokmålsforbundet 7, 55, 63
Bolivia 10, 256
Bond, James 148
Book of Judges 79
Bornholm 197
Bosnia, Bosnians, and Bosnian 165–168
Brande, Van den Luc 87
Brazil 9, 215, 217, 219, 221, 255–257
Breton 2021
Breydek, Jan 79–80
Brittany 147
Brooklyn and Brooklynese 154
Bruges 77, 79–80
Brussels 81, 87–91
Buenos Aires 216, 220–221
Bulgaria and Bulgarian 8, 33, 165, 174, 229
The *Bund* 16
Burgenland 196
Burns, Robert 148
Burton, Richard 141
Byelorussian (White Russian) 8, 33, 80–81, 163
Byron, Lord 227
Byzantine Empire, Byzantium, Byzantine civilization 9, 175, 179, 226–227

Cairo 210
Canaanites 236–237
Canada 3, 7, 51, 53, 55, 89, 116–122
Cape Dutch 130
Carthage 24, 68–69, 72
Caspian Sea 253
Castillian (Castellano) or Castillian Spanish 3, 5, 42–43, 77, 103–115
Catalonia, Catalans and Catalan 14, 15, 20, 42–43, 47, 104–111
CDU 197
Ceauşescu, Nicolae 175, 183
Celtic languages 7, 44–45, 47, 50, 52, 78, 94, 148–152
Charlemagne 78–79
Charleroi 80
Charles, Prince of Wales 143
Charlie, Bonnie Prince 151
Charrua Indians 220–221
Chinese 10, 103, 247
Chur 101
Church Slavonic 165
Churchill, Winston 48, 85, 116
Circassians 14, 209–210
Ciskei 133
CiU 107
Colonia del Sacramento 216, 218
Colorados (The Reds) 217
Condombé 216
Confessional Church 197
Congress Party 128
Conine de, Pieter 86
Constantine I, King of Greece 229
Constantine the Great 226
Coptic 233–236, 251
Corm, Charles 237
Corsica and Corsicans 20, 32, 67, 71, 100 106, 199
Crete 227–228
Crimea 36, 226, 229
Croatia, Croats and Serbo-Croatian 32, 80, 163–168, 248, 254, 256
Cronin, Sean 49
Crystal, David 146
Cuba 112, 114, 216, 256
Cyprus 225, 228, 230, 236, 243
Cyrillic alphabet 8, 165, 168, 174–175, 244
Czech Republic, former Czechslovakia and Czech 7, 8, 10, 38, 161, 165, 170–173, 176–177, 244, 248, 254–256
Czernowitz (Tshernovits) 15, 18

Index

Dacia 181
Danish, Danes and Denmark 8, 9, 40, 50, 55–64, 60, 80, 107, 153, 160, 179, 191–198, 254
Dante Aligheiri 157
Darwish, Mahmud 211
Deixonne Law 190
Demotike 9, 10, 228–231, 242
Densusianu, Ovid 182
De Valera, Eamon 48, 142, 249
Devanagari script 125
dialects 153–155
Diaspora 14–16, 23, 34–35, 41–42
Diglossia 41
Dijon 78
Dneister River 175
Doctor's Plot 36
Douglas, Neville 52
Dravidian languages 125, 140
Dreyfus affair 82
Druze 14, 220–221, 246
Dublin 50, 54, 60
Dunkirk 85–86
Dutch 50, 77–81, 84–85, 88–89

East Timor 249–250
Ebri (Judeo-Persian) 15
Edward I, King of England 139
Egypt and Egyptians 35–36, 205, 208, 210–211, 226, 232–240, 251
Ehrenfried Stoeber, Daniel 187
Eider River 195
Eilat 210
Elkind Group 34–35
English 3–8, 10, 15, 17, 19, 20–21, 29, 30, 32, 37–38, 41–42, 44–54, 61–67, 70–74, 81, 87, 89, 102–105, 109, 116–152, 210, 215, 227, 242, 246–247, 251, 253, 255
Eskildsen, Claus 191
Esperanto 17, 24, 28, 50, 253, 257
Estonia and Estonian 19, 22, 32, 35, 154
ETA 113
Ethiopia 70
Eupen-Malmedy 82, 88
European Community and European Union (EU) 25–26, 32, 44–45, 50–51, 58, 64, 71, 89–91
Eurovision 42, 52–53, 73, 77
Euskera *see* Basque
Evans, Gwynford 144

Faeroe Islands, Faeroese 57, 62, 82, 197
Falkland Islands 147

Fanagalo 133
Federalism 96–97
Ferdinand, Archduke 176
Ferdinand VII, King of Spain 216–217
Finland and Finnish 5, 9, 37, 179, 199–205, 254, 256
Finnish speaking Swedes, Finlanders (Swedish minority in Finland) 9, 199–205, 254
Fischer, Christopher Heinrich 193
Fishman, Joshua 138
Flanders, Flemings and Flemish 7, 21, 78, 80–91, 128, 197
Flatley, Michael 53
Flensborg Avis 195–197
Flensburg (Flensborg) 194–196
Florence 170
Franck, Helmar 50
Franco, Francisco 112
Francophonie 128, 133
France 3, 20, 77, 79, 82–85, 89–90, 94–95, 97, .109, 111, 114, 151, 187–190, 238, 254
French language 3, 9, 10, 15, 19, 21–22, 29, 32, 40, 42, 50, 77–88, 89–102 , 105, 107, 109, 111, 116, 118–123, 131, 139, 174–175, 197, 205, 215, 229, 237, 239, 242, 243, 246, 252, 254
Frumkin, Israel Dov 25
Fyn 194

Gaelic *see* Scottish Gaelic and Irish Gaelic (Erse)
Gaelic Athletic Association 52
Gaelic League 52–53
Gagauz 176
Gaidhealtachd 151
Galetacht 45–53
Galician (*Gallego*) 103–105, 111–112, 247, 252
Gandhi, Indira 127
Gandhi, Mahatma 127
Gandhi, Rajiv 127
Gardel, Carlos 220
Garibaldi 157
Gauchos 216
Geneva 50, 99
Genoa 158
Genootskap vir Regte Afrikaanders 130
German language (standard) 9, 10, 13, 15, 19, 20, 22, 25, 29–30, 36, 40, 50, 78, 87–89, 91–94, 99–102
Germany, Germans and German minorities 26, 40, 48, 77, 79, 81–86,

91-93, 95, 97-98, 166, 168, 171-172, 182-183, 188-198, 238, 243, 246, 248, 255-156
Ghent 77, 81-83
Gladstone, William 141
Glagolithic script 168-170
Glasgow 151
Globalism 63-64
Graubünden 101
Great Britain *see* United Kingdom
Greece, Greek and Greeks including *koine, demotike, katharevousa* 5, 9, 14-15, 45-46, 68, 96, 106, 167, 170, 175-176, 180, 223, 228-240, 242, 244, 250, 251 255, 261, 267
Greenland 191
Grossman, David 221
Guarani 220
Gujarati 124
Gunther, John 178
gypsies 178, 183; *see also* Roma language

Ha Aretz 26
Ha Mathil 26
Ha'Am, Ahad (Asher Ginsburg) 16
Habibi, Emile 211
Habimah Theater 39
Hahavatzelet 25-26
Haiti 3, 246
Haketia 15
HaKtiv HaMaleh 37
Halkin, Hillel 41
Hannibal 25, 67-68
Ha'Or 26
Hartshorne, Richard 5
Hasein, Taha 235
Hashkafah 28
Havana 112
Haykal, Muhammad Hussein 235
HaZvi 26
Hebrew 13-43, 114, 153, 168, 205-211, 223, 229, 233, 236-237, 242, 247-248, 250-251, 252-255
Hebrew Committee for National Liberation 23
Hebrew speaking Israeli Arabs 205-211
Hebrew University 17
Helsinki 199, 201, 204
Henry III, King of England 139
Henry IV, King of England 140
Henry VII, King of England 140
Herder, Johan Gottfried von 3, 6, 9, 132, 181, 246-247, 250, 253, 255
Herzl, Theodore 12
Hesse, Herman 100
Hindi 124-128, 249, 252
Hitler, Adolf 2, 4, 124, 136, 172, 189, 246
Hochdeutsch 198
Hourani, Albert 239
House of Orange 99
Huguenots 130
Hungary and Hungarian 9, 16, 20, 26, 165, 168, 171-173, 175, 181-190, 196, 246, 248, 253-254
Hussein, Saddam 238
Hyde, Douglas 47, 49
Hylland Eriksen, Thomas 160

Ibiza and *Ibicenco* 109
Iliad and Odyssey 44, 226
Illyria 189
India 6, 124-128, 262, 265
Indonesia 10, 259
IRA 46, 53
Iran *see* Persia
Iraq 221, 242, 248, 251
Ireland and Irish Gaelic (Erse) 5, 6, 7, 10, 21, 44-61, 73, 99, 155, 157, 162, 254, 256, 258, 260, 265-266
Irgun 25, 247
Israel 5, 13, 28, 38-48, 54, 99, 107, 188, 205-211, 241, 260, 264, 266
Italy, Italian (standard) and Italian dialects 7, 40, 50, 63, 66-68, 70-73, 79, 84, 92-95, 97-98, 100-102, 104, 105, 108-109, 111-112, 170-173, 185, 248, 254, 262, 264-265

Jabotinsky, Ze'ev 16, 20-22
James VI, King of England 147
Japan and Japanese 123, 246
Jewish Autonomous Oblast *see* Birobidzhan
Jews 13-43, 98, 106, 109, 151, 168, 189, 205-210, 215-222, 242, 247, 250, 256, 260
Jones, Tom 141
Jordan 126, 205, 210, 234, 236-237
Joyce, James 52

Kadar, Janos 183
Kalevala 48, 200
Kalinin 34
Kannada 124
Karamanli Christians 228
Kashmir and Kashmiri 124

Index

Katznelson, Rachel 16
Kazakhstan 243
Kells, Book of 45, 54
Kenan, Amos 211
Kerry 55
Khaddafi, Omar 72, 138, 149
Kiel 199
Knights of St. John 75
Koine 226-227, 251
Kol Yisrael (Israel Broadcast Authority) 26-28
Kolozsvar (Cluj) 184
Konkani 124
The Koran 9, 45, 232, 235, 238, 239, 241
Korea 4, 246-247
Kosovo 165
Kurds 135, 233-234
Kuwait 238
Kyrgyzstan 243

Ladino (Judezmo, Haketia, Sephardi or Judeo-Español) 15
Lallans 148, 150
Lammens, Henri 245
La Plata River and region 9, 215-217, 256
Latin America 11
Latin and Latin alphabet 8, 105, 125, 140, 157, 165, 174-176, 181-183, 188, 221, 229, 232, 142, 144, 148, 153
Latvia and Latvian 19-23, 35, 154
Lebanon 233-234, 233-234, 236-239
Lee, Joseph 52
Lega Nord 158, 161
Lehi (The Stern Gang) 25, 237
Lenin, Nicolai 35
Leon 116
Leopold III, King of Belgium 93
Levy, David 41
Lewis, Geoffrey 242
Lewis, Saunders 143
Libya 78, 80, 208, 234, 238-240
Liege 81, 87, 89
Lille 95
Linna, Vaino 37
Lithuania and Lithuanian 19-20, 22-23, 35, 154, 197
Llewelyn ap Gruffudd 139
Loazi 32-34
London 51, 72, 143, 148, 155
Lorraine 187-190, 193, 199
Louvain 96
Loyshen Kodesh 42

Luxembourg 109
Lucerne 92

Maastricht 95
Macedonia and Macedonian 165-168, 226, 229-231
Madrid 107, 114
Madrid Peace Conference 41
The Mafia 159
Maghreb 233, 239
Maharashtra 126
Majadla, Ghaleb 208
Major, John 79
Makeeba, Miriam 132
Malay 130
Malayalam 124, 126
Mallorca and *Mallorquin* 109
Malmedy 89
Malta and Maltese 66-74
Manchuria 36
Mandarin 10
Manipuri 126
Mannerheim, Carl Gustaf Emile, Marshall 202
MAR (Moldavian Autonomous Region) 175
Marais and Miranda (Josef Marais and his wife Miranda) 132
Marathi 124
Marxism 32-33
Masaryk, Thomas 171
Mazzini, Giuseppe 157
McClure, Douglas 150
McKay, Ross 122
McKinnon, Kenneth 137
Megali idea 227
Meir, Golda 36
Mexico 3, 10
Michael, Sammi 211
Milan 111, 172
Mintoff, Dom and Moyra 66, 71-72
Mizzi, Fortunato 67, 70
Mogul Empire 125-127
Moldavian and Moldavians 7, 8, 35, 163, 174-177, 184, 248, 253-254
Moldova 184-187
Moltke, General von 90
Mons 87
Montivideo 215-219, 221
Montreal 122
Morocco 44, 232, 234, 239
Mousa, Slama 244
Mozambique 249
Mussolini, Benito 78, 100

Namibia 131
Namur 97
Naples 157, 159
Napoleon and Napoleonic Wars 5, 56, 100
Nasser, Gamel Abdul 238
Natal Province 132
Nationalist Party, Afrikaaner 131–134
Nazi party 114, 172, 189, 195, 197
Nehru, Jawaharlal 125
Nepali 124
The Netherlands 132, 246, 252
Neuchatel 109
New Zealand 117, 132, 148, 246, 252
Ni Dhomnaill Nuala 49
Niemoller, Martin 197
Norn 148
Northumbria 150
Norway 7, 8, 13, 40–42, 55–65, 153, 157, 160–161, 197, 228–229, 232, 247–249, 251, 255–256
Norwegian (also Dano-Norwegian, Bokmål, Landsmål, Nynorsk) 14, 40, 47, 55–65, 251, 256
Nova Scotia 118, 150
Novi Sad 168

O Faoláin, Seán 51
O hEallaithe, Donnacha 51
Odense 194
Odessa 175, 230
O'Donnel, Peggy 49
Ontario 120
Oriya 124
Orkney islands 148
Oslo 42, 57, 58
Osmanlica 241–242
Ottawa 120
Ottoman Empire 210, 227, 233–234, 236, 241, 243
Outer Hebrides 148
Oz, Amos 37

Palestine and mandatory Palestine 14, 16–19, 21–26, 34–35, 41, 47, 49, 73, 229, 236–238, 240, 253
Pan-Netherlandish League 84
Parents' Movement Against Linguistic Unification 68
Paris 114, 138, 140, 151, 155, 168, 189, 228
Pashtu 234
Patai, Raphael 233
The Patriot 130

Pei, Mario 153–154, 157
Peres, Shimon 42
Persia (Iran), Persian (Farsi) 10, 32, 125–126, 132, 233
Perugia 158
Pétain, Marshal of France 116
Petrarch 157
Phanariots 227
Pharaohism (*fir'awniyya*) 235
Philippines 10, 107
Phoenicia 75–77, 233, 235–237
Pierlot, Premier of Belgium 85
Pirenne, Henri 79, 85
Plaid Cymru see Welsh National Party
Plato 227
Poe, Edgar Allan 22
Poirot, Hercule 84
Polaei Zion 17
Poland, Poles and Polish 19–20, 29, 44–45, 135, 178
Ponsonby, John Lord 217
Portugal and Portuguese 9, 10, 16, 140, 146, 171, 213, 215–220, 232, 246–250, 256–257
Portuñol 219–221
Prague 172
Prakim meSefer 21
Preca, Annibale 47, 77
Psicharis, Ioannis 228
Puerto Rico 114
Punjab and Punjabi 124, 127

Qawmiyya nationalism 238
Quebec and the Quebecois 108, 117–123, 246, 252, 256
Quixote Don 105–106

Rabin, Yitzhak 41–42
Remarque, Erich Maria 100
Renan, Ernest 136
Revisionist Movement 21
Rex 91–92
Reynaud, Premier of France 94
Rhine River 107, 188
Rhineland 91
Richardson, Michael 259
Robeson, Paul 39
Robins, Philip 252
Robinson, Mary 48
Roma language 183
Romandia 92, 99
Romania and Romanian language 8, 9, 20, 26, 163, 165, 174–179, 181–186, 229, 232, 248, 253–254

Index

Romansch (also Rhaeto-Romansch, Rhaeto-Romanic or "Lingua Svizra") 101–102
Rome 157, 159
Roosevelt, Theodore 114
Rosen, Haim B. 208
Rosetta stone 245
Rossini, Enzo 80
Roumanian *see* Romanian
RTE (Irish National Television) 51
Rumania *see* Romania
Russia and Russian language 5, 8, 10, 19, 20, 22, 25–26, 30, 33, 40, 105, 135, 154, 161, 163, 165, 167, 171, 174–177, 199–200, 205, 210–211, 227, 229–230, 243, 247–248
Rustow, D. A. 246

Sa'ada, Antoin 245
Sanskrit 124–127
Santiago de Compostela 111
Sardinia and Sardinian 106, 154
Scandinavian languages and "dialects" 153, 159–161
Scheveningen 86
Der Schleswiger 195, 197
Schoch, Bruno 108
Schwyzerdütsch 6, 99–102
Scotland, Scots, Scottish Gaelic and Scottish Nationalist Party 7, 44–45, 49, 51, 57, 106, 118, 135–139, 143–152, 256–262, 246, 253, 256
Scott, Sir Walter 148
Scottish Parliament 7
Sephardi Jews 16, 19
Serbs, Serbian and Serbo-Croatian 108, 165–168, 227, 248, 253–254, 256
Shalev, Meir 37
Shamir, Yitzhak 46
Shammas, Anton 205
Shaw, Bernard 59
Shetland Islands 148
Shibboleth 85–86
Sibelius, Jean 200, 203
Sicily 106, 147, 157–159
Sikhs 127
Silone, Ignacio 100
Sindhi 124
Singapore 10
Sinn Fein 142
Skopje 231
Slavic languages 14
Slovakia, Slovak and Slovaks 161, 163, 165, 168, 170–171, 248, 253–256

Slovenian and Slovenians 158, 165, 168
Socioloects 30
Sokolow, Nahum 49
Soloveichik, Max 23
Somaliland 78
Sønderjysk 194, 197
Sorbs 197
South Africa 7, 84, 124, 129–133, 253, 255
South Jutland 192–193, 197
South Slesvig and South Slesvigers 191–198, 254
Sovietish Heymland 35
Spain and Spanish 4, 21, 103–115, 170, 209, 215–218, 223, 232, 234, 247, 252, 255–256; *see also* Catalan, Galician, Basque and Valencian
Sparta 10
Spolsky, B. 27
SSNP 236
SSW 198
Strasbourg 187–190
Suez Canal 70
La Suisse Romande (French Switzerland or *Romandia*) 99
Sweden, Swedes and Swedish language 153, 157, 160, 179, 199–204, 206, 246, 248, 254–255
Swift, Johnathan 59
Swiss Nazi Party 98
Switzerland 3, 4, 6, 83, 92–102, 136–137, 158, 166, 188, 193, 221, 246, 252–253, 256
Syria 208, 210, 232, 232–2237, 247, 251
Syriac 233–234, 236
Szekely region and Szeklers 182

Talmud 42, 223
Tamil 124, 126
Tay River (boundary between Scottish highlands and lowlands) 147
TDR (Transdnistran Republic) 176
Teilifis na Gaelige 50
Tell, Wilhelm 91
Telugu 124
Tetum 249
Thailand 246
Thirty Years War 94, 188
Thomas, Dylan 141
Thrace 229
Ticino (Italian-speaking Switzerland) 93, 97, 100–102
Tin-Tin 84

Tønning 195
Transkei 133
Transvaal 132–133
Transylvania 181–186
Treaty of Tordesillas 215
Trieste 158
Tromsø 60
Trondheim 60
Turin 158
Turkey, Turks and Turkish 9, 10, 19, 25, 73, 166–167, 174, 176, 181, 182, 186, 210, 223, 227–230, 233–234, 237, 241–244, 251
Turkmenistan 243
Tuscany and Tuscan 155, 157–158
Tyrol and Southern Tyrol 158

Ukraine and Ukrainian 8, 10, 35, 123, 161, 174–176, 248
Ulpanim 29, 47
Ulster, Scotch-Irish and Unionism 46–48, 52–54, 147
UN 92
United Kingdom (UK) 4, 7, 48, 57, 81, 93, 103, 106, 135–152, 241, 248, 253
United States and American English 4, 60, 131, 135–137, 146, 150, 171, 109, 123, 151–154, 246, 257
Ural-Altaic language family 241
Urdu 124, 126
Uruguay 9, 215–221
USSR 35–38, 44, 175, 176, 201
Uzbekistan and Uzbek 234, 243

Va'ad HaAretz (Jewish National Council) in Lithuania 23
Valencia and Valencian 103, 106, 109, 111
Vatican 159
Vaud 93, 102
Venice 157–158
Verdinaso 84, 89
Versailles Treaty 2, 23, 167, 175
Vichy regime 116–117

Vienna 15, 196
Vienna Award 183
Vietnam 4
Vikør, Lars 62, 73
Vilna Gaon 23
Vlaams Blok 89–91
VNV 84–85
Volksgeist 3
Volksteile 194

Wadi Ara 207
Wales, Welsh and Welsh National Party 7, 24, 45, 49, 53, 139–145, 253
Wallachia 181
Waloons 75–81
Wardhaugh, Richard 141
Wataniyah nationalism 235–238
Waterloo 97, 147
Weuleresse, Jacques 237
White Russians *see* Byelorussians
Winter War (Russo-Finnish War 1940) 201
Wolfson, Shlomo 49
Xhosa 132–135
Xulu *see* Zulu

Yediot Ahronot 205
Yemen 5, 35, 232
Yevanic (Judeo-Greek) 13
Yevsektzia 37
Yiddish 5, 7, 12–48, 151, 154, 206, 247, 250
Yoash 27
Yugoslavia 8, 165–170, 231, 244, 254–255

Zagreb 166, 168
Zarphatic (Judeo-French) 13
Zionism and Zionist Congresses 12, 15, 17, 19–20, 54, 184, 186, 205, 211, 229, 237, 247
Ziyad, Qassem 218
Zug 93
Zulu 132–135
Zurich 93, 102